PERGAMON INTERNATIONAL LIBRARY
of Science, Technology, Engineering and Social Studies
The 1000-volume original paperback library in aid of education,
industrial training and the enjoyment of leisure
Publisher: Robert Maxwell, M.C.

The Education Dilemma
Policy Issues for Developing Countries in the 1980s

THE PERGAMON TEXTBOOK
INSPECTION COPY SERVICE

An inspection copy of any book published in the Pergamon International Library will gladly be sent to academic staff without obligation for their consideration for course adoption or recommendation. Copies may be retained for a period of 60 days from receipt and returned if not suitable. When a particular title is adopted or recommended for adoption for class use and the recommendation results in a sale of 12 or more copies, the inspection copy may be retained with our compliments. The Publishers will be pleased to receive suggestions for revised editions and new titles to be published in this important International Library.

Other Titles of Interest

BHALLA, A.
Towards Global Action for Appropriate Technology

CLARKE, J.
Population Geography and the Developing Countries

COLE, S. & LUCAS, H.
Models, Planning and Basic Needs

EPSTEIN, T. S. & JACKSON, D.
The Feasibility of Fertility Planning

FAGERLIND, I. & SAHA, L.
Education and National Development

FORD, B.
Health Education: A Source Book for Teaching

GOAD, L. H.
Preparing Teachers for Lifelong Education

HUSÉN, T. & KOGAN, M.
Educational Research and Policy — How do they relate?

LASZLO, E.
The Objectives of the New International Economic Order

LEGRAND, P.
Areas of Learning Basic to Lifelong Education

MENON, B.
Global Dialogue: The New International Economic Order

MITTER, W.
Secondary School Graduation: University Entrance Qualification
in Socialist Countries

SALAS, R.
International Population Assistance: The First Decade

SKAGER, R.
Organizing Schools to Encourage Self-Direction in Learners

THOMAS, R. M.
Politics and Education: Cases from 11 Nations

TRETHEWEY, A.
Introducing Comparative Education

The Education Dilemma

Policy Issues for Developing Countries in the 1980s

Edited by

JOHN SIMMONS
The World Bank

With a Foreword by

TORSTEN HUSEN

PERGAMON PRESS
OXFORD · NEW YORK · TORONTO · SYDNEY · FRANKFURT

U.K.	Pergamon Press Ltd., Headington Hill Hall, Oxford OX3 0BW, England
U.S.A.	Pergamon Press Inc., Maxwell House, Fairview Park, Elmsford, New York 10523, U.S.A.
CANADA	Pergamon Press Canada Ltd., Suite 104, 150 Consumers Road, Willowdale, Ontario. M2J 1P9, Canada
AUSTRALIA	Pergamon Press (Aust.) Pty. Ltd., P.O. Box 544, Potts Point, N.S.W. 2011, Australia
FEDERAL REPUBLIC OF GERMANY	Pergamon Press GmbH, Hammerweg 6, D-6242 Kronberg, Federal Republic of Germany
JAPAN	Pergamon Press Ltd., 8th Floor, Matsuoka Central Building, 1-7-1 Nishishinjuku, Shinjuku-ku, Tokyo 160, Japan
BRAZIL	Pergamon Editora Ltda., Rua Eça de Queiros, 346, CEP 04011, São Paulo, Brazil
PEOPLE'S REPUBLIC OF CHINA	Pergamon Press, Qianmen Hotel, Beijing, People's Republic of China

First edition 1980
Reprinted 1983, 1986

British Library Cataloguing in Publication Data
The education dilemma. — (Pergamon international library).
1. Underdeveloped areas — Educational planning
I. Simmons, John
379'.15'091724   LC2607   79-40071
ISBN 0-08-024304-5 (Hardcover)
ISBN 0-08-024303-7 (Flexicover)

The views and interpretations in this book are those of the authors and should not be attributed to the World Bank, to its affiliated organizations, or to any individual acting on their behalf.

Printed in Great Britain by A. Wheaton & Co. Ltd., Exeter

While millions of people from among the educated are unemployed, millions of jobs are waiting to be done because people with the right education, training and skills cannot be found. . . . [This is] one of the most disturbing paradoxes of our time.

> Robert S. McNamara
> *Education Sector Working Paper (1974)*

It takes a total of sixteen, seventeen, or twenty years for one to reach the university from primary school, and in this period one never has the chance to look at the five kinds of cereals, how the workers do their work, how peasants till their fields, and how traders do business. In the meantime, one's health is also ruined. Such an education system is very harmful indeed.

> Mao Tsetung
> *Talk at the Hangchow Conference (1965)*

A real humanist can be identified more by his trust in the people, which engages him in their struggle, than by a thousand actions in their favor without that trust.

> Paulo Freire
> *Pedagogy of the Oppressed (1968)*

TO THOSE ADULTS AND CHILDREN WHO CAN BENEFIT
FROM MORE HUMANE EDUCATIONAL POLICIES

Contents

ix

List of Tables and Figures

Foreword

The Education Dilemma challenges time-honored concepts and ideas about formal education and its usefulness as a panacea for social and economic ills. It raises profound questions about the adequacy of the Western European and North American model of formal schooling that has been exported wholesale to the developing countries where it may not be suitable.

During the early 1960s, confidence in education was at its euphoric high. Educational injections, formally conceived, were regarded as the main means of promoting development. Because development was to be reflected in gross national product, the main concern was with size and quantitative expansion, and, to this end, ambitious enrollment targets were set. Since then we have lived through a period of criticism and disenchantment with formal education. It has become increasingly evident that education does not operate in a social vacuum and that institutional arrangements should correspond to the wider societal framework which sets the limits to planning and reform. Quantitative planning has to go hand in hand with qualitative planning. Headcount alone does not suffice. What is in the heads—the outcomes of schooling—must be evaluated both in terms of individual competence achieved and the adequacy of education in the world of work. The shift in priorities over the last ten years entails more emphasis on distribution of educational services and equality of access to education and less emphasis on sheer numbers and formal schooling.

A decade ago we were far less aware than we are now of the role of politics in educational planning. The expert was perceived as a technician who presented policymakers with unequivocal "solutions" to problems posed by the latter. There are, however, no mechanical linkages between research and expert knowledge on the one hand and policy action on the other. The border between political a-rationality and expert rationality is seldom clear. Indeed, the relationship between them is apt to be a dialectical one. Increasing questioning about the proper role of the expert has already led to participatory planning involving local communities as well as top officials in the preparation of educational reforms.

It is now time for a basic reappraisal of the contribution of education to development. The present anthology, which includes essays by a number of the world's experts on education and development, is a major step towards this goal.

Torsten Husen
Institute of International Education
University of Stockholm

Acknowledgments

The authors reviewed their colleagues' chapters. They also appreciate the helpful comments on draft chapters by Bernard Braithewaite, Hollis B. Chenery, William Clark, Richard Edwards, Herbert Gintis, Aklilu Habte, Nagy Hanna, Frank Holmquist, Helen Hughes, Dean Jamison, Gloria Joseph, Nathan Kravitz, Raj Krishna, Michele Naples, Adele Simmons and Paul Streeten. Claire Chow, Richard Herbert, Helen Smith and Tony Phillips provided able editorial assistance. The Development Economics Department and the Education Department of the World Bank provided financial support.

We appreciate the permission to use extracts or revisions from the following materials that have already been published: Mark Blaug, *Education and Employment,* The International Labour Organisation; Edgar O. Edwards, "Investment in Education in Developing Countries", *World Development;* Marcelo Selowsky, "Preschool Age Investment in Human Capital", *Economic Development and Cultural Change;* and John Simmons and Leigh Alexander, "The Determinants of School Achievement", *Economic Development and Cultural Change.*

xv

CHAPTER 1

Introduction and Summary

JOHN SIMMONS

For the past decade, criticism of formal education has continued to increase throughout the world. The traditional school inputs, such as teacher training or expenditure per student, do not seem to be having the effect on student test scores that educators had anticipated. Graduates at all levels have had increasing difficulty finding the jobs they expected, whereas fifteen years ago planners predicted deficits in the number of school leavers needed to fill the expected job openings extending into the 1980s. And, finally, the rapid expansion of free schooling has not narrowed the distribution of income between the rich and the poor as planners had intended. While these problems are found to be serious in developed countries, they are even more serious in those developing countries where the resources available for the survival of the poor majority, let alone schooling, are meager. What has happened to the promise that schooling held out an equal opportunity to millions of people to develop their individual capabilities to their highest level and to climb out of poverty?

The purpose of this book is to review the evidence that is the basis for the growing criticism, and to draw the implications for policy-making in the 1980s. The contributors address the central issues that educators and planners who desire to reform their educational systems must face.

Since educational issues raise profound political questions, it is no wonder that few countries have successfully implemented major educational reforms. How many countries have launched reforms, only to have the vessels of implementation founder on rocky political shores? Not surprisingly most educators have responded by concentrating on the daily tasks of expanding enrollments, raising teacher qualifications and salaries, and making yet another curriculum innovation. Broader policy issues have not received the necessary attention.

A dilemma is a choice between alternatives which are equally unsatisfactory to people making the choice. Most developing countries are trying to cope with an educational dilemma in which the alternatives have become increasingly well defined. Should a country's leadership decide to continue the expansion of expensive secondary and higher education more rapidly than that of relatively cheap primary education? Or should major resources be shifted to expand the quantity and improve the quality of the first nine years of schooling, including nonformal education for adults? Nine years is probably the minimum number required to develop and sustain adequate levels of reading comprehension for most students under average school conditions. Nonformal education is organized learning outside of the traditional schools and university curriculum, for example, the upgrading of the proficiency of agricultural extension agents through short courses, or the raising of awareness of poor adults about the sources of their problems and how to organize to overcome them. Higher education is usually twenty to one hundred times more expensive per student than primary. Such a shift of resources to well-designed primary and adult education could both increase the rate of economic growth and reduce social inequality.

For many decisionmakers, neither alternative is satisfactory. If the expansion of secondary and higher education is continued, an increasingly large share of the nation's budget will go to education, leaving decreasing shares for investment in agriculture, housing, and health care. Ministries competing for budgetary funds will argue that the economic payoff is not justified if the social rate of return to other investments is higher (that is, if food, water, housing, and health care are higher priorities), and if the number of the educated unemployed is rising. If resources are shifted away from upper secondary and university education to the first nine years of schooling, how should the leadership handle irate upper income parents whose children will be denied access to the schooling deemed appropriate for their socioeconomic status, and upon whom the leadership depends for political support, as well as angry teachers' associations who see their job security threatened? This argument assumes that the State is the main source of capital and current expenditures while in some countries individuals and communities have met the financial obligations.

A shift in emphasis to primary and adult education then raises several other equally difficult policy issues. Does improving the quality of primary schooling include *both* boosting reading and arithmetic scores and adding exposure to employment and community skills? Should nonformal education be geared to the priority need of the rural poor and thus designed to elicit greater problem solving ability, self-reliance, and community participation, or should nonformal education maintain the narrow focus of most literacy and craft training programs? Should the curriculum for the nine years of primary education be made more practical; for example, by the inclusion of interpersonal and agricultural skills? Would "academic standards" fall as a result? Would the practical subjects be tested for entry into the university, or would only the more academic subjects be considered by the university admissions committees? If the practical subjects are not examined, is there any assurance that they will be effectively taught? Given the increasing evidence that supports a high payoff to investment in early nutrition, preschool education, and parent training to maximize rate of student learning, should some resources now being spent on primary education be shifted to these other areas? These few questions only begin to define the policy issues related to the dilemma.

The policy solutions to this dilemma and the related issues depend on the kind of "development" that the political leadership seeks to promote. If a country's main goal is economic growth, planners, using the results of economic profitability studies, might urge a reduction in public spending on higher education and upper secondary, and increase the proportion of spending on both primary education and vocational training for rural employment. In a few countries they might even reduce the percentage of the national budget which is allocated to formal education. The political leadership, as we have noted above, is not likely to receive support from the necessary middle and upper income groups for such a shift. If a country's primary development goal is to improve the standard of living of the poor majority of the population and the distribution of income, planners might promote an aggressive adult education program in community participation and problem solving and provide funds for villagers to organize to improve their circumstances. Planners could also set a quota on the proportion of students from lower and upper income families who would be admitted to higher education which would be consistent with their proportional representation in society. This solution may not be attractive to governments which wish to either maintain central control of relevant decisions or maintain the social status quo. Officials either may not trust the poor to make appropriate decisions about their own needs, or the officials fear that the increased self-confidence and organization of the poor will challenge the status quo. For those countries which wish to promote both growth and equality, the appropriate changes in educational policy may be some mix of these kinds of programs.

In summary, this analysis leads to a surprising conclusion. Usually, we are told by economists and other experts that some economic growth has to be sacrificed to achieve greater social equality. In education, we find that for most countries both the growth and equality arguments urge investment in primary education, while the more powerful interest groups urge expansion of higher education. Thus, we have the arguments for growth and equity arrayed together against the arguments of privilege. The educational dilemma of investment in higher versus primary education mirrors the political dilemma of how much growth and equity have to be *sacrificed* to maintain political stability.

In the past few years some countries, such as Pakistan and Colombia, have been trying to slip between the horns of the dilemma by reducing the rate of expansion of secondary and higher education without expanding primary education at a higher rate. They have undertaken modest expansion of investment in nonformal education, for example, the training of villagers for community development in the Pakistani Daudzai project, and the diffusion by radio of farm and family information in Colombia. Other countries, such as Brazil, fail 70 percent of the students in primary school in order to limit access to secondary education. China and Cuba are among a growing number of countries that appear to have not only faced the dilemma directly, but also implemented extensive reforms of their educational programs.

The Chinese and the Cubans have strictly limited the number of students who get more than ten years of schooling to those for whom jobs requiring higher education are available. The Chinese see student failure as a reflection of the teacher's ability, not the student's, and expect teachers and classmates to assist the slower students. The Cubans moved most secondary education to the five-day boarding schools in the countryside, to both facilitate the concentration of students on their studies and teach the importance of agriculture and manual labor. These two countries share the educational objectives of most developing countries to reach universal literacy, develop manpower to promote economic growth, and increase the economic payoff for groups previously excluded. One difference between these and other countries where the defense of privilege has so often obstructed educational progress is that not only have the Chinese and the Cubans been developing innovative solutions, they also have had the political will and organization to implement reforms. This is not to say that the costs in human terms which were incurred by revolution may not be as great as the costs incurred through mis-education in countries where educational reforms have not taken place. We simply note that these countries have undertaken genuine reforms to deal with the dilemma.

Where the class structure has been overturned, the educational policy issues are different. The Cubans have given priority to parental education about early child development, but are debating what is the best way to do it. Technical training is already as prestigious as academic training, but Cuban educators are concerned about creating a new elite which is isolated from the problems of the poor majority. Other countries such as Botswana, Ethiopia, Guinea Bissau, Somalia, Sri Lanka, Tanzania and Vietnam are making important efforts to meet the educational needs of the poor, but their programs may not have yet approached the critical minimum effort required for success. While the policy issues raised in these countries are important, and have been discussed elsewhere,[2] they are not the focus of this book.

The World Bank began lending for education in 1962 in order to provide the trained human resources needed to plan and implement development projects. Initially the objective was to supply schooling and training to provide middle manpower, which was thought to be in short supply at the time. More recently, Bank objectives have been expanded to support primary and some types of nonformal education.

The Bank's policies are described in more detail in the *Education Sector Working Paper,* published in 1979.

The essays in this volume are intended to forge the links between educational practice, research, and policy. The contributors have had long careers in research on either the economics or the sociology of education in developing countries. While they represent a wide range of views, they agree on the seriousness of the dilemma and the importance of reform. Since all the contributors have also assisted government policy discussion and formulation, they understand the kind of information that decisionmakers need and the hard choices they have to make.

Some observers have pointed out that educational research has not made the sort of contribution to development policy made by agricultural research. There is no "green revolution" in sight in education for most developing nations because the "product" is human, not vegetable, and can only be cultivated within a complex social, political, and economic field. Putting more resources into educational research may help, but no educational "high yielding variety" is expected to turn up—let alone one that removes the political constraints on educational reform. Although a theory of human learning comparable in rigor to the theory of plant growth is certainly lacking, we hope that these essays suggest in which directions policymakers can move with reasonable confidence.

The two chapters in the first section of this book provide an overview of the central issues faced by planners and educators in most developing countries. The next three sections—the twelve chapters which comprise the bulk of the book—deal with such topics as the efficiency of educational investment, the relation of employment, migration, and fertility to education, and the problems of allocation, equity, and conflict in educational planning. The final section suggests a planning and consultation process to study and promote educational reforms.

Major Problems of the Educational System

During the past ten years many observers have noted that formal education was failing to meet the needs of the poor majority. Formal education provided training for urban, white collar jobs while most jobs, and most skills required in development, tended to be manual and in rural areas. Moreover, students from poor families are usually unable to continue formal education to the university level. Instead of acquiring useful skills, the poor are usually taught by formal education that they are inferior. They fail to be promoted from one grade to the next in primary school, or they fail the entrance exam to secondary school. Educators, as the gatekeepers to job security and high incomes, reject them as unfit. In most countries, the poor are resigned to letting the educational establishment decide their fate and legitimize their poverty. Gunnar Myrdal, the Nobel Laureate in economics, has explained that "the poor are not educated to see their interests and they are not organized to fight for their interests". They lack the education for critical awareness and organization.

The central educational issues can be grouped into three categories: (1) inefficiency within the schools and the educational system, which can be measured by high dropout rates, illiterate graduates, and lack of paper, pencils, textbooks, and even teachers in the classroom; (2) mismatch between what the schools are producing and what employers, citizens, young people, and parents need—these problems are seen in unemployment of the educated, in the lack of critical awareness about problem definition and resolution and in the lack of information about sanitation and child care among parents and citizens from low income groups; and (3) inequities in the distribution of educational opportunities and results to the rural and urban poor.

These problems have been around for so long and appear so intractable that analysts have, however reluctantly, reached four main conclusions. First, neither the lack of knowledge nor the technical limitations of educational planning have been a major reason why educational systems have been so slow to change. A recent international meeting of educational planners concluded that even when better information is available it is not used; carefully prepared plans are shelved or only partially implemented.

Second, the outcome of planned changes in the system of education is shaped by the political and economic institutions of a country. The evidence suggests that educational reforms that seek to implement an egalitarian development policy can only be effective in the context of political and economic transformation. Even seemingly minor changes such as replacing the "irrelevant" academic curriculum with vocational training at the secondary level or reducing the "inefficiency" of a high rate of primary school dropouts will be resisted by the current leadership because both of these mechanisms tend to reinforce and legitimize the existing power structure.[3]

Third, as the Swedish educator and reformer Torsten Husen has acknowledged, within the past ten years "the mood has swung from the almost euphoric conception of education as the Great Equalizer to that of education as the Great Sieve that sorts and certifies people for their [predetermined] slot in society".[4] More of the same quality and quantity of schooling is unlikely to meet national objectives for social mobility and equality, nor the manpower development required for growth.

Fourth, as Blaug, Bowles, Carnoy, and Edwards have argued persuasively in this book, most educational investment enhances the power of those who already have social and economic advantages far more than it enhances the power or position of those who have not.

One of the solutions increasingly proposed—nonformal education—also raises additional issues. Many foreign experts from developed countries have recently reached agreement about the relevance of the type of nonformal education which teaches manual skills for developing countries. They urge the expansion of this type of nonformal education to reduce the mismatch between educational supply and employment demand. Most agree that the expansion of formal education at the secondary and higher levels should be stabilized at current rates of enrollment growth, or even slowly reduced.

World Bank authors wrote in 1974 that formal educational systems have been "irrelevant to the needs of developing countries for the past two decades".[5] The greatest economic need was perceived for training specialists in all aspects of rural development or self-employment. The Bank then urged a program of nonformal and vocational education. But educational establishments have been less enthusiastic about replacing formal education with an almost untried substitute. Ministers of education are understandably cool to such suggestions.

The difference of opinion over the relevance of formal education poses a major paradox. If the international experts agree that more practical education is good for economic growth, why are most of the national educators strongly opposed to it? While some of them are long on supportive rhetoric, they are short on implementing new priorities. The short answer is that the expansion of nonformal education that teaches rural and urban manual skills will cut into the funds allocated for formal education, which is more prestigious and in greater demand. But there is another equally serious consideration. The expansion of nonformal education will reinforce a dual system of education, with one side of the system training students for manual labor and the other for mental labor; one side preparing primarily for rural employment, the other for urban. Such a dual system will reinforce the social and political status quo, promoting neither the poor nor their interests. Thus, unwittingly, the nonformal strategy works against the poor, except in such countries as China and Cuba where both the reduction of poverty is the highest priority of the leadership, and nonformal strategy is applied to rich and poor alike. It appears that in nonsocialist countries, as well as some socialist ones, nonformal education streams poorer youth and adults into manual jobs and thus actually inhibits social mobility.

The extent of the opposition among educators and middle and upperclass parents to nonformal education is impressive. They feel that formal education *is* relevant to their occupational, personal and civic needs. Lower-income parents also object to a dual educational system that streams their children into manual jobs while still in primary school. At the same time, many national and multinational firms are glad to support a program of nonformal education that teaches future workers specifically what they need to know in order to perform well in semi-skilled or skilled jobs.

Although the Chinese acknowledge problems with their educational system, their educational program for economic productivity, community participation and cognitive skills comes closest to the World Bank's model program for a developing country as described in the *Education Sector Working Paper*. They have a curriculum that meets the needs of the mass of the population—an emphasis on language, maths, and practical training, ten years of schooling almost universally available, community management of the schools, a university selection process that minimizes discrimination against the poor, and an emphasis on raising awareness among adults about problems and their solutions through small study groups and self-criticism—all achieved at low cost within twenty years. Even countries with five times the per capita income of China's $250, and the same broad objectives in their development plans, have not achieved these results. I should again note that education programs that benefit the poor are emerging in other countries such as Botswana, Ethiopia, Somalia, Sri Lanka, and Tanzania, some with World Bank support.

Efficiency of Educational Investment

More research on the efficiency of educational investment has been done than on any other educational topic. The theoretical objective of efficiency is to obtain the optimum combination of inputs such as teacher training and expenditure per student to achieve at least-cost the desired outcome, such as a certain level of reading achievement. Ronald Dore provides an overview of the issue of the appropriateness of current school objectives. He suggests that certificates have replaced learning as the objective of formal education and argues that schools have become anti-educational as a result. Educators have tried to use schools as a replacement for apprenticeships in the transition of youth to adulthood and this, he maintains, is a step in the wrong direction. The concentration on mental and theoretical exercises, rather than manual and practical experience, has prepared most students for neither jobs, nor family, nor the responsibilities of citizenship. Even the few students who do get white collar jobs could benefit from an educational experience that combines theory and practice. The models that are being provided for the selection and training of all levels of health workers in China offer a good example of apprenticeships that combine theory and practice with the work study approach and refresher courses that the World Bank's *Health Sector Working Paper* emphasized. Dore also stresses the idea of replacing achievement tests with aptitude tests as a means to promote educational objectives, which are currently hampered by the importance placed on examinations, and to break the cycle of inflation of certificates, which requires increasingly higher certificates for the same job.

The issue of why some children learn more than others is reviewed by Leigh Alexander and myself as we examine the determinants of school achievement. We find that the studies in developing countries indicate that the school inputs tend to be less important in predicting student achievement on standard school tests than family and other out-of-school factors. The results are consistent with studies of developed countries. We suggest, for example, that the effectiveness of teacher training, as it is now practiced in most countries, in promoting student achievement may be a myth. While the studies show that inputs such as teacher selection or the provision of textbooks in some countries may affect what students learn in the classroom, experimental studies should be undertaken in each country before planners decide to modify their investment pattern.

The payoff of investment in children of preschool age is discussed by Marcelo Selowsky. The central hypothesis of his paper is that developing countries are overinvesting in formal schooling relative to preschool investment in human capital, basically nutrition and early environmental stimulation. The future effectiveness of investment in schooling will depend to a certain extent on the present investments in preschool age projects. According to Selowsky, this hypothesis rests on the following set of evidence: (a) growing empirical evidence shows that preschool age children of families of low socioeconomic levels tend to score worse in most ability tests; (b) to a large extent, those low scores are a product of a deficit after birth in environmental stimulation as well as nutritional intake, not genetic deficiency; and (c) future school enrollment will increasingly draw children from these socioeconomic levels. This means that the future effectiveness of primary schooling will depend on the present policies aimed at boosting—via a better quality of early environment and nutrition—the ability scores of those children.

Assuming the desirability of reaching more students at lower cost per student without lowering their test results, Joanne Leslie and Dean Jamison explore the use of radio and television in the classroom. They found that educational television (ETV) works no better than radio in teaching the desired subjects. ETV, however, is significantly more expensive to install and operate and more complicated to manage than radio. Compared to traditional classroom techniques, the radio approach can be less expensive and improve access to education of the remote populations.

Policymakers often wonder if the research methods used to reach some of the above policy implications are legitimate, especially those methods designed in developed countries. Ernesto Shiefelbein concludes that the research techniques are acceptable, given the usual reservations. He warns, however, that the conclusions reached from studies in the United States should not be used for policy in developing countries without first carrying out similar studies in less developed countries. He observes, for example, that in a few less developed countries school variables make a substantial contribution to explain differences in levels of achievement, while in the American setting schools having similar facilities and differences seem to have negligible effects on students' achievement. He suggests the existence of a threshold point for each one of the inputs; beyond that point no further improvement is obtained. Even the American research has not established the minimum threshold of schooling necessary for students to achieve and retain practical abilities such as the ability to read and understand a newspaper. Nor does the research show what could be accomplished if parents and their children between the ages of two and six were exposed to parent training or organized learning before the children entered school.

The Impact of Education on Employment, Migration, and Fertility

Traditionally, educators have been minimally concerned about what happens to students after they leave school. This was the responsibility of the family, the employer, and the ministry of labor. With the rising unemployment rate of school leavers and the dissatisfaction of employers with what students were learning, the mismatch between schooling and employment has become an issue.

Mark Blaug reviews the assumptions commonly held by many decisionmakers about the positive relationship between education and employment and finds that in most countries the assumptions are based more on myth than on fact. Investment in education does not create permanent jobs in the society, except for teachers. With some exceptions in countries that have widespread manpower deficiencies, the expansion of the educational system does not work effectively to eliminate poverty. Blaug suggests, in fact, that a policy of not expanding education, and assuming that the freed capital would be used for the direct creation of jobs, may at times be a more effective way of reducing poverty. And even when there are manpower shortages, closer examination often shows that the traditional economic solution of increasing the supply of educated people to drive down the wage rates has not been, and will not be, an effective solution to the problem. For example, the wage rates of plumbers are not allowed to rise which would encourage more people to take up plumbing; apprenticeships require five years, or there is really only a shortage of "good" plumbers. He also found that earnings differentials associated with higher levels of education are excessive. Blaug sees small-scale experimentation with new educational approaches as the only way to reduce the wasteful mismatch between education and employment.

Martin Carnoy notes that while the reports of manpower planners fifteen years ago predicted shortages of educated manpower in the 1970s and 1980s, particularly at the secondary and higher levels, most developing countries currently face an excess of educated manpower. He suggests that unemployment of the educated is not caused by the educational system itself but rather by an economic system in which employers benefit from high levels of unemployment since wages are thereby depressed. More education will not create jobs, outside of the education sector. One way to reduce the pressure for more schooling is to reduce unemployment at all levels of the labor force—with less unemployment there is less demand to continue schooling, since the income foregone by staying out of the work force increases.

Planners have been concerned about the effect of education on modernizing the population to become better citizens, parents, and workers. Remi Clignet uses evidence from the Cameroon to question the extent to which this has happened. Western-style education has not reduced polygamy as planners had expected. The more education the men have received, the more wives and children they acquire. Furthermore, schooling has discouraged students from entrepreneurial efforts: the more educated the school leavers, the more concerned they are with job security. Finally, because of the growing gap between the number of school leavers and the job opportunities for a given educational level, the income and status benefits of education have fallen. Clignet concludes that, far from promoting equal employment opportunities, the educational system tends to reproduce the inequalities found in society.

The rapid expansion of the number of school leavers has contributed to the massive rural-to-urban migration. It has created uncontrolled economic and social problems in the past thirty years that seem likely to continue. It is predicted that Mexico City will reach 25 million people by the end of the century and Bombay 20 million. Michael Todaro reviews the evidence and concludes that the rapid expansion of school enrollments has been a major cause of migration. There is human tragedy and economic waste in a system that channels the best of its rural youth into urban crime, unemployment, and underemployment. The control of urban migration requires adequate social services and wage rates in the countryside, plus legal sanctions. Planners have at least two strong tools available to begin dealing with the problems, but these require substantial political courage and organization. They include halting the expansion of post-primary education and sharply reducing wage differentials.

High levels of fertility and population growth have long been recognized as a major constraint on rates of development. Policymakers and some researchers have asserted that raising the level of education of both men and women would reduce fertility levels. Todaro points out that the relationship between education and fertility is not that simple. In fact, there is some evidence to show that an increase in education raises fertility levels. Research that has been done has often used simplistic models and statistical techniques that are not suitable for policy planning and investment decisions. Finally, no evidence shows how much fertility levels would be reduced if there were a large increase in education per capita. Todaro does not find very compelling the theory that more educated people have fewer children. He concludes that creating more full-time jobs for women is a much more realistic policy recommendation than increasing the years of schooling.

Allocation, Equity, and Conflict in Educational Planning

Given the problems that the authors raise about both the internal efficiency of past investments in education and the effects of education on employment, migration, and fertility, how should planners allocate funds both across the sectors of the economy and within the education sector? The art of planning such investments is not advanced enough to show what effect a dollar invested in textbooks will have on a student's test scores or on his future productivity, or whether a dollar invested in training agricultural extension agents is more effective than a dollar spent on fertilizer. At the same time, however, substantial lessons have been learned during the past twenty years about which approaches work better than others and under what conditions. Bowles, Edwards, and Harberger have had extensive experience in planning in different developing countries, and their conclusions exhibit both similarities and differences.

Does the demand for education of individuals and their families exceed the demand of society for educated people? Edgar Edwards cites the growing unemployment of the educated as an indication of a growing conflict between private and social signals. But jobs will not be created until unemployment of the educated becomes a threat to political stability. Some observers have suggested that public investment in education be cut, but the result would probably be an increase in private education. Edwards sees three ways to begin dealing with the problem, all of which require major reforms. First, wage differentials related to education should be narrowed, in order to cut the incentives students now have for more education and to untie the connections between hiring practices and school certificates. Second, the costs of education borne by the consumer should be increased, which should discourage students from wanting more education. Third, higher education, which is costly and reaches few of the people, should be financed from private sources. Students from poor families should be subsidized. Edwards is not optimistic that these changes can take place in most countries, however, because the powerful pressure groups desire the expansion of free public education at the secondary and higher levels.

Two economic approaches have been used to determine whether governments should spend more or less money on education: the manpower planning approach, which analyzes the supply of candidates trained for a specific occupation and the supply of jobs available in that occupation, and the rate of return to educational investment,

which calculates the profitability of such investment. Arnold Harberger
prefers the rate of return approach and maintains that where the
return to education is higher than that to physical capital, there is
hardly any question that investment in education should be expanded.
When the return to education is lower, the decision to invest depends
on the size of the shortfall and the nonincome benefits to education,
which the rate of return measurement does not capture. Concern
should be felt, he argues, only when the return falls below about
5 percent.

A major objective of planning investment in education has been to
improve the opportunities for social mobility of the poor and to narrow
the gap in the distribution of income. The expansion of rural primary
and secondary education is one of the results of this investment.
Samuel Bowles explains that the roots of social inequality in the capitalist countries lie in the class structure and in the uneven development
of the economy. Schools cannot directly affect such inequality.
Landlords and traditional elites have little interest in expanding the
educational system because they do not need educated workers, while
factory owners and government administrators do need them. Wage
workers want the benefits of education for their children, but oppose
universal education, which would expand the pool of potential wage
workers and keep wages down, as well as create the political unrest
that comes from unemployment of the educated. Because of the labor-
saving nature of imported technologies and generally high rates of
population growth, the capitalist sector does not generally face labor
scarcities. Capitalist employers have little motivation for extending
schooling beyond the limited employment needs of their own sector.

The resulting coalition of landlords, factory owners, administrators,
and urban wage labor effectively restricts the amount of education
available to the peasantry and uses school credentials to regulate the
flow of workers into the urban labor force. This reinforces a dual
educational system which permits only a small trickle of poor rural
children into the urban labor market, to assure that the children of the
middle and upper class get urban employment. Bowles uses evidence
from both socialist and capitalist countries to support his position.
He concludes that most proposals suggesting that schools might be
used to further social equality in the capitalist countries exhibit an

unwarranted optimism based on ignoring the realities of class relations and the power structure.

The final chapter reviews the reform strategies and policy options that most planners face concerning future investments in schooling and training. Specific questions are raised that could facilitate the planning of educational changes covering the topics of manpower analysis, equality, resource allocation, legal codes and systems models.

In conclusion, I review the policy issues that surround the dilemma in education. They are better understood and defined than they were ten years ago, when Philip Coombs first called attention to the seriousness of the problems in *The World Educational Crisis*. In many countries, however, better understanding has not led to the design and implementation of substantial improvements. There are two schools of thought as to why the record of educational change is not better. The first, the technical or incrementalist school argues that, until recently, available information about the problems of the educational systems and their causes has been insufficient for designing changes that can be successfully implemented, but that there are no major barriers to such success. The second, or structural school, argues that the political and economic forces which shape educational decisions are so strong that they must be changed before education can be expected to change. Both schools do agree, however, on the need for experimental efforts to try out various ideas, and select those that seem to work. But educational reformers are aware of the paradox that most educators, whose job it is to analyze, develop, and transmit ideas, are often reluctant to try out new approaches.

Notes

1. John Simmons, "The retention of cognitive skills acquired in primary school", *The Comparative Education Review,* February 1976, and World Bank reprint number 35.
2. Gerald Tannebaum and John Simmons, "The open door: lessons from educational reform in China", mimeograph (Washington, D.C.: World Bank, 1978), and Martin Carnoy and Jorge Werthein, "Educational reform in Cuba", mimeograph (Washington, D.C.: World Bank, 1978).

3. John Simmons, "Observations on educational reform: illustrations from more and less developed countries", mimeograph (Washington, D.C.: World Bank, 1978).

4. Torsten Husen, "Problems of securing equal access to higher education: the dilemma between equality and excellence", *Higher Education,* vol. 5 (1976), p. 411.

5. "Education Sector working paper" (Washington, D.C.: World Bank, 1974), p. 3.

CHAPTER 2

An Overview of the Policy Issues in the 1980s

JOHN SIMMONS

The expansion of investment in formal education has been pheno-
menal in the last two decades, and only in a few developing countries
are there signs that the rate of expansion may be diminishing. In
country after country, education has been the only sector to meet or
exceed planned investment targets. Demand has been fueled by critical
manpower needs, parental pressures for more years of schooling for
their children and thus better chances for high paying jobs, and the
conviction that education is a human right for all citizens. Further,
because the capital cost, including foreign exchange, of supplying new
school places is relatively low compared with the cost of creating new
job slots, the supply of educated personnel has often expanded more
rapidly than the supply of jobs.

The successful expansion of formal education has, however, created
a new generation of social and economic problems. Education is the
largest item in most countries' budgets; as a result, unless current
trends are dampened, an increasing number of countries will face
serious financial problems. Even foreign exchange costs become
serious when the expansion of secondary and higher education forces
the maintenance of ever larger numbers of expatriate teachers and
imported school equipment and supplies. At the same time, reducing
the rate of expansion creates serious political problems. Middle and
upper income parents are the most outspoken when reduced funding
for secondary or higher education is threatened, as their children
might be squeezed out of the public schools. And these parents are
usually the main source of political support for the government.
Teachers, usually the largest single group of wage earners in a poor

country, are also a politically potent element when changes in the educational system are proposed.

Finally, recent research suggests that schooling has not been as effective in promoting cognitive achievement, measured by school tests, as had been expected. Research results for Europe and the United States in the 1960s have been supported by studies in the 1970s for more than twenty developing countries.[1] Nonschool factors such as parental behavior, child health and nutrition, and peer group experience are more important than expected in predicting achievement scores. Traditional school inputs such as class size, length of teacher training, and expenditure per pupil are usually insignificant in determining differences in student scores. This research has important implications for future investment decisions.

Policymakers in countries that are considering increased efforts to reduce poverty through employment, income redistribution, and welfare measures are asking: What *is* the contribution of education to individual and social welfare? Should resources now used for formal education be shifted to other programs where they may have a higher marginal social product? Can allocations within the sector be made more efficient, effective, and equitable? These are the issues addressed by the authors of chapters in this book.

This chapter attempts an overview of the policy issues that will confront most planners and decisionmakers in the 1980s. It is meant to provide background for the problems covered in greater depth in the following chapters. Briefly, the following issues are reviewed: the nature of educational objectives, theories of learning and schooling, the magnitude of recent educational investment, the benefits and costs of education in its relationship to employment and income distribution, the efficiency with which the schools have combined the capital and labor inputs to achieve the desired student skills, and the net benefits from educational investment to the individual and society.

Objectives

Developing countries have invested in education to achieve a myriad of economic, political, and cultural objectives. Expanding free adult literacy and primary education would enhance the social mobility of the poor. Secondary school graduates were needed in expanding economies to perform technical and administrative functions, and to replace expatriates. University graduates were needed to supply professional and managerial skills needed in both the public and private sectors. Schooling would contribute to political socialization and cultural homogenization. Investment in formal education was considered an engine of economic growth and the more schooling per person the better; for poor parents, more schooling was perceived as the only hope for their children to join the urban middle class.

The transformation of systems of elite education, which trained only a small proportion of the school age population, to systems of mass education was the fulfillment of a preindependence promise to parents. Universal literacy was sought for adults. The importance to political leaders of achieving enrollment targets is illustrated by the fact that targets were achieved and exceeded in many countries. The educational sector was the only one with this consistent investment experience. The political pressures came from both low and high income groups, which realized that the more schooling and certificates their children accumulated, the better their chances of finding secure and well-paying jobs. Cultural objectives like expanding the use of the national language and deepening the understanding of national history were also important. These objectives were translated into a rapidly increasing demand for school places. In most countries, the supply of school places has not yet satisfied private demand.

These educational objectives must be seen in the context of each country's development goals. Because increases in the economic wealth of a nation, or even rapid expansion of education, have not necessarily brought higher standards of living for the poor majority, development might be best defined in terms of an investment process which contributes to a more humane society. This process requires political systems that are, or will be, more responsive to the needs of the poor. It also requires rising real income as well as a more equal distribution and management of wealth.

To what extent have the educational objectives been achieved, and to what extent were they realistic? Some critics have argued that the objectives are at the same time too diverse, vague, and even contradictory to the effective goals for policymaking. Before attempting to

answer these questions, it is necessary to sketch some of the major
features of the relationships between formal education and development. We begin with a discussion of the two major theories about the
function of schooling in development.

Theories of Learning and Schooling

While we may know the technically optimal proportions of capital
and labor to make steel, we do not know with the same precision how
people learn. If we did, there would not be the constant debate over
theories of learning and the reappearance of methods discarded
decades ago in some countries, like the resurrection of rote learning
in teaching machines. Schooling, as distinct from learning, is not
mainly a technical process. It is a human process with important political dimensions. Thus, even with advances in learning theory, other
factors will have to change to see the improvements reflected in the
schools. Because of our desire to focus on questions of investment
policy related to efficiency, effectiveness and equity, we concentrate
on the theories mainly developed by economists rather than those of
psychologists.

Before proceeding, several definitions are required in order to lend
precision to the discussion. *Schooling* and *formal education* refer to
what is taught in school and school-related experiences, such as sports
teams and theater groups. *Education,* without an adjective, refers to
learning that can take place outside the school as well as inside. *Nonformal education* refers to organized educational activities that occur
outside the school, such as adult literacy courses and agricultural
extension services. Learning that is not organized can be termed *informal education* and includes all forms of nonschool experiences,
including those on the job.

Countries have tended to limit their systematic investment in education to only the formal and nonformal areas. Mass media, activities
of political parties, and measures to alter the family environment have
been less frequently used systematically as tools for changing attitudes
and behavior of either the young or the old. Figure 1 outlines the
input/output and the feedback dimensions of a learning system. These
dimensions should be noted: first, the important range of early factors

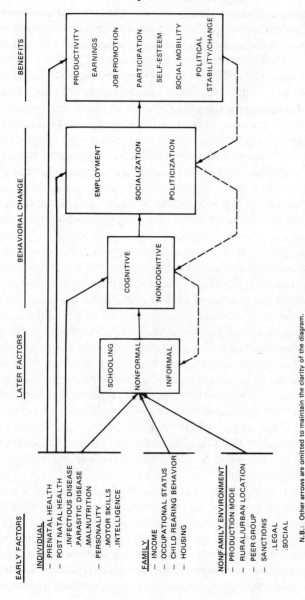

N.B.: Other arrows are omitted to maintain the clarity of the diagram.
For example, Family and Nonfamily Environment should have
arrows to Later Factors and Behavioral Change.

Fig. 1. The learning system: causes, consequences, and interaction.

like infant malnutrition, virtually all of which are now considered outside the scope of either formal or nonformal education in the poor countries; second, the important interactions (in Figure 1 dotted lines for feedback) that provide positive or negative reinforcement to behavioral change; third, the fact that formal and nonformal schooling appear as only two of the many factors in promoting behavioral change and benefits; and fourth, the diverse range of outcomes claimed for schooling. The input/output relationships among the factors will be discussed below.

To explore the possible reasons why the formal system of education has become so important in both poor and rich countries in less than 150 years, I now turn to a discussion of theories of schooling. Two basic theories—(1) the human capital or incrementalist, and (2) the structural—are used to describe the effect of education on individuals and the economy.

The human capital or incrementalist theory suggests that an invest- ment in education increases labor's productivity by embodying in that labor increased skills and knowledge. The schools are also sup- posed to develop the individual to his or her fullest potential. While different methods are used to measure human capital, they are all based on the cognitive effects of education, as captured by grades and tests of school achievement. In accordance with the neoclassical utilitarian paradigm, individual preferences are considered fixed or outside the realm of economic analysis. While preferences may change over time, the theory argues that consumption, investment and work preferences are not the outcomes of social institutions such as schools or individual experiences, but are considered only as inputs. The policy implications of this theory include the proposal that increased amounts of schooling for individuals with low schooling will increase their wages and also reduce social inequality.

The structural theory holds that educational systems are best under- stood not in terms of providing human capital to individuals or pro- moting economic equality, but rather in terms of their position in maintaining the status quo by reproducing the social order. While schooling does increase the productive capacity of workers, it also helps to diffuse the potentially explosive class relations which are generated by wide differences in wealth and authoritarian work relations. Structuralists argue, for example, that many of the supposed inefficiencies and perceived inadequacies of the educational system, like high dropout rates, functional illiteracy among primary and secondary school graduates, educated unemployment and the repeated failure of educational reforms, are, in fact, quite rational. They can best be understood in terms of the position the school plays in the reproduction of the society and the smooth integration of youth into the labor force. From this theory come five propositions.

The first proposition is that one cannot view educational policy as isolated from the context of an overall social policy. To change or improve, for example, the egalitarian aspects of schools requires an attack not only on education but also on political and perhaps economic life as well. The incrementalist, however, views schooling mainly as a technical process and therefore its recommendations are limited to technical recommendations like strengthening planning methods, improving teacher training, or raising teachers' salaries. In contrast, the structuralist assesses the feasibility of various policy recommendations with their compatibility with the reproduction of the social system.

The second proposition is that there are likely to be correspondences between the way the educational system operates internally and operation of the political and economic systems. That is, the basic structure of the social relations of the economy and its institutions—the degrees of inequality, the forms of authority, centralization of responsibility, and extent of subordination—are likely to be reproduced in the way the schools operate. The problem of student failure in school is a case in point. Incrementalists argue that students fail because teachers are inadequately prepared, textbooks are missing from the classrooms, teacher supervision is inadequate, teacher salaries are too low to attract the right kind of people into the profession, students lack intelligence, or parents are not sufficiently supportive of the efforts of their children to reinforce what the teachers are trying to accomplish. The structuralists argue that all of these points noted by the incrementalists could be improved, but their impact would not be substantial, as indicated by the systems analysis data in Chapter 4, compared to changing the factors outside of education which help determine educational policies and programs. They argue instead that education often acts so as not to maximize the full cognitive development of individuals, but rather to limit their development and leads to their leaving schools early. They argue that it is a major function of education to facilitate early school leaving to "cool people out". This experience legitimizes their relatively subordinate position in the economic system and justifies social inequality. Children who fail in primary and secondary school internalize their second-class citizenship for their lifetime.

The third proposition is that the primary role of schooling is to produce a work force, not to develop the capabilities of individuals to their fullest potential. Structuralists contend that the apparent returns to investment in human capital tend to be due more to the screening effects of schools in labeling prospective job candidates, rather than to the development of individual talent. Primary and secondary qualifications and university degrees are the pass keys to limited opportunities, especially in poor countries, for well-paying jobs.[2]

A fourth proposition is that whereas incrementalist theory tends to see schools having their primary function in generating skills and sees that a major problem of educational policy is being able to generate enough skills, the structuralists argue a different point of view. They say that the one conclusion that we can reach from the last thirty years of educational experience in both developing and developed countries is that school systems can quite efficiently and rapidly expand the supply of skills needed for entry into the labor force. The real problem, they argue, is the over-supply of skills. On the one hand, an over-supply of educated labor is a response to the necessity of political regimes getting support from middle and upper income parents regardless of the costs in terms of social inequality and inefficiency in manpower allocation. On the other hand, there is a tendency to produce over-supplies of labor adequate to the tasks at hand on all levels of the labor force in order to produce the surplus of job seekers who are necessary to keep the labor force in line.

The final proposition is that educational policy does not determine tradeoffs between various social objectives. The structuralists argue that political and economic forces shape both the tradeoffs within the education sector and among the social sectors. For example, when the obstacles to educational reforms are sufficiently removed, it will permit not only changes in the education system but also changes in health and welfare as well. Countries that have enjoyed successful educational reforms, like Cuba and China, also have experienced health and welfare reforms as well once the obstacles to the planning and implementation of reforms were removed. The structuralists' theory rejects the idea of there being a tradeoff between various social objectives.

The policy implications of the structuralist theory is that basic changes have to be made in the power relations of different interest groups and in the structure of the firm and other economic mechanisms before the dysfunctions of the school system will disappear. Evidence is available and will be presented in this book to support both theories. In the past few years, however, the balance of evidence appears to have tipped in favor of the structuralists' position. Professor Mark Blaug, who is not a structuralist, recently reviewed the theories in the *Journal of Economic Literature*. He concluded that the incrementalist or human capital theory is now in "crisis", and its explanation for education "increasingly unconvincing". He predicted that the incrementalist theory will never die, but will "gradually fade away".[3]

Magnitude of the Educational Investment

In order to expand enrollments, most developing countries increased the proportion of both the national budget and the national income that was spent on education. As shown in Table 1, public expenditures have grown rapidly. For the period between 1960 and 1968, public expenditures almost tripled in Asia and doubled in Africa and Latin America. Although declining somewhat for other regions, public expenditures doubled between 1970 and 1973 in the Arab States. These are public expenditures by ministries of education, and seriously underestimate the total cost of formal education, the inclusion of which could double the figure for public expenditure. Educational expenditures in other ministries and firms are usually not counted. Also excluded is the cost to parents of sending children to school, including income foregone, sending children to school, income foregone by children, and expenditures on private education, which are particularly high in Latin America.

TABLE 1

Public Expenditure on Education
(Per annum percentage increase)

	1960-1968[a]	1970-1973[b]
Asia	23	18.8
Africa	14	11.7
Latin America	17	12.6
Arab States	11	17.5
Mean	16	13.6
Developed Countries	-	12.1

Source: [a]Leo Goldstone, A summary statistical review of *Learning in the World,* International Commission on the Development of Education (UNESCO, Series A, No. 1, 1971), p. 25, Table 15.
[b]UNESCO, *Statistical Yearbook: 1975* (Paris, 1976), p. 70.

In most regions, per annum growth in educational expenditures during both periods doubled, and in some areas tripled, that of growth in gross national product (GNP). For example, from 1970 to 1973 the GNP of developing countries increased at an average annual rate of 6.3 percent. During this period, public expenditure on education grew at an average annual rate of 13.6 percent. No other sector showed a higher rate of increase in public expenditure. While reliable figures are not yet available, on a global basis, to indicate the proportion of total cost represented by capital cost, estimates range from 15 to 20 percent.

In the past, investment in formal education was seen as essential to high and sustained rates of economic growth. The experience of the United States, Japan, and more recently Korea, is often cited to support the causal link between education and growth. Furthermore, people with more schooling have higher incomes in all countries. Educational investment was also considered essential for achieving political socialization, occupational status, modernization, and other social objectives.

It has recently been observed that high rates of educational output followed rather than preceded initial spurts in economic growth in the

United States, Japan, and Korea. Other factors appear to be more significant determinants of growth. Some countries, such as India and Sri Lanka, have high levels of educational output but low economic growth. Beyond some minimum threshold, a high rate of investment in formal education cannot be considered to be a necessary condition for a high rate of economic growth.

Educational expenditures produced rapid increases in the number of students in developing countries. To illustrate enrollment trends, four representative countries with economies at different levels of development were selected—Afghanistan, Kenya, Colombia, and Brazil. The rates of increase per annum were highest for higher education, ranging from 11 percent in Brazil to 28 percent in Kenya. Primary education has the lowest rate of increased enrollment in almost all countries, ranging from 7 percent in Brazil and Venezuela to 11 percent in Afghanistan. The rate of expansion of secondary enrollment is similar to that of higher education. Even with massive investment efforts, countries, which more than twenty years earlier had espoused universal primary education were, by the mid 1970s, far from achieving it.

In any case, just how "massive" have inputs been to primary education? A disproportionate share of public educational expenditures has, in fact, gone to higher levels of education. The data in Table 2 show that while 70 percent of the total school enrollment in Asia was in the primary category, it received only 43 percent of the budget. Eighteen percent of the budget paid for 3.5 percent of the Asian students who were in higher education.

Barely fifteen years ago it was thought that the higher the rate of educational output, the better for both society and the individual. Universal primary schooling was a common goal across countries. Shortages in middle level manpower were projected for decades, and the demand for university graduates would not be satisfied in the planners' lifetimes. Insatiable demand for the output at all levels was the basic assumption.

These predictions of output needs now appear to be grossly naïve for four reasons. First, population growth among the school age cohorts was much higher than expected, forcing all but a few countries, such as China and Cuba, to delay or quietly abandon meeting the

TABLE 2
Distribution of Educational Budgets and Enrollments by Region
(circa 1973)

Region	Primary		Secondary		Higher	
	Percent of budget	Percent of enrollment	Percent of budget	Percent of enrollment	Percent of budget	Percent of enrollment
Africa[a] (excluding Arab States)	49	88.4	34	10.9	13	0.7
Asia (excluding Arab States)	43	70.3	30	26.2	18	3.5
Arab States[b]	40	74.3	36	22.5	20	3.2
Latin America	52	80.9	26	15.1	17	4.0
Mean	48	76.5	30	20.7	17	2.8

Notes:
[a]Percent of budget to primary education is the average of "Eastern" and "Western" Africa regions. Budget based on a sample that includes Sudan.
[b]Budget based on a sample that includes Turkey.

Sources: Manuel Zymelman, *Patterns of Educational Expenditures* (Washington, D.C.: World Bank, Staff Working Paper No. 246, November 1976); UNESCO, *Statistical Year Book, 1975* (Paris, 1976).

target of universal primary education. Second, actual rates of economic growth were often not as high as predicted, and jobs were not created as fast as needed to absorb the middle and higher level graduates. Third, planners assumed that new job slots could be filled by school leavers working as apprentices or clerks, whereas many of the jobs actually required experienced workers. And fourth, political pressure from upper income parents forced more rapid expansion of secondary and higher education than originally planned, and investment in primary education was reduced. Thus, manpower shortages and other early justifications for high rates of output are now seen in a different perspective.

Benefits and Costs of Education

While some economists feel that no reasonable measurement of educational benefits is possible, such an attitude is not shared by most students of the problem. They suggest that such measurements are useful for policy decisions, when combined with noneconomic information. These benefits include provision of manpower, cultivation and selection of potential talent, and reduced reliance on the market for services requiring basic cognitive skills. Educational benefits realized during the schooling process can be classified as consumption. After the period of formal education, the successive benefits can be thought of as deriving from prior investment, because schooling yields benefits in future time periods. Important external benefits of education, those that influence one's family, neighbors, and community may exist. These would include participation in community affairs, improved productivity from coworkers, lower law enforcement and insurance costs.[4]

I will now review the employment and income distribution benefits.

Employment

It was believed that a major reason for investing in schooling was that it would lead to increases in both the productivity of physical capital and in value added. But as more is learned about human capital and its relation to productivity, it can be seen that the cognitive benefits of schooling may not always significantly influence productivity.[5] Thus, the essential assumption of the human capital theory is in question.[6] This conclusion needs some explanation because it appears to be inconsistent with the early empirical research.

Early studies showed a modest correlation between the per capita income level of a country and the average amount of schooling of the population.[7] But correlation studies of this type are no indication of causality. The investment in schooling could just as well have followed as preceded the higher per capita income levels.

Other studies using macroproduction functions attributed the residual variance in output, which was unexplained by the value of capital and the quantity of labor, to the increase in quality of labor.[8] In other words, whatever was unmeasured was attributed to the effect of schooling. The research was not designed to examine the effects of education, and educational speculations which tried to explain the results were exaggerated. For example, attributing the residual to an improvement in human capital is an assertion for which there is no evidence. From microeconomic and sectoral data it could be expected that informal education outside the school, including on-the-job experience, would be more important than schooling in explaining this residual.[9] Other factors may be involved as well, like some behavioral traits that increase a worker's wage, but are not necessarily "productive".

The labor force in a growing number of developing countries is increasingly characterized by unemployment among the educated. Although there are limitations in the data[10] (in particular, the probable positive relationship between education and labor force participation, and consequent under-reporting of unemployment for those with the least education) Figure 2 nevertheless suggests some interesting observations. In Sudan, Peru, and Pakistan, for example, unemployment increases until it peaks at "secondary completed", and then declines somewhat at higher levels of education. (Mark Blaug has reported a similar "inverted U" pattern for Sri Lanka, Iran, Argentina, Venezuela, India, Malaysia, and Syria.)[11] However, unemployment at the "higher completed" level is still greater than unemployment among the illiterates. Kenya, however, has the opposite experience. Unemployment at the "illiterate" level is very high; it declines through "secondary completed"; it increases again at "higher completed".

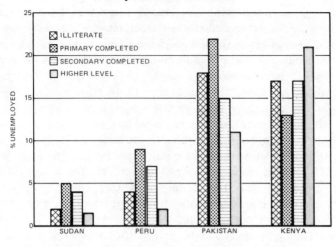

Fig. 2. Educated unemployment in four countries.

Note:

Sudan: Circa 1974 data for the Khartoum area only. "Higher completed" is defined as university completed; the sample size is very small. Years of schooling that correspond to a particular educational classification (for example, "primary completed") are not specified.

Peru: Circa 1970 data for urban areas only. "Illiterates" include kindergarden. Number of school years corresponding to educational classifications are not specified.

Pakistan: Circa 1972 data for rural and urban areas. "Primary completed" is defined as passing 5 grades; "secondary completed", 12 grades; "higher completed" 16 to 18 grades. Survey results (from which data was derived) are not official and several problems with the data make them not fully reliable.

Kenya: Circa 1970 data for Nairobi only. "Primary completed" is defined as 7 to 8 years; "secondary completed", 11 to 12 years; "higher completed", 13 to 14 years. Sample sizes for 11 to 12 and 13 to 14 years are small.

Source:

Sudan: Teshome Mulat, *Educated Unemployment in the Sudan,* Education and Employment Working Paper No. 5 (Geneva: ILO, July 1975), p. 13, Fig. 1.

Peru: Jan Versluis, *Education, the Labour Market and Employment, A Case Study for Peru,* Education and Employment Working Paper No. 4 (Geneva: ILO, December 1974), p. 5, Table 1.4.

Pakistan: *Housing, Economic and Demographic Survey,* 1973, Vol. II (Islamabad: Census Office, 1973), pp. 82 and 92.

Kenya: *Employment, Incomes and Equality, A Strategy for Increasing Productive Employment in Kenya* (Geneva: ILO, 1972), p. 59, Table 18.

The high unemployment rate among those who have completed schooling can be attributed (among other reasons) to rising expectations and greater discrimination in job selecting, as well as to financial security due to graduates' middle-to-high income parents. In Sudan, for example, unemployment was observed to be higher in groups that had finished schooling than in groups that had not. This suggests that while "incompletes" may lower their job expectations, those who successfully complete primary or secondary education may choose unemployment rather than a job they consider to be beneath their qualifications. In traditional societies, where private networks allocate a much higher percentage of jobs than even the "old school tie" networks of the developed countries, an unemployed high school or college graduate is simply passing time until his or her entry into an "appropriate" position is secured by friends or relatives. In addition, it is interesting to note that 60 percent of those unemployed were without previous job experience, or were working beneath their anticipated social status.

Underemployment of the educated is also becoming a problem of increasing magnitude; secondary school leavers now take jobs once effectively performed by primary school graduates. Expatriates often still hold high level jobs: until recently in Tunisia, 50 percent of the secondary and university teaching positions were filled by foreigners, while graduates financed by state scholarships were unemployed, underemployed, or had emigrated. Two reasons seem to explain this contradiction. First, incentives and streaming were insufficient to obtain enough math, science, and language teachers for secondary schools from the university graduates. Second, teachers of French nationality were offered to the government on concessionary terms.

Even in countries with high levels of unemployment of the educated in, say, engineering, there is often a great demand for places in engineering school.[12] This apparent paradox can be explained. Although the chances of getting a job as a secondary school teacher may be better than getting a job as an engineer, the higher lifetime earnings of an engineer mean that it is worth staying unemployed longer if there is a chance of getting an engineer's job. Because university leavers tend to come from upper income families, they can rely on the family for economic support while looking for a job. Thus the private incentive to get a job is much less for many of the educated unemployed.

Past observers have felt that there was a synergistic relationship between schooling and the creation of employment. More recent observers have determined that the evidence suggests that education cannot make a major contribution to reducing unemployment. There would be exceptions only to the extent that nationals were allowed to take the place of expatriates, and that jobs were created in the education sector.

Large wage differentials among occupations are seen by incrementalists as a major reason for unemployment of the educated and for the increasing inequality in income distribution. This chapter is not the place to review the inefficiencies of the labor market, particularly with regard to wage distortions.[13] But it is important to point out that the classical rationale of the need for the incentive provided by wage differentials no longer applies when, in many developing countries, a mechanic earns ten times as much as an agricultural laborer—or a doctor earns 100 times as much. An adequate supply of manpower can be achieved at much lower wages. This also suggests that the "market" forces seem to be out of line with national needs for lower labor costs among skilled and professional workers. Table 3 indicates the variation in income by amount of schooling for Uganda, India, and Brazil. In Uganda a secondary school graduate's average salary is twenty times the per capita income; in India it is about eight times. Brazilian university graduates earn more than sixteen times the average income of illiterates. While in the developed countries these differentials seem to be shrinking, in the developing countries there is some evidence to show that they are expanding.

The striking disparities in wage differences between developed and developing countries are illustrated in Table 4. In developed countries, the ratios of average annual earnings for those with higher education to those with primary education alone range between 2.13 in Norway to 2.63 in Canada. In developing countries, ratios range from a low of 2.24 in the Philippines to a high of 12.07 in Uganda. The same holds true for the "secondary over primary" ratio: the mean for developed countries is 1.43 with a high of 1.50; in the developing countries, however, the mean is 2.39 with a high of 4.28. Thus, the lifetime incentive of getting a certificate in developing countries may

John Simmons

TABLE 3

Average Yearly Salaries by Level of Education in Uganda,
India and Brazil

Educational level	Uganda (1965)	India (1960-61)	Brazil (1970)
		£	
Illiterates	-	-	114
Primary	-	-	243
Junior Secondary/Middle	209	131	-
School Certificate/Secondary	556	185	489
Higher Certificate/Indian Graduate/ Brazilian College	852	311	698
Ugandan Graduate/Brazilian Higher	1373	-	1731
Income per Head	28	25	175
Salaries as multiples of income per head			
Junior Secondary/Middle	7.3	5.4	-
School Certificate/Secondary	20.0	7.7	2.8
Higher Certificate/Indian Graduate/ Brazilian College	30.4	12.4	3.9
Ugandan Graduate/Brazilian Higher	49.0	-	9.9

Notes:

[a]The data refer to average earnings over all age groups.
[b]The data for Uganda refer to civil service earnings and those for India to average urban earnings.
[c]Indian earnings are converted from Rs to £s at the 1961 exchange rate.
[d]Under educational level, that for Uganda is shown first, followed by the roughly comparable Indian, then Brazilian level.
[e]Brazilian earnings are converted from NCr to £ and income per head from US$ to £ at the 1970 exchange rate.

Sources:

(i) Uganda: J. B. Knight, "The determination of wages and salaries in Uganda", *Oxford University Institute of Economics and Statistics Bulletin,* vol. 29, no. 3 (1967): 233-64.

(ii) India: Mark Blaug, Richard Layard and Maureen Woodhall, *The Causes and Consequences of Graduate Unemployment in India* (London: Penguin Press, 1969), Table 7.1. Data for India and Uganda were cited by Jolly and Colclough, "Africa manpower plans: an evaluation", *International Labour Review,* vol. 106, nos. 2-3 (1972): 230.

(iii) Brazil: I. M. Hume, "Notes on the distribution of income in Brazil", mimeograph (World Bank, 1972). Income per head is from 1973 World Population Data Sheet—Population Reference Bureau Inc., and is from World Bank data.

TABLE 4

*Mean Ratios of Average Annual Earnings of Labor by Educational
Level and Country*

	Educational levels compared				
Degree of developmenta	Primary over none	Secondary over Primary	Higher over Secondary	Higher over Primary	Higher over none
Developed	-b	1.43	1.68	2.39	-b
Intermediate	2.40	1.87	1.81	3.36	8.85
Less developed	2.43	2.39	2.67	6.39	17.31

Notes:

aDeveloped: United States, Canada, United Kingdom, The Netherlands, France, Norway.

Intermediate: Greece, Israel, Mexico, Chile, Colombia.

Less Developed: Malaysia, Philippines, Ghana, Republic of Korea, Uganda, Nigeria, India.

bData not available.

Source: G. Psacharopoulos, *Returns to Education* (San Francisco: Jossey-Bass Inc., 1973), p. 132.

be increasing. Economic incentives for more schooling may not be reduced until wages are realigned.

In short, two seemingly contradictory phenomena can be observed: (a) relative wage differentials between graduates of different levels are either widening or are relatively stable; (b) there is, in general, an oversupply of higher level graduates, as indicated by unemployment data.

Given this oversupply, why is the market mechanism not operating to reduce differentials? It is important to note that the labor allocation process in the more developed societies tends to be more impersonal than in the less developed countries where political and familial criteria are often applied to screen job seekers. Labor force surveys show that the majority of applicants get their job through a close friend or relative.

One interpretation is as follows: (a) a few more years of education does not by itself raise the productivity of labor. Job experience is required in addition to education. This appears to be borne out by age-income profiles for education levels. Beginning wages are, of course, higher for higher levels of education. More importantly, the rate of increase of wages over time is higher for higher levels of education. (b) Consider, then, the time path of a developing economy with a rapidly growing population, falling age structure, and rising enrollment rates at all levels. The growth rate of graduates from higher levels of the education system will significantly exceed the growth rates of the economy and employment in the urban sector. If the crucial modern sector inputs are capital and labor with schooling *and* experience, then rising wage differentials are consistent with high levels of unemployed graduates in the early years after graduation without work experience. This phenomenon is illustrated for India in Table 5, which shows that the average waiting period for employment of

TABLE 5
Year in which First Employment was Obtained: 1954 Graduates

Year of first employment	Percentage of graduates	Assumed average initial waiting period (years)	Col. (1) × Col. (2)
	(1)	(2)	(3)
Already employed	25.0	0	0
1954	25.0	¼	6.3
1955	18.2	1	18.2
1956	12.0	2	24.0
1957	6.9	3	20.7
1958	4.0	4	16.0
1959	1.7	5	8.5
1960	0.6	6	3.6

Notes:

[a]The table gives data for those graduates employed in 1960, and excludes the 9.8 percent unemployed. Percentages may not add up to 100: 6.6 percent are not available and, therefore, cannot be determined.

[b]In estimating column (2) it was assumed that students graduate at the end of June, when examination results become available.

Source: M. Blaug and others, *The Causes and Consequences of Graduate Unemployment in India,* p. 79.

university graduates has increased over time. (c) It is not surprising, therefore, that students continue to pursue higher levels of education despite the rising level of unemployment for graduates. Given that the cost of higher education is heavily subsidized, and that the foregone earnings of education levels without experience on the job are small compared to wages with education and experience, the risk of unemployment in the early years is less significant than the possible maximum return. (d) From a social standpoint, however, this private demand for more education is not optimal. It is unlikely that the modern sector will grow rapidly enough, given capital shortages, to provide the necessary employment for this high-grade manpower. Already, increasing waiting periods push back the time when high level graduates will have gained on-the-job experience, and have decreased the social returns. In general, therefore, it would be advisable for the government to suppress the demand based on low opportunity cost and high private returns, and to divert the capital so utilized into the creation of employment at the lower educational and skill levels. This would not only improve the income distribution immediately, it would also increase growth prospects by widening the base of the modern sector job pyramid, thus improving the productivity of the manpower employed at the top of the pyramid.

These technical arguments ignore the social and political aspects of the income distribution. Structuralists contend that professionals and administrators would not tolerate reductions in their wages simply because their children now wait a few more months before obtaining their first job than they did ten years ago. Such middle and upper income employees are in a position to exert some influence over their wages, so there is no political contradiction between rigid wages on the upper end of the scale and temporarily unemployed secondary and university graduates. In 1974 Robert McNamara called the education and employment problem one of "the most disturbing paradoxes of our time". With the benefit of recent data it appears that the paradox can now be seen as a dilemma whose solutions extend beyond the confines of the education system to political and economic causes. A central policy issue is, then, how can a useful dialogue be started among the different interest groups to explore and implement solutions.

Income Distribution

In most countries the poor quickly learn that schooling is an escape from poverty for only a few. They are the first to drop out because they need to work, the first to be pushed out because they fall asleep in class, and the first to fail their French or English tests because upper income children have better opportunities to learn at home. The hope brought to village parents by the construction of the primary school soon fades. The possibility of attaining enough schooling to secure a steady, even menial, job for their son, let alone for their daughter, seems just beyond their grasp. They are never one of the lucky parents. Before they had a school, any amount of schooling would have satisfied their aspiration. Now a primary school certificate is needed, and in some countries even those with some secondary schooling cannot get steady jobs; they could never afford to send their son away to town for secondary education.

Does schooling widen the gap between rich and poor? Given the objective that some people have for schooling to promote social mobility and to redistribute income, the answer, surprisingly, is "yes" for most developing countries. Better data and models for examining this question are only recently available.[14] The data indicate that children of upper income groups tend to receive more years of schooling than children of the poor. In Tunisia, 8.8 times the number of students whose fathers are of high socioeconomic status are receiving higher education than one would expect from the proportion of high socioeconomic status students in the population. Data from a study of students at the University of Karachi in Pakistan show that children of parents with a university education are over represented by twenty-seven times compared to children of illiterate parents. Research conducted in Brazil, India, and Colombia[15] has led to a similar conclusion: the educational process acts as a disequalizer of income. Government policies on educational expenditure and regressive tax systems have failed to adjust the inherent disequalizing forces and, in fact, have supported and reinforced them. The poor pay a higher percentage of their income in taxes than the rich. And it is tax and other public revenue which pay the cost of expensive higher education which mainly benefit the children of the rich. Table 6 illustrates the relationship between family income levels and educational attainment in

TABLE 6
*Distribution of Families of 1954 Graduates and of
All Families by Average Monthly Family Income*

Average monthly income of family (Rs)	Percentage of graduates families	Percentage of all families
500 and above	23.3	1.5
200-499	45.7	10.0
Below 200	29.1	88.5

Source: M. Blaug and others, *The Causes and Consequences of Graduate Unemployment in India*, p. 131.

India. Only 1.5 percent of India's families have 23.3 percent of the university graduates; these are the upper income families. And, when this process is repeated in the next generation, schooling becomes a factor for widening the gap between rich and poor.

While schooling is not the only factor which increases social inequality, it appears to be an essential one because it legitimizes the achievement of high-status occupations and increases the human capital of the rich. Students enter school with considerable differences in ability. Some of these abilities are genetically determined, but most are shaped after birth by the environment.[16] Children from upper income groups usually begin school better nourished, better cared for, and with more exposure to situations conducive to the development of cognitive and affective skills useful in school and in white collar work than children from low income groups. For example, in many developing countries, a second language is begun in primary school and even used as a language of instruction. Children coming from homes where this language is spoken obviously have a considerable advantage over children who do not.

Once the student enters school, promotion is based on performance in cognitive achievement and other personality skills. In contrast to the primary school system of the more developed countries, primary schools in many less developed countries do not have a system of automatic promotion from one grade to the next. Rather, children who do not get a minimum composite score for their courses (sometimes if they only fail one course) have to repeat the grade. This often encourages a syndrome of failure. Students who repeatedly find themselves scolded for failure and low marks learn to expect to fail. Their confidence and self-esteem is eroded, and they lose their hope of succeeding. This attitude of expecting failure in academic subjects is carried over into activities outside the school. Their poor performance in school legitimizes their low position in society. Upper income children who enjoy the combination of more developed cognitive skills before entering primary school and school promotion that immediately begins to reinforce their positive behavior have a higher probability of gaining more years of schooling.

Internal and External Efficiency of the Educational System

In order to discuss the internal efficiency of the educational system, the question should be asked: What is the relationship between the input of investment in formal education and the output, measured in terms of the quality and quantity of students?

School Inputs and Learning Outcomes

The members of the technical school of educational planners have measured inputs in terms of the quantity and cost of resources, including teachers, and output in terms of student test performance and grades. The structuralists have tended to emphasize the qualitative dimensions of inputs, such as what is taught and how, and the nature of the outputs, including personality traits and norms of activity learned in the classroom. The two schools of educators have come to very different conclusions about the efficiency of the educational system.

To analyze the question from the perspective of the incrementalists first, then, it might be expected that investment in certain types of physical or human capital, such as better buildings, science laboratories or teachers, would increase the quality of educational production. Have these improvements and increases in real costs per student been translated into increased achievement scores and other measures of school output? Western data suggest that they have not.[17] And the studies for developing countries are consistent with these findings.[18]

There are several explanations for this apparent anomaly. The first is based on the production function analysis, which suggests that nonschool inputs like parental influence and child health are more influential on test scores than the school inputs. Thus, replacement of existing school buildings, constructed from local materials, with others of reinforced concrete may make a more pleasing structure and place to work, but has little effect on achievement. Science laboratories cannot be used well when teachers are untrained and inexperienced and when test tubes are locked in closets to prevent breakage. Second, as enrollments have expanded under programs of mass education, a greater percentage of low income children are in school, particularly at the primary level. These students tend to have less encouragement at home, suffer brain damage as an effect of malnutrition, fall asleep in class as one result of low calorie intake, and receive less attention from middle class teachers than do students in upper income groups. The quality of new teachers usually suffers in mass expansion, partly because there are few incentives to keep good teachers in rural and low income areas, where they are needed most. Thus, achievement test scores for a district or a country may fall as a real unit cost rises.

Production function studies relate both school and nonschool inputs to the types of output like reading achievement that schooling is supposed to influence.[19] Earlier studies consistently demonstrated internal *in*efficiency between inputs and outputs among educational systems, and two national studies completed in 1967 and 1966 (the Plowden Report for England and Coleman's report for the United States) provided further evidence. Jencks and his colleagues summarized the literature in 1972, and Bowles and Gintis provided new insight in 1975.[20] Chapter 4 in this book by Simmons and Alexander reviews the literature for developing countries. While the methods and findings of these studies have been criticized, little contradictory evidence has been published.

The findings are quite specific. They show that the current technologies of formal education are inefficient in their promotion of learning, in both the developing and the developed countries. Additional marginal inputs of capital or labor with these current technologies, like the quality or quantity of teacher training or reading curricula, may have little or no influence on the amount that students learn in school, as measured by achievement tests and grades. What seems to be more important in learning the subjects tested in school are family environment, peer group interaction, personality, and nutrition. The findings do not study the minimum efforts required to reach a learning threshold, which could permit self-teaching.

Students in classes of twenty-five learn no faster than those in classes with forty. Teacher training courses of two or three years produce results no better than courses of one year. There is some evidence to suggest that length of teaching experience affects student's cognitive behavior, but not in all countries. Students who have access to well-stocked libraries and well-equipped laboratories in school perform little better than students with poor facilities.

The research is not comprehensive. It is not known if classes of ten students perform better than classes of twenty-five to forty, because schools in the surveys did not have less than twenty-five students. Private schools often have class sizes that are half the size of public school classes. It is not known if this size is more effective. Cutting the size of public school classes by half would mean, however, almost doubling school costs in developing countries because teachers' salaries are 90 percent of current expenditures. While it appears that an increase in unit cost does not significantly improve cognitive achievement, it is not known what would happen to the progress of student learning if the unit cost of capital or labor inputs was substantially lowered.

Surprisingly few data are available on the functional nature of learning outcomes. While studies exist which compare math and reading scores across countries,[21] they do not indicate what the score is equivalent to in terms of everyday functions such as reading and understanding a national newspaper. UNESCO has maintained that four years of primary schooling would be necessary to achieve adequate literacy. Data for Tunisia, however, suggest that six grades of primary education may not be enough for a large percentage of students to reach an adequate level for reading and understanding the newspaper. These data show that 73 percent could not read French adequately, 62 percent could not read Arabic adequately, and 77 percent did not have adequate arithmetic skills.[22] Although the students surveyed were sixth graders, they had been in school for an average of eight years. The primary system in this country, moreover, has high quality inputs compared with those of many other developing countries. Reading test results in other countries support this conclusion.[23]

School Wastage and Costs

Wastage rates, including dropouts, pushouts and repeaters, are an important dimension of internal efficiency. (A dropout occurs at the student's volition while a pushout is the result of school action.)[24] Most developing countries do not have systems of automatic promotion from one grade level to another. Quotas and examinations select the desired number of students to pass to the next grade. Some students may be promoted to the next grade or the next level (cycle), but decide for economic or other reasons not to continue. Both types of students are measured by wastage rates, the causes of which are the subject of debate. Questions have been raised regarding (1) the adequacy of internal factors such as the content, organization and structure of the education system, especially the treatment of village children by urban teachers, and (2) the impact of external factors such as social, economic, political, and cultural constraints. Poverty is a major reason why students leave before completion. Table 7 gives data on the rates of dropout and repetition in primary school. Data from Latin America and Africa suggest that more than 50 percent of the students who start primary school drop out before finishing. Dropout rates for Africa and Latin America range from 26.2 to 81.3 percent and from 33.1 to 74.7 percent respectively. Several of the Asian countries in the sample have automatic promotion systems, thus raising the mean level. Secondary school dropout rates are only slightly better, as shown in Table 8. Repetition rates, on the other hand, are somewhat lower. Africa has the highest rate at the primary level with 20 to 54 percent of all students repeating. The rate in Africa remains comparatively high during the first cycle of secondary education, but dips below that of Asia during the second cycle. Repetition rates in Latin America are low at the primary level with a range of 1.7 to 11.6 percent and continue to decline during the first and second cycles of the secondary level.

Table 9 illustrates wide interregional and intraregional variations in

John Simmons

TABLE 7
Primary Wastage Rates, Cohorts Entering
Primary School Around 1960
(Median value of percentage of total in
school)

Countries in major regions	Dropouts and pushouts	Repeaters
Africa	54.0	40.7
Latin America	61.6	5.3
Asia	20.2	10.3
Europe	18.3	3.6

Sources: Leo Goldstone, *A Summary Statistical Review of Learning in the World* (Paris: UNESCO, 1972), p. 15.
International Bureau of Education, *A Statistical Study of Wastage at School* (Paris: UNESCO, 1972), p. 20.

TABLE 8
Secondary Wastage Rates, Cohorts Entering General Secondary
School Around 1960
(Median value of percentage of total in school)

Countries in major regions	First cycle		Second cycle	
	Dropout/Pushouts	Repeaters	Dropout/Pushouts	Repeaters
Africa	30.8	26.5	41.9	24.2
Latin America	33.6	9.4	18.5	3.5
Asia	11.8	20.7	18.1	37.7
Europe	20.1	2.5	11.4	_ a

Note:

[a]Data not available.

Sources: Leo Goldstone, *A Summary Statistical Review of Learning in the World* (Paris: UNESCO, 1972), p. 15.
International Bureau of Education, *A Statistical Study of Wastage at School* (Paris: UNESCO, 1972), p. 20.

TABLE 9

Approximate Education Survival Rates
(for 1960 Cohort; both sexes)

Regions	Percentage of enrollment in grade 1 in 1960 that reached grade 4	
Mean for all regions	47	
East Asia	95	
Japan		99
Other East Asia		91
South Asia	48	
Middle South Asia		44
South-East Asia		54
South-West Asia		67
Africa[a]	66	
Western Africa		60
Eastern Africa		63
Middle Africa		47
Northern Africa		85
Latin America	34	
Tropical South America		29
Middle America		35
Temperate South America		56
Caribbean		36

Note:

[a]Excluding Southern Africa.

Source: UN World Population Conference, *Educational Development: World and Regional Statistical Trends and Projections until 1985* (Paris: UNESCO, 1974), Annex II, p. 1.

education survival rates for grades one through four. Overall, Latin America has the lowest survival rate, particularly in Tropical South America with only 29 percent of enrollment in grade one reaching grade four. Asia, on the other hand, has wide intraregional differences ranging from a survival rate of 95 percent in East Asia to only 44 percent in Middle South Asia.

If the dropouts occur late in the cycle, could it not be argued that students get sufficient benefits? In a few countries, dropouts may be

concentrated at the end of the cycle. But in most, the wastage proportion is either constant at each grade or bunched near the beginning of
the cycle. The data in Table 10 are for an African country with a per
capita income of $130. It shows that for the last year that was measured

TABLE 10
Wastage Rates by Primary Grades

Grade	Enrollment in the first grade reduced to 1000		
	1959/60	1961/62	1965/66
1	1000	1000	1000
2	651	608	674
3	424	428	489
4	292	304	345
5	96	127	170
6	64	97	145

Source: Philip H. Coombs and Jacques Hallek, *Managing Educational Costs* (London: Oxford University Press, 1972), p. 75.

(1965-66), only 15 percent of the entering class reached the sixth grade,
while 51 percent dropped out before reaching fourth grade. This is
nonetheless an improvement over earlier years where, for example, in
1959-60 only 6 percent of the entering class reached the sixth grade.

   Why are the wastage rates higher for developing countries than for
developed countries? There are four possible explanations, but these
remain speculative because there are little good data on the determinants
of wastage in developing countries.[25] First, the supply of school places,
expressed as a percentage of the school age cohort, is higher in developed
countries, thus obviating the need to reduce the number seeking admission, as is necessary in the developing countries. Lack of finance and
of local self-reliance are the main constraints to expanding enrollment.
Second, individuals in developing countries generally have less motivation to obtain more years of schooling. While the poor of the
Brazilian Northeast are aware that the Paulistas of the South enjoy
high standards of living, in part because of their length of schooling,
the probability of the children of the poor reaching second grade is

about one in two and that of getting a university degree about two in 1000. This is not encouraging to most parents. Furthermore, children of the rural poor, unlike most upper and middle income children, have responsibilities beyond doing well in school. They have errands to run, animals to tend, and siblings to look after. By the time boys and girls reach age twelve or so, they must do the work of adults. Third, parents of poor children are not as understanding or supportive about doing homework or learning foreign languages as are parents of upper income children. In fact, the behavior of low income parents is often dysfunctional, if the objective is to keep the child in school as long as possible.[26] They may punish their children severely for school failure, a behavior which encourages the children to quit school. Thus, the link between motivation and wastage rates across countries is closely related to the proportion of the poor in those countries. Finally, the costs of education, both direct and in earnings foregone, are often too great for the poor to afford. And, as can be seen in Table 11, the

TABLE 11

Ratios of Social Costs by Educational Levels per Student per Year (primary = 1)

Degree of development	Secondary/Primary	Higher/Primary
Developed[a]	6.6	17.6
Intermediate[b]	6.6	20.9
Less developed[c]	11.9	87.9

Notes:

[a]New Zealand, United Kingdom, United States.
[b]Chile, Colombia, Israel, Mexico.
[c]Ghana, India, Kenya, Republic of Korea, Nigeria, Uganda. Social costs are defined as direct costs plus earnings foregone.

Source: George Psacharopoulos, *Returns to Education* (1973), p. 126.

higher the level of education, the higher the cost. The social cost of higher education is 87.9 times higher than primary in a sample of less developed countries.

If analysis of the functional reading data and the wastage data are combined, surprising economic *hypotheses* can be reached about efficiency at the primary level. First, a significant proportion of primary school students quit school before completing the primary cycle, thus yielding low or insignificant private benefits. Second, even if they complete the primary cycle, students may not have achieved even the minimum cognitive skills like newspaper reading to have economic utility. And third, if the real economic benefits of the skills learned in primary school are minimal, the high social rate of return to primary education may be largely a measure of the effect of requiring a certificate in the employer's selection process, rather than of an increase in productivity resulting from primary education.[27] If these hypotheses can be supported by further research, they provide a basic challenge to the human capital theory. It can also be a result of the affective traits they learn like deference to authority.

Unit costs are another dimension of internal efficiency, and are an essential factor in rate of return calculations, discussed in the next section. The data in Table 12 suggest that (1) the average social cost, or public expenditure in developing countries for a year of schooling, rises rapidly from the primary to the higher levels and (2) students who

TABLE 12

Index of Social Unit Costs per Student Year

(100 = direct public expenditures)

Degree of development	Primary	Secondary	Higher
Developed[a]	100	172	660
Intermediate[b]	100	272	1439
Less developed[c]	100	498	5033

Notes:

[a]United States, United Kingdom, New Zealand.

[b]Puerto Rico, Mexico, Venezuela, Colombia, Chile, Brazil, Israel, N. Rhodesia.

[c]India, Malaysia, Philippines, Republic of Korea, Nigeria, Ghana, Kenya, Uganda.

Source: George Psacharopoulos, *Returns to Education* (1973), p. 177.

stay in school longer receive a significantly greater share of public resources.

High wastage rates can make the unit cost of producing one graduate many times higher than the cost per student at the outset, or during the course of schooling. For example, Table 13 illustrates the unit cost of producing one graduate of the UNESCO World Functional Literacy Programme in four countries. These costs are higher than six years of primary schooling in the same conditions. "Enrolled" participant is defined as any student who has ever been enrolled in the program, including dropouts and pushouts. "Final" participant is defined as any student who actually finished the program, but may or may not have passed the final examination. "Graduate" includes only students who have passed the final examination. As can be seen, the dropout and failure rates were very high, particularly in Sudan where costs per participant who passed the final examination were

TABLE 13
Cost of Participant and Graduates of Functional Literacy Projects [a]
(US$)

Country	Cost per enrolled participant	Final participants as a percent of initial enrolled	Total estimated cost per final participant	Graduates as a percent of initial enrolled	Estimated total cost per participant passing final exam
Tanzania	7	63	10	21	32
Sudan	7	32	272	8	269
Ecuador	70	57	123	23	300
Iran	49	48	100	14	332

Note:

[a] Costs are unweighted and do not take into account country-to-country variations in definitions of literacy. Cost estimates are of varying reliability. Depending on the country, cohort entered program between 1967 and 1969. For the Sudan it appears that the cost per final participant is higher than the cost per participant passing the examination, but the source offers no explanation.

Source: UNDP, *The Experimental World Literacy Program A Critical Assessment* (Paris: The Unesco Press, 1976), pp. 174 and 185.

thirty-eight times higher than the cost per student when enrolled. In Iran the cost per successful participant was $332, hardly a figure to encourage a government to undertake a mass literacy campaign.

A Critique of Efficiency

Concerning internal efficiency, educators and planners assumed in the past a direct, if not linear, relationship between school inputs and improvements in reading comprehension and other cognitive skills. For example, they believed that the more years of teacher training, the better the students' achievement scores. Higher unit cost should mean better scores. Failing a quota of children from each year of the primary school was seen as essential to the successful operation of the entire system and the society.

More recently, data have suggested that the relationship between many school inputs and outcomes tends to be weak. Student motivation and self-esteem, however, the result of many factors including personality, parental behavior, and the probability of access to higher education, may be more important determinants of student achievement that previously thought. The school can no longer be considered a lathe shaping better students in direct relation to the quality of the curriculum and the intentions of the teacher. Furthermore, to extend the analogy, the craftsman or teacher can damage the material rather than develop it to the fullest potential as the school experience can with particularly students from low income groups. Finally, the available evidence on efficiency suggests that if major improvements in rates of learning are to be achieved, much more effort is required in shaping and combining the nonschool inputs. Implicit in these evaluations of the efficiency of education is the notion that cognitive achievement, as developed by schools, is an important component of human capital and thus has a positive impact on job performance. Furthermore, it is assumed that schools' only function is the technical role of teaching people mental skills. Members of the structuralist school have used recent research to challenge these assumptions, and in turn call into question the apparent *in*efficiency of educational systems in the developing countries.

In addition to the effects of various quantities of inputs on the education students receive, recent research has studied the effects of the process of classroom learning on the students.[28] It has been found, for example, that the school reinforces the norms of independence and competition, which imply a certain isolation, as opposed to the family's or community's reinforcement of mutual dependence, cooperation, and solidarity. Also, schools teach children that they will be judged and evaluated in accordance with their achievements, without reference to ascriptive characteristics, like parental social position, or emotional needs. This means that children have to be able to compartmentalize themselves into different dimensions, and to accept the teacher's and later the employer's unidimensional treatment of them, for example, in terms of their performance on school tests and work tasks, not in terms of their friendliness. Day-to-day experience in the classroom teaches children to accept being dealt with as members of a group or category (for example, as first graders), rather than to expect to be addressed as individuals with a unique set of needs and abilities.

This type of behavioral education, often referred to as the "hidden curriculum", is not simply a matter of threshold inputs and outputs: certain types of behavior are continually reinforced by testing and grading. First, students learn to respond to the *external* rewards of grades and appreciation by the teacher, as distinct from any *intrinsic* pleasure from the educational process and control over it. Second, in school students learn to obey the teacher, and to accept the authority embodied in his or her position, in explicit rules, and in the "facts" that are the ultimate standard for right and wrong answers. Empirical studies in primary and secondary schools in more developed countries have shown that the better the work orientation, perseverance, discipline, subordination to the rules, even when students of the same cognitive ability as measured by achievement tests are compared, then the higher the student grades. In other words, teachers will give higher grades to the students who show these traits, even though these students receive the same scores as students who do not show these traits. At the same time students showing creativity, problem solving, mental flexibility, and spontaneity are penalized by grades as well as by the process of rote learning.[29]

Whereas at first encounter this evidence may be discouraging, upon

further investigation it appears that these kinds of norms and personality characteristics are coincident with the behavioral skills that
workers need for securing and retaining employment, particularly at
the lowest end of the job ladder. Thus, social mobility can be inhibited
by schooling. Studies of American workers have shown that such
traits as rules orientation, dependability, and internalization of the
norms of the firm strongly predicted supervisor evaluations of
workers.[30] While few parallel studies have been implemented in the
less developed countries, it is most likely that, for instance, consistent
performance, respect for authority, and general dependability would
be more important characteristics of a rural manual laborer in a poor
country than would the ability to read a newspaper.

Thus, not only is the "inefficiency" of the inputs to education
called into question by these process-oriented evaluations of the
educational system, but the "wastage" resulting from high dropout
rates takes on a new aspect. In societies where on the one hand social
mobility is stressed, while on the other hierarchical firms provide for a
stratified labor force, it is necessary that some mechanism mollify
those who are effectively rationed out of the best jobs. Educational
systems with failure rates in the range of the figures cited earlier legitimate nonpromotion and school failure in two ways: first, individual
achievement and merit are society's standards for grades, advancement, and success in general (this prepares people to accept treatment
on the job as being fair within the meritocratic dimension of the job);
second, in societies with unemployment and underemployment rates
double or triple those in the advanced industrial countries, school
systems which teach young people to accept failure and nonpromotion
in school because of an inadequate supply of school places are actually
an efficient means of selecting them out of the school system, preparing
them for jobs where schooling is not important, and even conditioning
them to accept passively future unemployment and poverty. In short,
if the relations of the labor process are hierarchical, then the workers
must be socialized to accept that. If different social relations exist,
then different traits may be useful. This means, however, that efficiency can only be defined within a system of social relations, not as a
universal characteristic across systems.

Adherents to the structuralist theory are consequently more favorable in their interpretation of the efficiency of education in the developing countries. Preparation of the poor majority of the population for economic life in those countries means preparation for authoritarian work relationships, few possibilities for advancement within a firm, and frequent unemployment. Thus schools that are more successful in teaching students to become accustomed to failure and to the norms of industrial society than they are in teaching them to read, are efficiently fulfilling their role of creating the manpower, mainly semi-skilled and passive, that society and firms consider appropriate.

The Economic Impact of Schooling

I now turn to the issues concerning the effects of schooling on individual productivity and national economic growth, often described as the external productivity of education. Members of the technical school have relied primarily on rate of return analysis based on human capital theory. Recently certain economists have challenged the early estimates, arguing that they are biased upwards, and that more accurate figures were much lower. The structuralists, however, argue that, if the job structure in developing countries is relatively rigid, the social opportunity costs of education are much less than the incrementalists' estimate, so that the existing rate of return figures are too low.

Most of the data for the incrementalists' measures of rates of social return to investment in education are based on the lifetime earnings of school leavers, discounted by a suitable interest rate, and subtracting the individual and social costs of the school.[31] Private rates of return include only the costs to the individual, including income foregone by not working, and thus exclude social expenditures. But both these social and private rates tend to overestimate the economic rate of return, because they are not adjusted for the cognitive abilities and affective traits that students gain before entering school, or for skills gained after leaving school, such as work experience. The rate of return data are usually aggregated by level of schooling, for example by secondary, and thus combine variance across individuals. The few studies which do make some of these corrections suggest that the rates need to be discounted up to 50 percent.[32] Furthermore, the available estimates cover only one point in time and cannot give useful information on trends. Given these considerations, the rate of return data require careful interpretation.

Important findings of the rate of return studies are shown in Table 14. First, the private returns are consistently higher than the social returns, despite the fact that the private rate accounts only for personal earnings after deducting income tax while the social rate includes earnings before taxation. The reason for this is that the total resource cost of education exceeds the cost that individuals and their families must bear themselves. Second, the highest returns are to primary level graduates; returns to secondary and higher education are usually quite close, but significantly lower than to primary. To further illustrate this point, a social benefit to cost ratio has been calculated based on data similar to that of Table 14.[33] At the primary level, the benefit to cost ratio is 9.5. The ratio decreases sharply to 2.37 at the secondary level, and declines again at the higher level to 2.00. Third, the social rates of return for secondary and higher education are for most countries surprisingly close to the social rates for investment in other sectors.[34] However, if corrections for nonschool abilities, especially family background and work experience, are made by discounting the education return rate as suggested above, the rate of return would be sharply reduced. For example, the average social rates of return for the countries in Table 14 are 25 percent in primary school, 14 percent in secondary, and 11 percent in higher education; if the proper corrections would reduce them by 50 percent then the rates would be *lower* than returns to investments in other sectors. Fourth, given that these rates of return are several years old and that unemployment rates among school leavers and unit costs per student, in real terms, have been rising, it is very likely that the current rate of return to education is even lower. Based on this analysis, the past estimates of the social and private profitability of investment in education may have been exaggerated. Given such a high level of economic profitability for investment in the rapid and sustained expansion of primary schooling, a central policy issue is why planners concerned with promoting economic growth allowed investments in primary and literacy to stagnate and increased the rate of investment in higher education which has a much lower benefit cost ratio?

The above analysis of the technical school, however, is based on the

assumption that the social opportunity costs of education are substantial. In the United States—where the best data are available—the
direct private and social costs of secondary and higher education are
typically less than or equal to the estimated opportunity costs of
income foregone, in other words, what people could earn if they were
not in school. However, many economists, ranging from those who
developed theories of job competition and a labor queue to those
whose theories of the wage and employment distribution are based on
class analysis, argue that the employment structure and supply of jobs
is relatively fixed in both developed and developing countries, and
therefore does not respond to changing supply schedules for labor
with different amounts of human capital.

The structuralists' assumptions imply that, whereas on the margin
one worker foregoes income by going to school, it cannot be asserted
that all secondary students, for example, are foregoing good jobs by
attending school. There are simply not that many middle income
jobs (witness the relatively high levels of unemployment among recent
graduates). If all secondary schools closed tomorrow, sending former
students to the labor market, whatever jobs primary school graduates
could obtain would be at the expense of the less-educated former
occupants of those positions. Observers who take seriously the notion
that education is primarily a means for providing the credentials that
ration an inadequate number of good jobs, realize that the social
opportunity costs of education are nil in countries with substantial
levels of unemployment at any or all levels of the job structure. In
the aggregate, the society foregoes no productive labor by having
children in school, since the alternative is unemployment.

The structuralists conclude that the initial estimates of the costs of
education were inflated, and thus that real rates of return are actually
much higher than the initial figures cited in Table 14. For example,
members of the technical school would estimate for India that an
eighth-grade student foregoes 500 rupees per year by staying in school.
This is almost ten times the total public cost of his or her education
which is 54 rupees/year for primary.[35] If the social opportunity cost
is close to zero, however, assuming there would be no increase in the
number of jobs in the economy simply because an eighth grader left
school, the social cost of 554 rupees should really be closer to 54 rupees.

TABLE 14

Social and Private Rates of Return by Educational Level and Country
(percentages)[a]

Country	Year	Social			Private		
		Primary	Secondary	Higher	Primary	Secondary	Higher
United States	1959	17.8	14.0	9.7	155.1	19.5	13.6
Canada	1961	..	11.7	14.0	..	16.3	19.7
Puerto Rico	1959	17.1	21.7	16.5	> 100.0	23.4	27.9
Mexico	1963	25.0	17.0	23.0	32.0	23.0	29.0
Venezuela	1957	82.0	17.0	23.0	..	18.0	27.0
Colombia	1966	40.0	24.0	8.0	> 50.0	32.0	15.5
Chile	1959	24.0	16.9	12.2	..	..	..
Brazil	1962	10.7	17.2	14.5	11.3	21.4	38.1
Great Britain	1966	..	3.6	8.2	..	6.2	12.0
Norway	1966	..	7.2	7.5	..	7.4	7.7
Sweden	1967	..	10.5	9.2	..	..	10.3
Denmark	1964	..	..	7.8	..	..	10.0
The Netherlands	1965	..	5.2	5.5	..	8.5	10.4

Country	Year						
Belgium	1967	..	..	9.3	..	..	17.0
Germany	1964	..	..	..	..	..	4.6
Greece	1964	..	3.0	8.0	..	5.0	14.0
Turkey	1968	16.5	..	8.5	27.0	24.0	26.0
Israel	1958	20.2	6.9	6.6	24.8	6.9	8.0
India	1960	9.3	16.8	12.7	..	19.2	14.3
Malaysia	1967	6.6	12.3	10.7	..	..	..
Singapore	1966	7.0	17.6	14.6	7.5	20.0	25.4
The Philippines	1966	..	21.0	11.0	..	28.0	12.5
Japan	1961	12.0	5.0	6.0	..	6.0	9.0
S. Korea	1967	30.5	9.0	5.0	56.0	..	..
Thailand	1970	24.1	13.0	11.0	> 100.0	14.5	14.0
Hawaii	1959	23.0	4.4	9.2	30.0	5.1	11.0
Nigeria	1966	..	12.8	17.0	..	14.0	34.0
Ghana	1967	18.0	13.0	16.5	24.5	17.0	37.0
Kenya	1968	21.7	19.2	8.8	32.7	30.0	27.4
Uganda	1965	66.0	28.6	12.0	..	..	..
N. Rhodesia	1960	12.4	..	..	..	..	..
New Zealand	1966	..	19.4	13.2	..	20.0	14.7

Notes:

a"..." denotes data not available.

Source: George Psacharopoulos, *Returns to Education*, p. 62.

Thus the rate of return to education at that level should be substantially higher. The figures the human capital theorists present for the return to education are too low because of their overestimation of social opportunity costs.

However, the critique based on a fixed employment and wage structure must call into question the cause of the higher income earned after schooling as well as the supposed social. opportunity cost of education while in school. A rigid job structure means that the income earned after schooling does not reflect returns to human capital, but to certification; in other words, a person's productivity is affected relatively much more by the requirements and characteristics of his or her job than it is by individual skills. The actual manpower, cognitive, and social development that takes place in school cannot therefore be evaluated by a rate of return analysis that hinges on the premise of a flexible job structure and of productivity embodied in a person rather than an occupation. Instead, direct inspection of what is learned in school and the private and real social costs of that education is required in order to analyze the benefits derived from different amounts of education.

The policy question is: How strong is the evidence for selectively reducing the rate of new investment in formal education, although not eliminating it? Planners assumed in the past that high social rates of return could justify high rates of public investment in formal education. More recently it has become clear to members of the technical school that the figures do not necessarily support past policy decisions, partly because of unexpectedly lower rates of return to secondary and higher education, which were thought to be the priority especially when adjusted, and partly because of measurement difficulties in comparing potential investment across sectors. Given this information, plus the rising rates of unemployment of the educated, strong adherents to this school of planners have concluded that the economic evidence suggests the transfer of new investment from secondary and higher education to primary, as well as the stabilization of the total educational investment at existing levels, in most countries.

Yet the structuralists, positing a relatively fixed supply of jobs, and concerned with the cumulative "job-bumping" that might follow cutbacks in secondary and higher education, have urged continued public support of post-primary education. They argue that in most countries reductions in funding for secondary and higher education will not necessarily lead to either greater expenditures on modes of primary education that will develop self-reliance and social equality, or greater expenditures on direct creation of jobs. In those few countries with the political will to shift expenditure from upper secondary and higher education to primary schooling and jobs that meet the needs of the poor, such a shift is justified.

Conclusion

In this overview I have tried to sketch the major issues of educational systems found in most developing countries. More detailed discussion of these and related issues is provided in the following chapters. I did not review the experiences of countries such as Cuba, China, or Tanzania, which have made major changes in their educational systems, often in response to the problems described.[36]

I began with several issues which have preoccupied educational planners and researchers for more than two decades. Expressed as questions, these were:

- Do children learn more as a result of schooling?
- Can allocation within the sector be made more efficient, effective, and equitable?
- Should resources now used for formal education be shifted to other sectors where they would have a higher economic rate of return?
- Can education bring basic reforms to the structure of the economy, such as the redistribution of income and assets, or does redistribution have to come first?

While neither the information presented in this chapter, nor in those that follow, pretends to respond to these questions other than tentatively, the data and analysis should leave the reader with one strong conclusion: the assumptions which were used in the past to make the investments in formal education in the past need to be seriously questioned. Few planners and educators can say that the outcomes of the educational investment of the past two decades have made the contribution to either growth or to development that they had expected. Schooling has not contributed to student learning in many of the ways which had been assumed. This growing doubt is also shared by observers in the developed countries about their systems.

There are two ways of explaining these unexpected outcomes. Some observers assert that the systems of formal education in developing countries are irrelevant to the countries' needs. They argue that reforming the countries' educational system to meet the needs of both the poor and the rich, including greater efficiency, can be done without a shift in political and economic power. Others, however, argue that while the existing education systems are not addressing the priority needs of the poor majority, they *are* addressing the priority needs of the elites to maintain political and economic power, especially over the poor. This explains why so many plans for educational reforms to increase the benefits to the poor have never been implemented. Thus the educational systems can best be defined by the groups that established and maintain them. These groups are doing very little, in the words of Gunnar Myrdal, to educate the poor to see their interests, and organize them to fight for their interests.

While neither school may not have enough evidence to "prove" its theory of the relationship between education and development, the number of converts from the first to the second school is growing. Adam Curle, recently director of international education at Harvard University, is one of the more recent. He has worked and lived in more than twenty developing countries as a teacher, researcher, and consultant. For half his life, he writes, he supported the idea that formal education would open men's minds, shape their skills, and would thus become a great force of social equality and economic development. Reviewing his experience, he now sees that "education, *as it is mostly practiced,* does not so much free men from ignorance, tradition, and servility, as fetter them to the values and aspirations of a middle class which many of them are unlikely to join".[37] Except for the few who reach the elite, he feels that "education enslaves; men and women become free through their own efforts". In the following chapters, authors belonging to both schools of thought provide a more detailed discussion of the issues.

Notes

1. John Simmons, *The Effectiveness of Schooling in Promoting Learning: A Review of the Research,* Working Paper No. 200 (Washington, D.C.: World Bank, 1974); Chapter 4 in this book by Simmons and Alexander; and Ernesto Schiefelbein and John Simmons, *"The Determinates of School Achievement: A Review of the Research for Developing Countries"* (Ottawa: International Development Research Centre, October 1978).

2. For an elaboration of the theories and evidence. See Lester Thurow, *Inequality; Mechanisms of Distribution in the U.S. Economy* (Basic Books, Inc.: New York, 1975); Peter B. Doeringer and Michael J. Piore, *Internal Labor Markets and Manpower Analysis* (Lexington, Mass: D.C. Health, 1971); Ronald Dore, *The Diploma Disease: Education, Qualifications and Development* (Berkeley: University of California Press, 1976); and Kenneth Arrow, "Higher education as a filter", in K. G. Lumsden, ed., *Efficiency in Universities: The Le Paz Papers* (Amsterdam: Elsevier, 1975); and the references in note 6 below.

3. "The empirical status of human capital theory: a slightly jaundiced survey", *Journal of Economic Literature,* September 1976, pp. 849, 850.

4. See Burton A. Weisbrod, *External Benefits of Education: An Economic Analysis* (Princeton, N.J.: Princeton University Press, 1964) for an extensive treatment of externalities.

5. There are few data for developing countries. The evidence for the United States is derived from studies measuring the relationship between the level of cognitive achievement of students and their productivity measured by lifetime earnings or occupational status. Cognitive achievement is measured in various ways, including national examinations, rank in class, and grade point average. Controls are usually made for years of schooling and parental socioeconomic status. IQ is usually not controlled since it is a measure of cognitive ability and thus strongly correlated with other measures. The results tend to show that the relationships between cognitive achievement and productivity are minimal. See Randall Collins, "Functional and conflict theories of educational stratification", *American Sociological Review* (December 1971), and Samuel Bowles and Herbert Gintis, *Schooling in Capitalist America* (New York: Basic Books, 1975) for reviews of the literature. IQ and income show a very modest relationship. The incomes of American men with IQ genotypes above the 80th percentile in the IQ genotype distribution were compared with men below the 20th percentile. The incomes of the top fifth IQ genotype were only 35-40 percent higher than the lowest fifth. This is not a major difference when considering that the men in the top fifth of the income distribution earn 600 percent more than the worst paid fifth. Individuals with the same IQ genotype show, at most, only 3 percent less income inequality than in the enti.e U.S. population. Christopher Jencks and others, *Inequality, A Reassessment of the Effect of Family and Schooling in America* (New York: Basic Books, 1972), pp. 220 ff.

6. See Theodore W. Schultz, "Investment in human capital", *American Economic Review* (August, 1961), and Gary S. Becker, "Investment in human capital: a theoretical analysis", *The Journal of Political Economy,* supplement (October 1962) for a description of human capital theory. See Samual Bowles, "Towards an educational production function", in *Education, Income and Human Capital: Studies in Income and Wealth,* vol. 35 (New York: National Bureau of Economic Research, 1970); Richard C. Edwards, "Alienation and inequality" (Ph.D. Dissertation, Harvard University, Department of Economics, 1972); Herbert Gintis,

"Education, technology, and the characteristics of worker production"; Christopher Jencks and others, *Inequality;* and Mark Blaug, *Education and the Employment Problem in Developing Countries* (Geneva: International Labour Organisation, 1973), for syntheses of the evidence which challenges the theory.

7. For example, F. Svennilson, F. Edding, and L. Elvin, *Target for Education in Europe in 1970* (Paris: OECD, 1962).

8. Robert Solow, "Technical change and the aggregate production function", *Review of Economics and Statistics* (August 1957), and Edward F. Denison, *The Sources of Economic Growth in the United States and the Alternative Before Us* (New York: Committee for Economic Development, 1962).

9. When labor and capital inputs were unchanged, output increased at 1 percent per annum at a firm in Horndal, Sweden, and is attributed to experience. See Kenneth Arrow, "Learning by doing", *Review of Economic Studies* (June 1962) for the Hornal effect. See also Jacob Mincer, "On the job training: cost returns and some implications", *Journal of Political Economy* (October 1972 supplement); E. N. Zhil'tosov, "Statistical methods of evaluating the complexity of labor", in Harold J. Noah, ed., *The Economics of Education in the U.S.S.R.* (New York: Praeger, 1969); and John Simmons and Henry Noerenberg, "Schooling, income and satisfaction" mimeograph (Washington, D.C.: World Bank, 1978) for studies on the effects of informal education. Other evidence suggest, for example Ivar Berg, *Education and Jobs: The Great Training Robbery* (New York: Praeger, 1970), that for each occupation there is an optimum amount of formal schooling. Thus, in some cases, labor productivity declines as schooling increases.

10. Mark Blaug, *Education and the Employment Problem* (Geneva: International Labour Organisation, 1973), pp. 7-11. The employment data required to understand the full dimensions of this problem need to be cross-tabulated by age, schooling, length of unemployment, and hours worked per week, and are virtually unavailable. For exceptions, see the ILO reports on Kenya and Ceylon, *Employment, Incomes, and Equality: A Strategy for Increasing Productive Employment in Kenya* (Geneva: International Labour Organisation, 1972) and *Matching Employment Opportunities and Expectations: A Programme of Action for Ceylon* (Geneva: International Labour Organisation, 1971).

11. Mark Blaug, *Education and the Employment Problem in Developing Countries* (Geneva: International Labour Organisation, 1974), pp. 9, 7-11.

12. Mark Blaug, Richard Layard, and Maureen Woodhally, *The Causes and Consequences of Graduate Unemployment in India* (London: Penguin Press, 1969).

13. See Richard C. Edwards, Michael Reich, and David Gordon, *Labor Market Segmentation* (Lexington, Mass.: D.C. Heath, 1975) for a review of the issues and data.

14. For a review of the methods and data see Asim Dasgupta, "Education, income distribution and capital accumulation", mimeograph (Washington, D.C.: World Bank, 1973).

15. See Asim Dasgupta, "Education, income distribution and capital accumulation", and Jagdish Bhagwati, "Education, class structure and income equality", *World Development*, vol. 1, no. 5 (1973), and Jean Pierre Jallade, *Public Expenditures on Education and Income Distribution in Colombia* (Baltimore: Johns Hopkins University Press, 1974).

16. For an excellent review of the evidence and controversy, see Christopher Jencks and others, *Inequality,* Appendix 1. See also Richard Herrenstein, "I.Q.", *Atlantic Monthly* (September 1971).

17. The data refer to large populations, such as whole cities or regions, rather than to separate schools. While data for individual schools are useful for experimental purposes, they are less useful for policy purposes, since the resources may not be duplicated quickly or the benefits extended to a large population due to resource constraints. For examples of the Western approach, see Harvey A. Averch and others, *How Effective is Schooling? An Initial Review and Synthesis of Research Findings* (Santa Monica, California: The Rand Corporation, 1972); L. C. Comber and John P. Keeves, *International Studies in Evaluation. I: Science Education in Nineteen Countries* (Stockholm: Almqvist & Wiksell, 1973); and John Simmons, "The effectiveness of schooling in promoting learning: a review of the research", Working Paper No. 200 (Washington, D.C.: World Bank, 1974).

18. For an early exposition of this concept see J. R. Walsh, "Capital concept applied to man", *Quarterly Journal of Economics* (February 1935); and further refinements by Theodore Schultz, "Investment in human capital", *American Economic Review* (1961); and Gary S. Becker, "Investment in human capital: a theoretical analysis", *The Journal of Political Economy,* supplement (October 1962).

19. See Chapter 4 for a discussion of the techniques.

20. James S. Coleman, *Equality of Educational Opportunity* (U.S. Department of Health, Education and Welfare, 1966); Christopher Jencks and others, *Inequality;* Bridget Plowden, *Children and Their Primary Schools: A Report of the Central Advisory Council for Education* (London: Her Majesty's Stationery Office, 1967). For a critique of Coleman see Samuel Bowles and Henry Levin, "The determinants of scholastic achievement—an appraisal of some recent evidence", *The Journal of Human Resources* (Winter 1968); and Frederick Mosteller and Daniel P. Moynihan (eds.), *On Equality of Educational Opportunity* (New York: Random House, 1971). For a critique of Jencks et al., see the Special Issue of the *Harvard Educational Review,* 1973.

21. T. Husen, ed., *International Study of Achievement in Mathematics* (New York: John Wiley and Sons, 1967), and L. C. Comber and John P. Keeves, *International Studies in Evaluation I.*

22. John Simmons, "Retention of primary school cognitive skills", *Comparative Education Review* (February 1976) and World Bank reprint No. 35.

23. L. C. Comber and John P. Keeves, *International Studies in Evaluation I,* and Robert L. Thorndike, *Reading Comprehension in Fifteen Countries: International Studies in Evaluation III* (Stockholm: Almqvist & Wicksell, 1973).

24. For a review of the literature, see Russell Beirn, David Kinsey, and Noel McGinn, *Causes and Consequences of Early School Leaving* (Cambridge, Mass.: Harvard University, Graduate School of Education, 1972).

25. Russell Beirn, David Kinsey, and Noel McGinn, *Causes and Consequences of Early School Leaving* (Cambridge, Mass: Harvard University, Graduate School of Education, 1972).

26. Eric Fromm and Michael Maccoby, *Social Character in a Mexican Village: A Socio-Psychoanalytic Study* (Englewood Cliffs, N.J.: Prentice Hall, 1970).

27. Ronald Dore, *The Diploma Disease.*

28. For further information about the effective impact of education see Nobuo Kenneth Shimahara and Adam Scrupski, eds., *Social Forces and Schooling: An Anthropological and Sociological Perspective* (New York: David McKay Co., Inc., 1975); especially articles by Yehudi Cohen and Adam Scrupski; Joan I. Roberts and Sherrie K. Akinsanya, eds., *Schooling in the Cultural Context—Anthropological Studies of Education* (New York: David McKay Co., Inc., 1976), especially the article by Jules Henry; C. H. Patterson, *Humanistic Education* (Englewood Cliffs, N.J.: Prentice-Hall, Inc., 1973); Herbert Gintis, "Education, technology, and the characteristics of worker productivity", *American Economic Review*, May 1971; and Samuel Bowles and Herbert Gintis, *Schooling in Capitalist America: Educational Reform and the Contradictions of Economic Life* (New York: Basic Books, Inc., 1976), pp. 138-9 and Appendix II.

29. Ralph Hoepfner et al., eds., *Test Evaluations: Tests of Higher Order Cognitive, Affective and Interpersonal Skills* (Los Angeles: Center for the Study of Evaluation, Graduate School of Education, University of California, 1972).

30. Richard C. Edwards, "Personal traits and 'success' in schooling and works", *Educational and Psychological Measurement,* in press, 1975; and "Individual traits and organizational incentives: what makes a 'good' worker?", *Journal of Human Resources,* in press, 1976.

31. For a review of this method, see Mark Blaug, "Economic planning of education in developing countries", Working Paper (Washington, D.C.: World Bank, 1967); and Samuel Bowles, *Planning Educational Systems for Economic Growth* (Cambridge, Mass.: Harvard University Press, 1969).

32. For examples of two developing countries where an attempt has been made to correct some biases, see Marcelo Selowsky, "The effect of unemployment and growth on the rate of return to education: the case of Colombia", Economic Development Report No. 116 (Cambridge, Mass.: Center for International Affairs, Harvard University, 1968); and Mark Blaug and others, *The Causes and Consequences of Graduate Unemployment in India*; Christopher Jencks and others, *Inequality,* p. 222, corrected the U.S. earnings data for preschool ability and parental socioeconomic status and lowered the private rate of return by 40 percent.

33. See Chapter 14 for details.

34. The data in Table 14 use a social discount rate of 10 percent for data on thirty countries.

35. Mark Blaug, Richard Layard, and Maureen Woodhall, *The Causes and Consequences of Graduate Unemployment in India,* p. 21 and p. 202.

36. For a review of their experience, see John Simmons, "Lessons from educational reform", mimeograph (Washington, D.C.: World Bank, 1979).

37. Adam Curle, *Education for Liberation* (London: Tavistock, 1973), p. 1, italics added.

*Efficiency of Investment
in Education*

CHAPTER 3

The Future of Formal Education in Developing Countries

RONALD DORE

These days, it is fashionable to smile at the naïve optimism of the Victorians who believed in the inevitability of progress. Civilization, as they saw it, was advancing to ever greater degrees of perfection and refinement. From the metropolitan centers, it was reaching out to illuminate the darkest corners on the earth. Macaulay looked forward to the day when India would be a cultural outpost of Europe, its inhabitants not a whit "lower" in their level of civilization than those of the metropolis. Oh, the simplicity and arrogance of it all!

Yet, under the skin, most of us are still, like the Victorians, children of the Enlightenment. We still believe that learning, knowing, understanding, and thinking "civilize"; that education—the cultivation of human minds and spirits—is the foundation of a good and economically productive society; and that the improvement of education is a means to a better society.

The deschoolers notwithstanding, there is little likelihood of abandoning the schools and universities. Unfortunately, schooling cannot be automatically equated with education. Much of it is qualifications-earning, and more and more of it is becoming so. Everywhere, in Britain as in India, in Russia as in Venezuela, more schooling is qualifications-earning than it was in 1920, or even in 1950. Qualifications-earning is ritualistic, tedious, suffused with anxiety and boredom, destructive of curiosity and imagination; in short, anti-educational.[1]

In many places this problem can be endured a while longer. A certain amount of educational vitality remains in those school systems capable of resisting the ritualizing disease of qualifications-earning. But for the more fragile school systems of the developing countries, where the stress of dualistic development increases the virulence of the disease, the problem leads to not only disenchantment but disaster.

Such a perspective on education is a product of the gloomy 1970s. No one argued this way in the optimistic 1950s, when economists and statisticians first paid attention to education and offered to show in quantifiable terms how much of the growth of advanced economies had been due to educational expansion. Implant education, and growth would follow. The mood was set by the grand conferences at Karachi and Addis Ababa, which looked forward to universal primary education in Africa and Asia by the early 1980s. Manpower planners discerned the strategic importance of middle and higher-level manpower and urged the rapid expansion of secondary and tertiary training institutions.

The Sources of Disillusionment

The mood today is different. Hope has given way to disillusionment. The pacesetting international agencies are now seeking a new key to the doors of progress. Nonformal education has been discovered as more likely to deliver the development goods than the traditional panoply of primary, secondary, and tertiary institutions. Within the formal system, basic education rather than occupational training is to receive priority.

The sources of disillusionment are fairly clear. It has proved easier to build modern school systems than modern societies. Educational qualifications, eagerly sought as a means to modern sector jobs, lead often to unemployment. In 1960 a Kenyan child in the 13 percent who finished seven years of primary school could be reasonably certain of a "good job". Ten years later, 60 percent of even larger age cohorts were finishing primary school, and 8 percent were getting Form IV secondary certificates. Meanwhile, the economy was providing wage or salary employment for only 15 percent of the 200,000 young Kenyans who reached working age each year. Less than half of those were getting jobs offering the security and income of the modern sector. The school system generated frustration rather than confident achievement. Massive unemployment came to the Kenyan secondary school leavers in 1968. In countries further along the road, unemployment had long since reached the higher levels. In the late 1960s India counted those of its jobless with technical degrees in the tens of thousands. Two factors reinforce the process. First, in the escalation of qualification requirements, secondary leavers take jobs which formerly went to primary school leavers, and gradually a secondary certificate becomes necessary for the job. What were once secondary leavers' jobs become graduate jobs, and so on. Second, in response to the qualifications spiral and because there is nothing else to do, the unemployed primary leavers redouble their efforts to get into secondary schools, the unemployed secondary leavers press on to the university, and the unemployed graduates flock to masters programs. The result has been a near-exponential increase in secondary and tertiary provision. This has been most rapid in countries such as the Philippines, where private entrepreneurs meet the market demand with more and more private schools and universities, and not much less rapid in countries such as India, where the political pressures from the articulate middle class parents prove irresistible in their demand for state funds.

The social frustrations and political dangers of unemployment of the educated are only one aspect of the problem. The demands for more higher level schools press heavily on government budgets. Education's share of government expenditure has grown steadily in many countries despite the fact that those extra resources, which might have gone to creating jobs for the impoverished, will produce more unemployed graduates.

At the same time, primary school enrollments mark time, partly because political demands for the expansion of secondary and tertiary places are more potent than the peasants' demand for primary schools, partly because in too many societies the primary school has become not the place where one is educated for a useful life, but the place where one competes for an exit visa from rural society. Small wonder that so many disadvantaged children in the villages, with little chance of getting into secondary school, simply drop out. What is the use of school if there is no job at the end of it?

These problems are the consequences, in the educational sphere, of the dualistic bridgehead strategy which has dominated development thinking in past decades. Development was seen as a matter of creating and gradually expanding an outpost of modernity within a basically traditional society, as if one were reclaiming a swamp, creating a bridgehead of solid land, and gradually enlarging it until the whole swamp is filled in. The developed sector naturally had to be thoroughly modern: with the latest technology in the factories and hospitals; with universities up to world standards; and with engineers, doctors, and professors trained on a par with their peers in the most advanced countries.

The flaws of that strategy are now glaringly apparent. The modern sector expands so slowly (except in a few favored oil-rich countries) that it may be centuries rather than decades before it can accommodate the whole of the labor force. Meanwhile the salaries and wages of modern sector workers, pulled up by the demonstration effects exerted by their developed-country professional peers, are out of proportion to traditional sector incomes. As inequalities grow, rather than diminish, so too do social tensions.

Only in the health field has this strategy been widely challenged. Thanks in large measure to the Chinese example, it has been realized that there are alternatives to the bridgehead strategy: putting resources into rural health centers rather than into kidney machines, or training thousands of paramedical personnel rather than a few heart surgeons. These actions contribute to the broad-based build-up of overall health standards rather than a slow expansion of an enclave of modern health services.

A similar approach to education is only beginning to take root. Schools had a dual function in traditional development thinking. At the primary level, they were to improve overall levels of skills and intellectual sophistication, thus raising the productivity of farmers, fishermen, and traditional craftsmen. At the same time, they were the recruitment agencies for the modern sector, auditioning aspirants to the favored 10 or 20 percent of each age group to be welcomed into the enclave of the modern sector, and providing training for that elite. Vocational and professional training were for a minority of students; academic secondary and tertiary education were for the majority who sought administrative and clerical jobs.

Inevitably, the second function triumphed over the first. Schools belonged unmistakably to the modern sector. Timetables were adjusted to the city week, not to the rhythms of the traditional agrarian calendar.

Teachers were hired and paid in accordance with the canons of modern bureaucracy, not indigenous custom. Furniture, layout, and curriculum design explicitly mimicked imported models. Schooling was socialization into modern sector life—in anticipation of a future which only a small minority could enjoy. Hence, an overwhelming importance was attached to examinations, which determined who should belong to that minority.

A modern assumption of the advanced industrial societies is that preparation and selection for careers is best done in schools. It was not always so. A century ago most occupations were entered through some form of apprenticeship; progress was earned by the demonstration of competence in one's work. Education was concerned with intellectual and moral improvement, not the pursuit of qualifications to unlock the doors to closed professions. But gradually, for a variety of reasons not wholly creditable either to the professions or to educational institutions, precareer qualifications have become essential for the professions. Certificates of general education are increasingly the means by which each generation is sorted into social slots.

The developing countries adopted this emphasis on precareer qualifications as if there were no alternatives. That a government clerk needed a secondary school education, while a night watchman could "qualify" with six years of primary school, was taken as part of the order of nature rather than as contingent product of the affluence of developed societies.

With the schools' screening, sifting, and qualifying functions came also the disease of qualifications ritualism, but in a more virulent form. In Western societies, as more and more students are chalking up the necessary credits for a chosen occupation, so complaints increase about the declining quality of education and the anti-educational nature of examination-dominated schooling. In developing countries, the "backwash effect" of this type of schooling is much worse, for four reasons. First, so much more is at stake for the individual. In a developing country, the difference between a pass or honors degree may mean a 20:1 differential in personal income. In developed societies, with narrower differentials and more fluid labor markets, the outcome has a less pronounced effect. Second, there is a greater gap between the modern culture of the school and the culture of the home and village. The alien curriculum content is highly susceptible to codification for the purposes of ritual cramming. Third, schools in the developing countries are impoverished. Without libraries or science equipment, teaching often consists of "chalk and talk", the imparting and memorizing of dry facts. Fourth, schools in many developing countries have, since their initiation, been qualification-oriented. Where they lack certain idealistic preindustrial traditions it is harder to sustain the guise that education is aimed at personal development and spiritual enrichment rather than money-earning opportunities, a fiction which in older societies derives some strength from traditional ideals and mitigates the effects of the qualifications disease.

There are increasing doubts about whether the schools are successful even in their function of producing a modern elite. Economists count educational investment in years of schooling. But the sixteen years of schooling which yield a university graduate can be sixteen years of intellectual excitement and personal maturation, developing a zest to tackle and solve problems, or sixteen years of dutiful grind, learning how to please examiners and avoid risk, how to get a good salary and the status that goes with it. It is not surprising that there should be disillusionment with the school system. Not only is there a growing army of failures, dropouts, and unemployed, but "successes" who do get employment are often ill-equipped or motivated to make the contribution to their country's development that is expected of them.

Is There an Alternative?

What alternative is there to the present system? One view argues that the worse evils can be slowly mitigated. Somehow one has to select the tiny percentage of children who will be the future elite and the larger percentage to become middle-level personnel. A system using educational certificates is better than one judging by birth and patronage. Reduced salary differentials would minimize the desperate struggle for grades. Other suggestions include: increase the price of secondary and higher education; give loans rather than state subsidies in order to reduce the pressure to continually climb up the educational ladder, as well as to reduce the subsidy of the children of the rich by the poor; get the civil service to pay less attention to qualifications and more to job performance in making promotions; switch, as fast as is politically possible, resources from secondary and higher education to the primary sector; introduce relevant curricula into the primary schools, for in most countries, most students are inevitably destined to make their livelihood in traditional self-employment; and improve specific vocational education at the secondary level, not only for modern sector jobs but also for farming and other forms of self-employment. Slowly, intellectual capital will be built up. Greater maturity and sophistication, from the second and third generation elite, will be spread through the system, raise standards, and set up countervailing forces against tendencies which are deplored today.

The alternative view is that none of these measures can succeed, that built-in pressures exacerbating present failures of the system are too strong. The only solution is to cut the Gordian knot which links job opportunities to the results of school and university achievement tests. This could be done by (a) substituting apprenticeships for formal precareer courses as a means of training for occupations, and (b) using selection methods which cannot be easily prejudiced, such as aptitude tests and special short-term teaching-and-testing courses. It might imply selecting future civil servants after nine or ten years of basic schooling, identifying future administrators by further internal tests and work performance, and sending them for tertiary education and training in mid career. A medical career might begin with brief training and some years of work as a paramedic, followed by gradual upgrading through a combination of work and study.

Relieved of the burden of selection and qualification, schools could be used for education. Primary and lower secondary schools could concentrate on the needs of the majority who will not proceed to the modern sector, and there can be increased numbers of practical courses. If apprenticeship replaces graduate entry to the professions, tertiary institutions will no longer be filled with students concerned only with getting a bachelor's degree to compete for jobs. University students will be men and women truly intent on gaining the knowledge required for their jobs, rather than just the qualifications necessary to get them. This implies a restriction of enrollments in tertiary institutions to the real job opportunities, which will release resources for the building of a universal and effective primary school system.

These two alternatives were labeled by the special report on education and employment of the Economic Commission for Asia and the Far East (ECAFE)[2] as the "marginal incrementalist package" and the "structural reform package", respectively. The difficulties of the second proposal were noted, not least the pedagogical revolution required if teachers could no longer rely on their pupils' bread-and-butter motives ("learn this or you will fail the exam and stay a peasant all your life") and had to find new ways to inspire pupils. Given the uncharted difficulties of such a system, the radical nature of the change, and the number of established interests which would be adversely affected, it is unlikely that many countries would be eager to embark on such experiments.

These seem to be the lines along which China has restructured its educational system in recent years, as the report noted.[3] Given the growing influence of the Chinese model in the health field, more of these ideas may be heard in future. Perhaps it is only in an extreme crisis that such reforms would ever be contemplated. Sri Lanka has already had an abortive revolution which sprang from the frustrations of its educated but alienated youth. But as the pressure for secondary and higher education mounts, and with it the figures for educated unemployment and the size of educational budgets, many countries may find themselves not far from such a crisis.

Notes

1. For a full discussion of these and related issues, see Ronald Dore, *The Diploma Disease: Education, Qualification, and Development* (Berkeley: University of California Press, 1976).
2. Economic Commission for Asia and the Far East, *Economic Survey of Asia and the Far East: Education and Employment* (Bangkok: UN, 1973). This kind of "structural reform package" was also advocated in the ILO employment mission's report on Sri Lanka. *ILO Matching Expectations and Opportunities: A Programme of Action for Ceylon* (Geneva: ILO, 1971).
3. The preliminary version of the report, presented at the ECAFE conference in March 1973, contained references to China that were deleted from the final edition.

CHAPTER 4

Factors which Promote School Achievement in Developing Countries: A Review of the Research*

JOHN SIMMONS and LEIGH ALEXANDER

Officials in developing countries are concerned with the efficient allocation of educational resources, since education represents their largest and most rapidly increasing budgetary expenditure. The efficiency of an educational system can be defined partly by the net benefits—lifetime earnings, labor productivity, or personal satisfaction—accrued to individuals with more education than those accrued to individuals with less. Educational institutions provide their graduates with these advantages by instilling in them attributes considered necessary to obtain such advantages. These attributes are both cognitive—academic achievement and manual skill—and effective—self-esteem, dependability, creativity, and motivation.

The purpose of this paper is to review studies concerned with school inputs, subject to policy control, which influence student cognitive achievement. First, we discuss the educational production function, a statistical analysis often used in these types of studies. Second, we review studies which have tested the specific effect of a schooling input on achievement. Third, we present a comparison of school inputs relative to other variables. Finally, we list recommendations to policymakers in the developing countries based on the results of these studies.

We conclude that increasing the quality or quantity of most of the traditional inputs, such as teacher training or expenditures per student,

*An earlier version of this chapter was published as an article in *Economic Development and Cultural Change,* vol. 26 (January 1978): 341-67.

is not likely to improve student achievement. Although our review does not cover affective skills which schools also teach, the evidence suggests that they may be more important than cognitive skills in obtaining benefits after going to work, such as higher earnings and satisfaction.[1]

This review is not concerned with linking cognitive and affective attributes to their ultimate benefits, but with identifying the factors which promote cognitive achievement, as measured by school examinations. The major tool of analysis used to measure the relationship between the school inputs, like teacher quality and school facilities, and cognitive achievement, is the educational production function (EPF).

The Educational Production Function and Its Limitations

The "production function" is used to determine the maximum product which can be derived from a given combination of inputs within the existing state of technical knowledge. Its nature and underlying assumptions, as a dimension in the theory of the firm, have been extensively examined. Used for education, it can be generally expressed as:

$$A_{it} = f\,[F_{i(t)}, S_{i(t)}, P_{i(t)}, I_{i(t)}] \tag{1}$$

where i refers to the ith student, t refers to time, and (t) refers to an input cumulative to t. A denotes educational output, usually academic achievement, and the input categories F, S, P, and I represent family background characteristics, school inputs, peer group characteristics, and preschool age abilities, respectively.

To maximize output it is necessary that the marginal product of the last dollar spent be the same for all inputs. The policy prescription which emerges from this condition is to equate the ratios of marginal product to price, over all inputs. However, if this prescription is applied to the input coefficients which emerge from an estimated EPF, efficient allocation of educational resources will almost certainly not result. This is because the estimated coefficients will be biased estimates of the marginal products of the true EPF.

There are five major sources of error which can bias the equation:

(a) *Multiple output interaction.* The educational system produces multiple and interacting outputs; for example, higher self-esteem may also improve a student's academic achievement. Therefore simultaneity bias will arise in the estimation of any single equation by ordinary least squares.[2]

(b) *Misspecification of the functional form of EPF.* There is no established theory of education which can serve as a guide to either the correct form of the EPF, or a priori limits on its coefficients. In practice, an additive linear function has most commonly been used. However, in some schools this may be unacceptable since it implies that the marginal products of the inputs are constant.[3]

(c) *Data limitation.* Inaccuracy can arise from measurement bias due, for example, to a student's inaccurate recollection of family background characteristics, or can arise from specification error due to the omission of a correlated input variable.[4] For example, although student ability may be closely related to socioeconomic status of the family, the exact relationship may be difficult to measure. Similarly teaching methods, frequently related to teacher experience, are usually omitted. Finally, the student's ability upon entering school is seldom measured and thus is not controlled for.

(d) *Multicollinearity.* When the independent variables are highly correlated as they often are among the block of school resources, this can lead to unreliable estimates of the coefficients. Limitation of sampling and measurement error can improve reliability.

(e) *Technical inefficiency of schools.* There is no evidence to suggest that schools are efficiently managed, yet the policy prescription of equating ratios of marginal products to input prices assumes that schools are operating at maximum efficiency. Since this is a false assumption, adherence to the policy prescription for the estimated coefficients from an EPF would not result in optimal resource allocation. Furthermore, the degree of inefficiency is likely to vary among schools. Therefore estimates will reflect an "average" production function.[5] If the coefficient estimates were used as a policy guide, and affected more and less efficient schools, the results would possibly decrease the efficiency of educational allocation as a whole.

One must conclude that these deficiencies prohibit automatic policy recommendation based on EPFs. Depending on the actual limitation in each set of data, the EPF may still be a useful analytical tool for improving, rather than optimizing, the allocation of educational resources, if the improvements are first tested experimentally before being adopted as policy. Since schools may not be running at maximum efficiency, it is more accurate to speak of a cognitive achievement function than an EPF. For example, the affective outcomes of education are not included in the cognitive measures. While the technical inefficiency in schools in combining inputs may not be an important practical problem, the unavoidable bias in the input coefficient estimates will remain, and will prevent them from being used as point estimates of the true marginal products.

A sensitivity analysis is therefore essential, in which the cost effectiveness, or achievement gains per unit cost of a given input, is calculated for a range of values around the estimate of marginal achievement. Since additional assumptions must be made in determining unit input costs, testing a range of unit costs is also desirable. Cost-effectiveness ratios for different inputs can then be compared and used as the basis for policy decisions.

Valid EPF Studies and Inputs to Cognitive Achievement

Student cognitive achievement, as measured by examinations, has been the educational benefit most extensively studied in developing and developed countries. A review of statistically valid EPF studies of primary and secondary level student achievement in developing countries will suggest the effect of various inputs on achievement.

There are at least nineteen EPF studies on developing countries which tend to be comparable since they follow accepted procedures of regression analysis using the ordinary least squares technique and some of the same measures.[6] In contrast to simple correlation analysis, multiple regression permits, for example, the age and family background to be held constant across different students in order to examine the effect of different amounts of teacher training on how much students learn. The authors rejected studies which were not readily available in English, did not examine cognitive achievement as a dependent variable, and did not test a wide range of input variables. The acceptable studies, with their sample statistical procedures and dependent variables, are listed in Table 15.

The independent variables tested cannot be listed in detail since they range from five in the Thias-Carnoy upper secondary school study, to approximately 500 in the International Association for the Evaluation of Educational Achievement (IEA) studies. However, they can be summarized according to the category to which they belong, as shown in equation (1) above.

The most revealing characteristic of family background is usually considered to be the family's socioeconomic status, often measured by parental education, occupation, and income. Some studies also include student, family, and local community expectations and attitudes toward education. Other studies place these variables in a separate block of "kindred variables" which modify the effects of the socioeconomic status. The school inputs listed were variables which describe the learning conditions in the school. While these variables include both school facilities and teacher characteristics, the study is designed in such a way that potentially important effects on learning may not be revealed. For example, studies which use an average of teacher characteristics for the school as a whole cannot detect the influence of teacher-student relationships operating in the classroom. The Carnoy-Thias study[7] and the IEA studies by Comber-Keeves[8] are an exception.

Simmons'[9] and Schiefelbein-Farrell's[10] study of peer group characteristics measured the influence of other students' attitudes and performances on the individual's achievement. Finally, the last category of input, initial endowments, considered variables such as IQ or reading ability at school entry, age, and sex. No study includes a direct measure of ability such as IQ. However, some studies of upper secondary achievement used a secondary entrance examination as an approximation of ability. This attempts to summarize the impact of all prior influences, including IQ, on performance.

TABLE 15

Description of Educational Production Function Studies Explaining Student Cognitive Achievement in Developing Countries

Author(s) and publication date	Country	Sample		Statistical procedure	Measure of student academic achievement
		Primary or lower secondary grade	Upper secondary grade		
Carnoy 1971	Puerto Rico	182,000 students in grades 3, 6, 9 and 12 of all public schools		OLS and two-stage least squares multiple regression	Average student score on a Spanish reading examination for each school*
Youdi 1971	Congo	...	1450 students in grades 11 and 12 selected randomly from 25 secondary schools	Stepwise OLS multiple regression	Individual scores on IEA†multiple choice tests in French and mathematics
Simmons 1972	Tunisia	44 students from a village and 80 students from an urban suburb, all in grades 4-8	...	Stepwise OLS multiple regression	Individual scores on multiple choice tests in Arabic, French, and arithmetic
Beebout 1972	Malaysia	...	7674 students in grades 10 and 11 in a random sample of 89 secondary schools	OLS multiple regression using both a quadratic and linear functional form	An index of individual student performance relative to that of his peers; performance defined as the difference between secondary entrance and final examination scores
Comber-Keeves 1973 Thorndike 1973	Chile, India, Iran, Thailand	258,000 students in 9700 schools randomly selected in 15 developed countries and 4 developing countries. Three populations were tested— primary students aged 10, lower secondary stu-		Stepwise OLS multiple regression	Individual scores on internationally developed multiple choice tests in science and

				native language reading comprehension‡
		dents aged 14, and students in the terminal upper secondary year		
Schiefelbein-Farrell 1973	Chile	353 randomly selected grade 8 classes in both primary and secondary schools with an average response of 10 students per class	OLS multiple regression and commonality analysis	Individual scores on national grade 8 test in Spanish and arithmetic
Ryan 1973	Iran	797 grade 2 students selected randomly from 66 rural schools in 2 provinces	OLS multiple regression and commonality analysis	Individual scores on multiple choice tests in Persian and arithmetic
Thias-Carnoy 1973	Kenya	3405 rural primary students in grade 7 in a random sample of 89 primary schools	OLS multiple regression	Average student score on Kenya Preliminary Examination for each school
Thias-Carnoy 1973	Kenya	Students in 115 rural and urban schools in form IV (grade 11)	OLS loglinear multiple regression	Average student score on Cambridge School Certificate Examination for each school
Carnoy-Thias 1974	Tunisia	6195 students in grades 7-11 randomly selected from rural and urban secondary schools	Stepwise OLS multiple regression	Individual student grade point average on school examinations

Note—OLS = ordinary least squares.
*Other endogenous variables in the simultaneous equation model were the student's expected level of schooling, self-esteem, and desire to transfer to another school.
†IEA = International Association for the Evaluation of Educational Achievement.
‡Other subjects tested were literature, French as a foreign language, English as a foreign language, and civics.

School Inputs

Understanding the influence of schooling inputs on achievement, both absolutely and in relation to other variables, is of primary importance in policy decisions. Some of the policy variables are easier to change than others. These include, for example, allocation of resources with regard to teacher quality, student-teacher ratio, school size, availability of boarding accommodations, and the size of library facilities. Other policy variables, such as those concerning the amount of time an individual is exposed to a learning environment, are more difficult to control. They may be subject to policy control in the future—for example, allowing the student to obtain more education by changing the size of the educational system.

The findings of the studies in Table 15 reveal that some school inputs do have an important and statistically demonstrable effect on academic achievement. However, many inputs, especially those subject to policy control and traditionally thought to be important, have no effect on achievement. There is such inconsistency in the effect of a given policy variable on achievement across countries that we can tentatively suggest only a few which might be used to improve the internal efficiency of education in countries for which there are data. These recommendations will be made in a later section of this chapter. Given the limitations of methods and data, experimental and longitudinal studies of the country in question should be undertaken before policy decisions are made.

A Comparison of the Importance of Schooling Inputs and Home Background

Home background, or parental socioeconomic status, generally has a stronger influence on student performance at primary and lower secondary grades than the policy controlled schooling variables. This premise is supported by the results of the Simmons study for Tunisia. Also, the IEA study by Thorndike of reading comprehension at primary grades in Chile, India, Iran, and Thailand found that home background variables explained between 1.5 percent and 8.7 percent of the variance in test scores, while most policy controlled schooling variables were not statistically significant and accounted for little of the total variance. The remaining variance is due to either factors which have not been measured or a more accurate measurement of the variables already included. The only exception consistent across several countries was the number of hours of homework done each week. However, it accounted for only 0.6 percent of the total variance. There are exceptions to this general finding, depending on the composition of the sample and on the subject being tested.

The Ryan study for Iran,[11] covering only rural and village students, found that the combination of school and teacher variables explained more of the variance in achievement scores than did home and peer group variables combined. Of course, the variance in family socio-economic status for the rural sample is small, and the contribution of home background may thereby be reduced. The IEA study of primary students showed that both home background and policy controlled school variables explained between 0 percent and 4 percent of test score variance. Finally, it is possible that the relative influence of schooling variables is underestimated by single equation estimation of the EPF. The structural form results of the Carnoy study for Puerto Rico[12] indicate that home background has a smaller influence, and schooling variables a larger influence on achievement compared to the reduced form results.

Although home background is important in the primary and early secondary grades, its influence diminishes as the student moves upward. In the upper secondary grades, policy controlled schooling variables have the greater influence. This is demonstrated by four studies which cover many grade levels—Carnoy-Thias for Tunisia, Carnoy for Puerto Rico, Thorndike,[13] and Comber and Keeves. In Comber and Keeves' study of terminal secondary science achievement (the last year of secondary school), the average contribution of home background is between 0 percent and 2 percent, while schooling policy variables explain over 4 percent of total variance. Only the Beebout study[14] of upper secondary students receiving instruction in the Malay language indicates that socioeconomic status is important.[15]

Furthermore, IEA studies for reading and science concluded that home background accounted for more of the variance in primary and lower secondary scores in the developed countries than in the developing countries. However, this greater contribution of home background

TABLE 16

Results of Educational Production Function Studies for Developing Countries

Variable and expected sign of its relationship to student performance	Statistically significant with expected sign	Not statistically significant, or with opposite sign
Boarding at secondary grade (+)	Thias-Carnoy (grade 11); Carnoy-Thias; Youdi	Beebout
Grade repetition(-)	Thias-Carnoy (grade 7); Simmons-Youdi	Beebout
Double sessions (-)	Beebout	Schiefelbein-Farrell
Size of school enrollment at upper secondary grades(?)	(+) Thias-Carnoy (grade 11); Comber-Keeves	(-) Beebout; Youdi
Performance and attitudes of classroom peer-group (+)	Carnoy-Thias; Schiefelbein-Farrell(?)	…
Per pupil expenditures on school facilities or teachers (+)	…	Thias-Carnoy (grade 11); Beebout
Average class size, or pupil : teacher ratio (-)	Carnoy; Beebout; Ryan	Thias-Carnoy (grade 7); Schiefelbein-Farrell; Comber-Keeves; Thorndike
Teacher certification and academic qualification at primary and lower secondary grades (+)	Carnoy	Ryan; Thias-Carnoy (grade 7); Schiefelbein-Farrell

Factor		
Teacher certification and academic qualification at upper secondary grades (+)	Beebout; Youdi; Comber-Keeves	Carnoy-Thias; Carnoy
Teacher contract (tenure) at upper secondary grades (+)	Carnoy	Carnoy-Thias
Teacher experience at primary and lower secondary grades (+)	Thias-Carnoy (grade 7); Schiefelbein-Farrell; Carnoy	Carnoy-Thias
Teacher experience at upper secondary grades (+)	Beebout	Carnoy-Thias; Carnoy; Youdi
Teacher sex—males at primary and lower secondary grades; females at upper secondary grades (+)	Carnoy-Thias; Beebout; Comber-Keeves; Thorndike	Thias-Carnoy (grade 7); Carnoy; Youdi
Teacher motivation (+)	Ryan; Comber-Keeves	
Textbook availability at primary grades (+)	Schiefelbein-Farrell; Comber-Keeves	
Availability and use of library (+)	Beebout; Thorndike	
Homework and free reading at home (+)	Schiefelbein-Farrell; Simmons; Comber-Keeves; Thorndike	

could be explained largely by exposure to educational experiences rather than by the influence of policy controlled schooling inputs. Parents in the developed countries may tend to show more interest in educating their children and in providing them with educational materials than parents in the developing countries.

This finding suggests that formal education does improve cognitive achievement in the developing countries, but that it is effective primarily through the length of a student's exposure to schooling. Fiscal policies attempting to alter schooling inputs, such as the length of teacher training, are likely to have little effect on student achievement at primary and lower secondary grades. For the upper secondary grades, while exposure to the educational system is still important, policy controlled schooling variables have an equivalent or greater effect on achievement. This indicates that the physical efficiency of existing educational systems in the upper secondary school could be improved substantially. Since cost-benefit analysis has not yet been performed with these data, we do not know whether or not such improvement would yield net benefits, thus improving economic efficiency. A school system might be able to increase student reading ability by a few percentage points by increasing the amount of time spent on books by 100 percent. Unless the benefits in terms of more income or productivity that accrued to the worker and the society were greater in value than the cost of the books, the physical efficiency had gone up but the economic value of the change was negative.

The Effect of Schooling Variables on Achievement

The findings of all studies reviewed by this chapter are summarized in Table 16, while Table 17 shows where the studies were done. Table 16 shows which studies find a given schooling input to have a statistically significant impact on achievement, on the basis of the traditional expectations of educators and economists, and which studies do not. Table 16 suggests several important findings.

One policy variable which also intensifies the exposure to learning environment is the provision of boarding facilities at the secondary school. This is demonstrated by the Carnoy-Thias studies for Kenya and Tunisia and in the Youdi study for the Congo.[16] The studies show

TABLE 17
Location of the Studies

Author	Country
Beebout	Malaysia
Carnoy	Puerto Rico
Carnoy and Thias	Tunisia
Comber and Keeves	Chile, India, Iran, Thailand
Ryan	Iran
Schiefelbein and Farrell	Chile
Simmons	Tunisia
Thias and Carnoy	Kenya
Thorndike	Chile, India, Iran
Youdi	Congo

that "boarding", independent of home background, has a greater influence than any other policy controlled variable. We should note, however, that boarding may be a substitute for more study time, fewer distractions, and increased financial motivation. The Beebout study for Malaysia, on the other hand, found that boarding is not statistically significant. The provision of more boarding facilities may or may not lead to higher achievement.

It is obvious, therefore, that no general recommendations on boarding can be made to developing countries without further study. It can only be regarded as *potentially* important in aiding student performance. Furthermore, it should be determined whether or not the learning environment associated with the boarding schools can be provided without incurring the expense.

Other policy variables are shown to have a positive influence on performance by some studies, but negative or no influence in others. Collectively, the results again stress the need for individual EPF and experimental studies of a given educational system before policy recommendations can be made. One of these ambivalent variables is the use of double sessions at primary and early secondary grades in order to extend formal education to more students. Schiefelbein-Farrell find that double sessions have a positive influence on achievement, whereas Beebout finds the opposite.

A larger school size at the upper secondary level was found to be important by both Thias-Carnoy and Thorndike, possibly because larger schools have better teaching aids and facilities. However, Beebout and Youdi found a larger enrollment to be detrimental to performance, perhaps because smaller schools in Malaysia and the Congo have superior facilities.

A variable traditionally considered important to the internal efficiency of schooling, as argued by the educators, is class size or the student-teacher ratio within the range twenty-five to forty-five students. The larger the class size or higher the student-teacher ratio, the lower the student achievement. Four studies, including those of Thorndike and Comber-Keeves in Chile, Thailand, and elsewhere found this assertion to be incorrect. However, in Puerto Rico, Malaysia, and the Congo, a larger class size did in fact have a negative impact on performance. These countries were not in the IEA sample.

Recommendations on Schooling Variables

The influence of teacher characteristics on student performance is a central issue. Although no general policy recommendations for these variables can be made, each of the following conclusions is suggested by the majority of studies.

- Teacher certification and academic qualification are not important at primary and lower secondary grades. But they do appear to be important at upper secondary grades in *some* subject areas, such as science, given the consistency across developed and developing countries in the IEA science study regarding the significance of post-secondary schooling of teachers.
- The percentage of teachers on permanent contract (tenure) has no effect on student achievement in primary and lower secondary grades. However, it may have a positive or negative influence on upper secondary grades depending on the country being examined. Examples of this agnostic conclusion are seen in the IEA science study and the Thias-Carnoy Kenya study.
- Teacher experience tends to have a positive influence on academic achievement in primary and lower secondary grades. For example, teacher salary is significant in the Thias-Carnoy Kenya study, and

this reflects teacher seniority and experience. In upper secondary grades, teacher experience is not important.

Teacher sex has a variable influence on performance, depending on grade level. Male teachers tend to positively influence male students in grades five to eight, but have a negative influence on students of both sexes at the upper secondary level. However, the negative influence of male teachers is evident in the Carnoy Puerto Rico study by the eighth grade. At higher levels, female teachers positively influence female student performance.

Finally, there are a few policy variables which tend to give consistent results across the countries in which they were tested. These are the variables that should receive the greatest attention of policymakers. However, we do not imply that choosing the variables mentioned below will guarantee an improvement in student achievement or in reducing cost. The studies indicate that for the developing countries: (a) Gross expenditures such as the cost of school facilities per student or the average teacher salary are not important influences on student performance. Thus, unit costs, particularly at the secondary and higher levels, could be lowered significantly without affecting performance. (b) Teacher motivation, as indicated by time spent in lesson preparation or membership on curriculum reform committees, is a positive influence on performance. Policy research should identify highly motivated teachers and discover methods for motivating the rest of the staff. (c) Textbook availability at the primary level may be an important influence on performance. An associated factor is the availability and use of a library at primary and early secondary grades. The policy implications include supplying a minimum number of texts or reading materials to all students. (d) The amount of homework done by students, the physical conditions of home study, and the amount of reading done at home are important predictors of student achievement.

These observations indicate that the more a student is exposed to a learning environment in the home, the greater his academic achievement will be. Policymakers could ensure that teacher training courses promote the use of homework as a teaching method, and that students are at least provided with adequate conditions, such as good light and a quiet room for home study and with opportunities for extracurricular reading. Programs should be developed to educate parents on early child development.

Thus, the only changes that could possibly be recommended to improve internal efficiency of the educational system in those developing countries for which there are data concern the reduction of unit costs, teacher motivation, textbooks and other reading materials, and homework. These recommendations are offered simply as a starting point. They may be useful to policymakers interested in experimenting with a limited number of schools to see if improvements could be made. No guarantees of success are made.

We can recommend certain methods for conducting this research. In contrast to most of the reviewed studies, future EPF studies should examine a variety of schooling outputs rather than isolating one, such as achievement, for analysis. Variables such as academic achievement, drop-out rates, individual modernity, motivation, and self-esteem should be treated as simultaneously produced outcomes. Ordinary least-squares estimations and path analyses offer the most attractive statistical procedures. Also, efforts should be made in cooperation with other disciplines such as psychology and anthropology to improve measurement of these variables. Refining the measures for student and teacher motivation and schooling outputs is possibly the first step in this process.[17] Finally, data on preschool age cognitive ability are essential. This information would allow the researcher to determine what effects education alone had on later achievement.

Results from these procedures should provide data for sensitivity analysis of the cost effectiveness of the inputs suggested by EPF research. However, given limited resources, it may be more fruitful for countries where EPF research has already suggested important schooling inputs to test the cost effectiveness of these inputs by experimental and longitudinal research techniques rather than by repeating the cross-sectional EPF approach.

Conclusion

This review concludes that the determinants of student achievement appear to be basically the same in developing and developed countries.[18] This view is supported by the consistency of the influence on achievement of the variables tested in the IEA studies, which compared four developing countries with nineteen developed countries. Studies which summarize the data from educational production functions conducted in the United States, such as that of Keisling, have also reached this conclusion. However, an important difference arises because home conditions in the developing countries are not as conducive to learning, and reading materials are not as readily available. But it is important to realize that factors which have traditionally been considered essential to better education—higher quality teachers, more expensive facilities—do not seem to increase achievement at lower grade levels, even in the poorest countries. Instead, the greatest gains occur simply because the student is moved from the home into a school environment. Therefore, policies which are aimed at increasing the individual's exposure to the educational system could, on average, have a positive influence on his cognitive achievement.[19] By the time the student has reached upper secondary grade levels, he has already been exposed to a learning environment and therefore other variables—such as teacher quality—might have a greater influence on his achievement. This will be true to a greater extent in some countries than in others.

Finally, regardless of the grade level, policies designed to improve educational efficiency must be as cost-effective as possible, given the limitations imposed by data and available techniques of analysis. The educational production function can assist in identifying potential policy controlled determinants of achievement in a specific educational system. When used in conjunction with cost-benefit analysis and experimental design, it can indicate those which have the greatest net social benefits.

Notes

1. See Herb Gintis, "Education, technology, and the characteristics of worker productivity", *American Economic Review,* vol. 61 (May 1971): 266-79, for a discussion of the relationship between cognitive and affective traits, and the ultimate benefits of each; and for data on developing countries, see John Simmons and Henry Noerenberg, "Psychological determinants of earnings", mimeograph (Washington, D.C.: World Bank, 1977).

2. Simultaneous equation models for the United States include Henry Levin, "A new model of school effectiveness", in *Do Teachers Make a Difference?* (Washington, D.C.: U.S. Dept. of Health, Education, and Welfare, 1970); and Anthony E. Boardman, Otto A. Davis, and Peggy R. Sanday, "A simultaneous equations model of the educational process", working paper (Pittsburg, Pa.: Carnegie Mellon University School of Urban and Public Affairs, September 1973).

3. Harold S. Beebout, in "The production surface for academic achievement: an economic study of Malaysian secondary education" (Ph.D. dissertation, University of Wisconsin at Madison, 1972), tests eleven functional forms for use as educational production function surfaces and chooses the quadratic form on a priori grounds.

4. These limitations are discussed in more detail in Samuel Bowles, "Towards an educational production function", in *Education, Income, and Human Capital* ed. W. L. Hansen (New York: Columbia University Press, 1970); and Herbert J. Keisling, "Multivariate analysis of schools and educational policy", mimeograph (Santa Monica, Calif.: RAND Corporation, March 1971). Also see Carl F. Christ, *Econometric Models and Methods* (New York: John Wiley & Sons, 1966), p. 338.

5. Since schools are not maximizing it may be more correct to replace the term "educational production function" with the term "cognitive achievement function" if cognitive achievement is the output being examined.

6. We have reviewed only two of the studies made by the International Association for the Evaluation of Educational Achievement (IEA) because of the comparability of science and reading achievement with the rest of the literature. We would appreciate readers' suggestions of studies we have omitted.

7. Martin Carnoy and Hans H. Thias, "Draft report of second Tunisia education research project RPO248", mimeograph (Washington, D.C.: World Bank, 1974).

8. L. C. Comber and John P. Keeves, *Science Education in Nineteen Countries* (New York: Halsted Press, 1973).

9. John Simmons with Erkut Sumru, "Schooling for development? Students and workers in Tunisia", mimeograph (Cambridge, Mass.: Harvard University, Department of Economics, 1972).

10. Ernesto Schiefelbein and Joseph Farrell, "Factors influencing academic performance among Chilean primary students", paper presented at the Annual Meeting of the International Society of Educational Planners and the American Association for the Advancement of Science, Mexico City, June 1973.

11. John W. Ryan, "Educational resources and scholastic outcomes: a study of rural primary schooling in Iran" (Ph.D. dissertation, Stanford University, 1973).

12. Martin Carnoy, "Family background, school inputs and students' performance in school: the case of Puerto Rico", mimeograph (Palo Alto, Calif.: Stanford University, 1971).

13. Robert L. Thorndike, *Reading Comprehension in Fifteen Countries* (New York: Halsted Press, 1973).

14. Harold S. Beebout, "The production surface for academic achievement: an economic study of the Malaysian secondary education" (Ph.D. dissertation, University of Wisconsin at Madison, 1972).

15. Ernesto Schiefelbein and Joseph Farrell, "Factors influencing academic performance among Chilean primary students", argue that for the lower secondary grades, peer group influence is greater than home background. A commonality analysis indicates that the observed contribution of peer group variables is twice

that of student background characteristics. However, the "average possession of a TV set in the home per class" has a high Beta coefficient and is included in the peer group variable. Since this variable should probably be included in home background, the strong influence of peer group variables is doubtful. Also, no other study indicates peer group influence to exceed that of home background.

16. Robert V. Youdi, "An exploratory study of achievement and attitudes of high school students in the Congo: an aspect of socialization for national development", Ph.D. dissertation, Stanford University, 1971.

17. A study which attempts to define a measure of academic motivation for eleventh-grade Puerto Rican students is W. M. Farquhar and E. W. Christensen, *Motivational Factors Influencing Academic Achievement of Eleventh Grade Puerto Rican High School Students* (East Lansing: Michigan State University Press, 1968). Its aim is to determine the influence of child rearing and other psychological-sociological factors on motivation and thence on academic achievement. Some psychologically interpretable instruments are suggested. For a catalog of these measures for the United States, see Ralf Hoepfner et al., *CSE-RBS Test Evaluations: Tests of Higher Order Cognitive, Affective, and Interpersonal Skills* (Los Angeles: Center for the Study of Evaluation, Graduate School of Education, University of California, 1972).

18. For a review of research on the developed countries see John Simmons, "Does schooling make a difference?", Working Paper (Washington, D.C.: World Bank, 1974).

19. Because we do not have EPF data on the effect of nonformal education on changing behavior, we cannot draw inferences from the data on formal education.

CHAPTER 5

Preschool Age Investment in Human Capital

MARCELO SELOWSKY

It is true that schools have "inputs" and "outputs", and that one of their nominal purposes is to take human "raw material" (i.e. children) and convert it into something more "valuable" (i.e. employable adults). Our research suggests, however, that the character of a school's output depends largely on a single input, namely the characteristics of the entering children. Everything else—the school budget, its policies, the characteristics of the teachers—is either secondary or completely irrelevant.[1]

This widely held view in the current discussion about the effectiveness of schooling in the United States is a good way to introduce the subject of preschool age investment in human capital into the discussion of human capital formation in general. The thrust of this chapter is that this idea articulated by Christopher Jencks ought to be a working hypothesis of prime importance in the discussion of human capital formation in developing countries. The relevance of preschool age investment in human capital to the process of human capital formation in general and to formal schooling in particular, rests heavily on the following evidence: (a) The fraction of children from low income families in the elementary school system will increase over time. (b) There is growing empirical evidence to show that preschool age children from poorer segments of the population in developing countries do worse on most ability tests than matching controls from higher income groups.[2] (c) There is a growing literature in the medical field which attempts to show that early malnutrition, a phenomenon that characterizes a large fraction of children in developing countries,[3] adversely affects mental performance as well as children's psycho-motor activity.[4] (d) The recent literature in the field of education and psychology suggests that although heredity explains an important fraction of children's intelligence scores (Jensen), environment is still crucial in such explanations (Jencks), particularly at early ages of life (Bloom).[5]

If considerations (a) and (b) are accepted, elementary school systems in developing countries will face an increasing deterioration of its "raw input". On the other hand, if the productivity of school inputs in the production of abilities, however defined, is largely dependent on the quality of that "raw input", the effect of schooling might in the future be highly sensitive to current policies concerning preschool age types of investment in human capital. Considerations (c) and (d) suggest some determinants of low ability scores which might be mani-pulated by public policy.

A Model for Examining Preschool Age Abilities

In order to focus on the economic questions of the earlier discus-sion, it would first be important to analyze the effect of preschool age public actions on cognitive and affective performance at adult age (or at the age the individual enters the labor force), as measured by available tests. The economic problem becomes how preschool age investment in human capital can contribute to a "least-cost solution" in the accumulation of cognitive and noncognitive skills by adulthood.

A glance at the literature on educational psychology suggests the use of some familiar tools. Assume that the production of cognitive and noncognitive performance at adult age (π) can be written as:

$$\pi = F(A, S) \tag{1}$$

where A represents the abilities of the child as he or she enters the school system, and S represents the school (and nonschool) environ-ment inputs to which he or she is exposed during schooling age. Let us treat S as a vector of school inputs.

Some of Jencks's findings also allow the mathematician to say something about the form of equation (1): not only has A an impor-tant independent contribution to π, but it also determines the magnitude of the contribution of S.[6] This means that equation (1) could be written as:

$$\pi = A^{\alpha} S^{1-\alpha}. \tag{2}$$

From expression (2) it is clear that the contribution or marginal productivity of school inputs (MPS) now becomes a function of the level of ability of the entering child:

$$MPS = \frac{\delta \pi}{\delta S} = (1-\alpha)\left(\frac{A^{\alpha}}{S}\right). \tag{3}$$

Jencks's statement now implies that the more important A in the production of π, which implies a "large" value of A, the more important the quality of the raw input in determining the contribution of schooling to adult abilities.

On the other hand, considerations (c) and (d) of the previous section suggest that A is itself a function:

$$A = Gf(O, E) \tag{4}$$

where G is a genetic endowment; O is an index of inputs affecting organic and physical growth; and E is environmental inputs characterizing the milieu of the child.

For policy purposes, some of the explanatory variables of the above expression can be further detailed:

$$A = Gf[N, H, E_h, E_o] \tag{5}$$

where N is an index of the quality of nutrition during preschool age, H is an index of health services the child receives during preschool age, E_h is an index of the quality of the child's home environment during preschool years; and E_o is an index of the quality of the child's out-of-home environment during preschool years.

The question, "Are developing countries overinvesting in schooling relative to preschool age investment in human capital?", can now be summarized in Fig. 3, in which π_1 and π_0 represent different levels of ability. Answering such a question will require: (a) information about α, or the contribution of A to π. To a certain extent this can be obtained through "educational production function" studies where A is introduced explicitly into such a function;[7] (b) information about the coefficients of those explanatory variables of equation (5) which

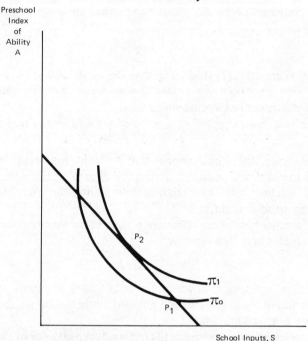

Fig. 3. Preschool ability and school inputs in the "production" of abilities at adult age.

can be affected by public policy; and (c) calculating the resource cost of inducing changes in those variables affecting π, per unit change in π.

The developing country will be overinvesting, given the relative costs of A and S, if it is situated at a point such as P_1, rather than P_2, which represents the optimum.

To date, virtually no research attempting to separate the "value added" of schooling from the effect of the ability of the entering child has been undertaken in developing countries. Most of the research on this subject has been conducted in the United States by researchers with noneconomic perspectives.

An estimate of preschool ability requires measurement of abilities in long individual follow-ups (at least fifteen years), as well as data on all environmental variables in the interim period. Almost no study combines both requirements. Some of them, particularly those under-taken by psychologists, consist of long follow-up studies of IQ measurements, with little recorded data on environmental variables to which the individual was exposed between these measurements.[8]

I now review some of the research which suggests that early ability (at ages four and six) is an important determinant of an adult's level of ability, as measured by current IQ tests.

Bloom's interpretation of the results of major longitudinal studies undertaken in the United States in the last sixty years,[9] finds that the correlation coefficient between IQ at any age (*T-t*) and IQ score at maturity (*T*), increases. Such a relationship appears to be quite similar across studies "done with different groups of children, in different parts of the country, with different examiners, and at different times".[10] Figure 4 illustrates these findings.

Bloom concludes that "in terms of intelligence measured at age 17, at least 20 percent is developed by age 1, 50 percent by about age 4,

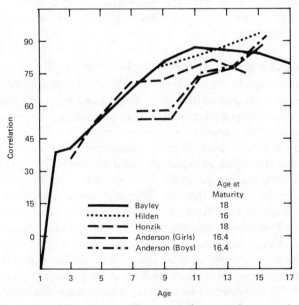

Fig. 4. Correlation between IQ at an early age and at maturity.

80 percent by about age 8 and 92 percent by age 13."[11] If Bloom is correct, it is possible that the regression coefficient obtained by using an IQ score at age eleven would represent an upward bias estimate of the contribution of an earlier IQ score (at preschool age).

Research by John Conlisk, using longitudinal data on students' IQ scores, found the following regression equations:[12]

$$IQ_{18} = 4.77 + 4.90\,IQ_{1\text{-}5} + 1.514\,\text{years schooling}$$

$$(6.44)\quad (.099)\qquad\quad (.358)\qquad\qquad R^2 = .45;$$

$$IQ_{18} = 8.11 + .527\,IQ_{6\text{-}8} + 1.051\,\text{years schooling}$$

$$(5.75)\quad (.093)\qquad\quad (.367)\qquad\qquad R^2 = .49.$$

The subscript of IQ denotes the age range at which the test was administered, and standard errors are in parenthesis.

According to these results, three points of IQ at ages below five are a substitute for one year of schooling; for IQ at later ages (between six and eight), two points of IQ are a substitute for one year of subsequent schooling.

Nongenetic Determinants of Preschool Ability

It is important to identify those variables which determine a child's preschool abilities and which can be manipulated by policy instruments usually available to governments. Very possibly the nongenetic variables fall into this category.

By now it is well accepted that an important fraction of children's intelligence scores can be explained by inheritance. The recent discussion has centered on the order of magnitude of such explanation. In this respect I quote Jencks: "Whereas Arthur Jensen and others have argued that 80 percent of the variance in IQ scores is explained by genetic factors, our analysis suggests that the correct figure is probably more like 45 percent."[13]

The question remains to what extent these studies would show less variance explained by genetic factors if undertaken in developing countries. It is probable that there is a much greater variation in nongenetic variables across children in developing countries than in the

United States. If this is true, and if these variables do influence the level of preschool abilities in the theoretical model, the results obtained for the United States would not be applicable to the developing countries, where nongenetic variables have a greater effect on variance in IQ scores. This is an important conclusion; it means that those variables subject to governmental manipulation assume an even greater importance than may have been previously believed.

At this stage, it is worth asking a pragmatic question: Is it worthwhile to disentangle the effect of the different nongenetic variables to which low income group children are exposed, and which, as a package, contribute to low preschool ability scores? If it is true that children from lower income groups, subject to a package of nutritional, health, and environmental deprivation, score worse on mental tests, why not deal directly with the whole package of these variables?

Two considerations reject such a proposal. First, some of the variables in that package are difficult to manipulate from an institutional point of view, and it is not known to what extent the variables are the true determinants of children's performance. In such a case, manipulating the rest of the package would not have a great effect on performance.

Second, it is realistic to assume that the resources available for such public programs would be highly constrained, particularly because they involve sharp redistributive policies. Therefore, it is necessary to identify those variables which have the greatest effect per dollar spent. This necessarily requires an estimate of the net effect of such a variable. The following is a discussion of the literature which provides information on the net effect of nongenetic variables.

The Effect of Early Malnutrition

The way in which early malnutrition, especially a deficiency in the intake of high quality proteins, affects mental functioning is basically physiological: nutrient deficiency damages the central nervous system, because early brain growth is largely a process of protein synthesis.[14] This has been confirmed in experiments with animals, and by preliminary findings of reductions in the number of brain cells in children who had suffered severe malnutrition.[15]

The relevant issue is the extent to which these organic changes affect learning and behavior, as measured by available test scores. J. Cravioto and E. De Licardie review the experiments undertaken in various countries which tend to support the connection; what should be emphasized here is the fact that some particular types of abilities that seem to be affected by malnutrition also appear to be crucial for further learning. If this is true, early malnutrition would condition the effectiveness of school inputs at later ages. For example, Cravioto and De Licardie found in 1969 that problems with auditory-visual integration could lead to impairment of reading abilities.[16]

Almost all studies have recognized apathetic behavior as one of the clearest consequences of malnutrition. Cravioto and De Licardie have an interesting hypothesis about the further effects of apathy: "It should be recognized that the mother's response to the infant is to a considerable degree a function of the child's own characteristic of reactivity. Apathetic behavior in its turn can reduce the value of the child as a stimulus and diminish the adult's responsiveness to him. Thus, apathy can provoke apathy and so contribute to a cumulative pattern of reduced adult-child interaction."[17]

Other causal mechanisms by which early malnutrition is thought to affect learning have been advanced in the literature. There is some evidence showing that infectious diseases are likely to be more severe and more frequent among malnourished children.[18] To the extent that an infectious disease affects the child's responsiveness to his environment, it affects his cognitive development.

The Effect of Early Environment

The effect of early environment on later achievement is a subject about which much has been written, and which has yielded many contradictory interpretations. One phenomenon is striking: little research has been done in developing countries.

One approach to this problem is oriented toward policy. There are basically two types of environment which the child is exposed to at preschool age, home environment and out-of-home environment. The policy options are to change the quality of both types of environment and to change the amount of time that the child is exposed to a particular environment.

Figure 5 shows, under two different settings, a hypothetical distribution of the time spent in both environments; the older the child the larger the fraction of time he spends (or can spend) away from home. On the same graph is plotted an index of Bloom's development curve (BDC); the shaded area represents the limit of variation that the quality of the environment can produce at different points in the child's development.[19]

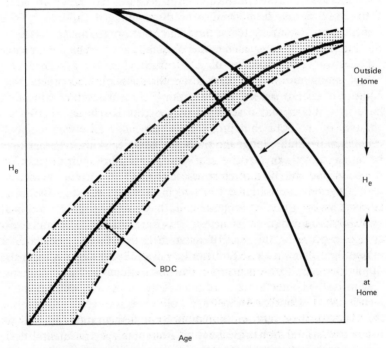

Fig. 5. Changing the mix of environments of the child. (H_e = hours per year exposed to the environment; BDC = Bloom's development curve.)

Changing the Out-of-home Environment

The best examples of changing the out-of-home environment are the large-scale programs of preschool compensatory education (between ages three and five) undertaken in the United States, particularly the Head Start program. The Rand Corporation has surveyed almost all the research evaluating such programs.[20] Although there is wide disagreement over the interpretation of such evaluations, it would seem that results have not been encouraging.

These preliminary findings concerning large-scale compensatory programs in the United States have led researchers into two new areas of study. First, they hoped to determine the extent to which programs such as Head Start were unsuccessful because they failed to adapt themselves to the characteristics of disadvantaged children. To a large degree, some features of the Head Start program were based on the nursery and kindergarten model originally adopted by high income families whose aim was free play. Hunt concluded that, "Headstart is not synonymous with compensatory education. Compensatory education has not failed. Investigations of compensatory education have now shown that traditional play school has little to offer the children of the poor, but programs which made an effort to inculcate cognitive skills, language skills and number skills, whether they be taught directly or incorporated into games, show fair success."[21]

The second line of research stresses the fact that current compensatory programs are initiated too late in a child's life. If Bloom is correct, by age three or four the child has already been conditioned by the environmental deficiencies of his family life.[22] The main constraint in pursuing this line of research is that there is probably a minimum age at which a child can be physically withdrawn from the family in order to be exposed to an institutionalized environment.

Outside the United States, I found a piece of research which must be mentioned.[23] Undertaken in Cali, Colombia, it attempts to identify the types of intervention (nutritional supplementation as well as behavioral stimulation) necessary to overcome specific mental deficiencies in three-year-olds from the lowest economic levels of the city. This research is important because: (a) the children analyzed are not characterized by extreme malnutrition and tend to represent the more typical and therefore more relevant situation of low income families in urban areas; and (b) particular emphasis was placed on analyzing the effect of a specific type of intervention on mental tasks, important to later learning. Preliminary findings showed that particular types of stimulation and nutritional intervention at age three can boost certain mental capabilities above the performance of well-nourished children from similar income groups.

Home Environment Before Age Three

Bloom's hypothesis, together with the fact that there are probably institutional constraints on the earliest age that a child can be drawn away from the family, has led some researchers into another area of study: the effect of different rearing practices and different mother-child interactions on the child under age three. I quote Jerome Kagan: "A final strategy, not exclusive of the first two (school and preschool years 2½ to 5), is to change the mother's relationship with her infant. The idea for this suggestion rests on the assumption that a child's experience with his adult caretaker during the first 24 months of life are major determinants of the quality of his motivation, expectancy of success, and cognitive abilities during the school years."[24]

In an experiment with 140 infants of different socioeconomic classes, Kagan found significant differences in fixation time, vocalization, and fear responses. In another experiment, sixty ten-month-old girls from two different socioeconomic groups were studied.[25] The families were visited and the child-mother interactions were recorded. In the higher socioeconomic group, the mother "spent more time in face-to-face posture, more time talking to her and issued more distinctive vocalization to the infant. They were more likely to entertain their children with objects, to encourage walking and to reward them for mastery."[26] Behavior of the infants at the laboratory showed that those belonging to the upper group were better able to differentiate meaningful from nonmeaningful speech and its source. At the same time, they showed a stronger will to resolve acoustic differences between different voices.

The Ypsilanti Carnegie Project discovered an important effect on the mental growth of young infants in programs where specially trained teachers worked with the mother and the infant at home. The main objective of the program was for the teacher to affect the child through the mother.[27]

Research Implications for the Future

Research implications for the developing countries drawn from these hypotheses are enormous, and priorities should be established. I have chosen the following criteria in such a selection: (a) research that can be helpful in guiding policy instruments available in the short run; (b) research requiring the cooperation of the existing logistics of the educational system; and (c) research whose policy implications are directly relevant to existing educational systems.

Level of Abilities of the Entering Student

Three questions concerning the levels of abilities of entering students appear to warrant further exploration: (a) How large are the differences in abilities across socioeconomic and ethnic groups on a country-wide basis? Until now, this information has been obtained through isolated samples and by a variety of scientists in different disciplines, making it hard to analyze. Is it possible to institutionalize a generalized test of abilities to be administered to all entering children? What questions should be asked in these tests? What could the educators suggest in this report? (b) Which socioeconomic and ethnic groups will be incorporated into the elementary school system of a given country during the next decade? How would they perform on the test outlined in question (a) above? (c) If the level of entering abilities will be changing, what are the implications for changes in the quality and types of school inputs? Are certain types of school inputs better substitutes for entering abilities than others?

Affecting the Determinants of Ability

Policies to change the out-of-home environment through wide-scale preschool compensatory programs seem to be difficult to undertake in the short run, unless these programs are thought of as simple extensions of the existing elementary school system, which would draw children into kindergarten programs one or two years earlier. The United States' experience has shown, however, that simple extensions of kindergarten are not sufficient or properly designed to compensate for the environmental deprivation low income children have already suffered. A more complex type of program appears to be required.

Short of that, a short run second-best solution is a policy which attempts to correct for the fact that lower income students enter primary schools at a later age (one and three years later) than higher income students. This evidence is at least clear for Latin America. An important research topic is to study how parents decide at what age their children should enter school.

How can the logistics of the existing educational system be used to shape the determinants of entering ability that take place in the home before the child reaches three years? In the short run, improvised educational programs for young parents concerning child rearing practices would provide one type of solution; it is a kind of education for which economists never compute rates of return!

In my analysis, two types of educational program with clear research implications appear to be important. First, a program should be designed to teach parents sound nutritional practices, emphasizing infant and breast-feeding. There is growing evidence that the decline in breast-feeding in low income families of urban areas is a primary cause of infant malnutrition. The resource cost of substituting formula milk for breast milk appears to be quite large. Preliminary estimates by Berg suggest that if 20 percent of the mothers in urban areas of developing countries do not breast-feed, the loss in breast milk is around $365 million per year. If half of the other 80 percent do not continue breast-feeding after the sixth month, the total loss reaches $780 million.[28] This is an important area to be researched; it must be asked what determines the length of breast-feeding and how could it be lengthened through educational programs.

The second line of research involves education on child rearing practices, with particular emphasis on early stimulation. Designing this type of program requires some preliminary research which, to my knowledge, has not been undertaken on a wide scale in developing countries. How different are child rearing practices across families in developing countries? What determines these differences? Are they related to income groups or to particular ethnic groups of the population? These types of questions should be answered if the developing countries are to begin making wise preschool age investments.

Notes

1. Christopher Jencks et al., *Inequality: A Reassessment of the Effect of Schooling in America* (New York: Basic Books, 1972), pp. 256.
2. For such evidence see: F. Monckeberg, F. Donoso, S. Valiente, A. Arteaga, A. Maccioni, and N. Merchak, "Analisis de las condiciones de vida y estado nutritivo de la poblacion infantil de la provincia de Curico", *Revista Chilena de Pediatria*, vol. 38 (1967); V. Kardonsky et al., "Cognitive and emotional problems of Chilean students (7 to 10 years) in the northern section of the City of Santiago", mimeograph (Department of Psychology, University of Chile, 1971); B. Robles, "Influencia de ciertos factores ecologicos sobre la conducta del Nino en el medio rural Mexicano", IX Reunion, Asociacion de Investigacion Pediatrica, Cuernavaca, Mexico, 1959.
3. See surveys by C. W. Woodruff, "An analysis of the I.C.N.N.D. data on physical growth of the pre-school child", in *Preschool Child Malnutrition* (Washington, D.C.: National Academy of Sciences-National Research Council, 1966); R. Revelle and R. Frisch, "Distribution of food supplies by level of income", in *The World Food Problem* (Washington, D.C.: White House, 1967); R. Frisch, "World food supplies", in *World, War, and Hunger* (hearings before the Committee on Agriculture, House of Representatives, Serial W, Part I, Washington, 1966), pp. 41-51; M. Guzman, "Impaired physical growth and malnutrition in malnourished populations", in N. Scrimshaw and J. E. Gordon, eds., *Malnutrition, Learning, and Behavior* (Cambridge, Mass.: M.I.T. Press, 1967).
4. For surveys on this issue, see: A. Berg, *The Nutrition Factor: Its Role in National Development* (Washington, D.C.: Brookings Institution, 1973); J. Cravioto and E. De Licardie, "The effect of malnutrition on the individual", in A. Berg et al., *Nutrition, National Development, and Planning* (Cambridge, Mass.: M.I.T. Press, 1973).
5. A. Jensen, "How much can we boost IQ and scholastic achievement?", *Harvard Educational Review*, vol. 39 (Winter 1969): 1-123; Benjamin Bloom, *Stability and Change in Human Characteristics* (New York: John Wiley & Sons, 1964); C. Jencks, op. cit.
6. "We have therefore abandoned our initial belief that equalizing educational opportunity would substantially reduce cognitive inequality among adults. This does not mean that we think cognitive inequality derives entirely from genetic inequality, or that test scores are immune to environmental influence. It simply means that variations in what children learn in school depend largely on variations in what they bring to school, not on variation in what schools offer them." C. Jencks, op. cit. p. 53.
7. Samuel Bowles, "Toward an educational production function", in L. Hansen, ed., *Education, Income and Wealth* (New York: Colombia University Press, 1970).
8. Benjamin Bloom, *Stability and Change.*
9. Ibid.
10. Ibid.
11. Ibid.
12. Samuel Bowles, op. cit.
13. Christopher Jencks, op. cit., p. 65.
14. "High quality" proteins provide all of the so-called essential amino acids. Proteins of animal origin provide all such amino acids.

15. M. Winick and P. Rosso, "Head circumference and cellular growth of the brain in normal and marasmic children", *Journal of Pediatrics*, vol. 74, no. 5 (May 1969); K. Ambrosius, "El comportamiento de algunos organos en ninos con desnutricion de tercer grado", *Bol. Medico Hospital Infantil* (Mexico, 1951); and R. Brown, "Decreased brain weight in malnutrition and its implications", *East Africa Medical Journal*, vol. 42 (1965).

16. J. Cravioto and E. De Licardie, "Infant malnutrition and later learning", paper presented at the Symposium on Dysnutrition in the Seven Ages of Man, University of California Program for Continuing Education, no date.

17. Ibid.

18. N. Scrimshaw, "Nutrition and infection", in J. Brock, ed., *Recent Advances in Human Nutrition* (London: J. Churchill, 1961).

19. One of the major conclusions of Bloom's study is that "variations in the environment have greatest quantitative effect on a characteristic at its most rapid period of change and least effect on the characteristic during the least rapid period of change".

20. H. Averch et al., *How Effective is Schooling? A Critical Review and Synthesis of Research Findings* (Santa Monica, Calif.: RAND Corporation, 1972).

21. J. M. Hunt, "Has compensatory education failed? Has it been attempted?", *Harvard Educational Review*, vol. **39** (Spring 1969): 278-300.

22. D. Weikart and D. Lambie, "Early enrichment in infants", V. H. Denenberg, ed., *Education of the Infant and the Young Child* (New York: Academic Press, 1970).

23. H. McKay, A. MacKay, and L. Sinisterra, "Behavioral interventions studies with malnourished children", Western Hemisphere Conference on Assessment of Tests of Behavior from Studies of Nutrition, Puerto Rico, October 1970.

24. Jerome Kagan, "On class differences and early development", in V. H. Denenberg, ed., *Education of the Infant and the Young Child* (New York: Academic Press, 1970).

25. The socioeconomic groups were characterized as follows: in the upper groups, one or both parents had graduated from college and the father had a professional job. In the lower group, either or both parents had dropped out of high school, and the father was working at a semiskilled or unskilled job.

26. Jerome Kagan, op. cit.

27. D. Weikart and Lambie, op. cit.

28. A. Berg, op. cit.

CHAPTER 6

Policy Implications of Instructional Technology: Cost and Effectiveness*

JOANNE LESLIE and DEAN T. JAMISON

The educational systems of developing countries around the world share many or all of the following familiar problems: (a) rising total and unit costs; (b) relatively poor access for rural children; (c) low quality instruction, which often results in children from developing countries acquiring less cognitive training than children from developed countries; (d) slow response in providing education relevant to development goals; and (e) adverse effect on income distribution, in part because children from high income families tend to receive a disproportionate share of educational and economic opportunities. In recognition of these problems, a range of suggestions for educational policy has been proposed. Some have argued that the problems are sufficiently intractable so that the best course is simply to cut back on educational expenditures to the extent politically feasible. Others have argued for a vast expansion of "nonformal" education—outside existing educational establishments—in order to alleviate these problems. Still others argue that reform within educational systems can respond, at least in part, to these problems.

Continued international experience with instructional radio and television has led an increasing number of advocates of reform to consider seriously the expanded use of these technologies in order to reduce costs, improve quality, or improve access to education. Previous claims that the electronic media would quickly influence educational practice seem, in retrospect, far off the mark; nonetheless there has been an ever-growing number of successful uses of instructional technology, particularly of radio and television. These successes suggest

*See footnote on page 134.

the importance of increasingly careful consideration of technology in planning the future growth of educational systems. In this chapter we will consider some of the recent and more successful Latin American experiences with instructional radio and television. Although instructional technologies can serve both formal and nonformal education, this chapter considers those technologies used only for formal education.

By formal education, we refer to education with the following two characteristics. First, its curriculum is primarily concerned with the acquisition of cognitive skills. At the elementary and secondary levels these skills include effective use of the national language, mathematics, social and natural sciences, and second languages; at the higher level specialized skills such as agronomy, engineering, and medicine would be included. Inculcation of societal values may also be an important implicit objective of formal education.

Second, formal education typically leads to certification that is readily understood internationally: one can label the product of a formal education system as having a university degree, or having completed primary school. Although research is under way to find more meaningful descriptions of educational attainment than those currently used (based on time in school or examination scores), it is reasonable to expect that traditional methods of describing educational attainment will remain important for the foreseeable future. There is nothing in this definition of formal education to imply that it need employ traditional pedagogical techniques; such learning systems as Radio Santa Maria in the Dominican Republic can provide formal education by nontraditional techniques.

The following section of this chapter reviews aspects of the literature dealing with uses for and the effectiveness of instructional technology. Three case studies of instructional technology projects in Latin America are then presented, and a concluding section draws some policy implications from these studies.

Uses for Instructional Radio and Television

Uses for instructional technologies can be divided into three broad categories: improving educational quality and relevance; lowering educational costs (or the rate of increase of costs); and improving access to education, particularly in rural areas. In this section we briefly discuss reasons to believe that increased use of technology has the potential to improve education in each of these three ways.

Improvement of Educational Quality

Early innovators in the field of educational technology were perhaps most strongly motivated by their belief that educational technology had the potential to improve quality. Early results, however were almost uniformly disappointing. Reports of research on the instructional effectiveness of the media tended to conclude overwhelmingly that there were no significant differences between, for example, student performance in a class taught by an instructor and by the same instructor on television or audio-tape.[1] Jamison, Suppes, and Wells concluded that:

> Though there is a substantial past history in the use of instructional radio, few studies of its effectiveness exist. A number that do exist were, however, carefully done and they indicate that instructional radio, supplemented with appropriate printed material, is about as effective as traditional instruction. Despite this potential, the extent to which instructional radio can be substituted for traditional instruction remains to be tested. There is a much more extensive research literature on the effectiveness of instructional television, and excellent surveys of that literature already exist. There is strong evidence that instructional television, used in a way that closely simulates traditional instruction, is as effective, on average, as traditional instruction for all grade levels and subject matters. There is very little evidence concerning the effectiveness of instructional television used in ways that utilize the unique capabilities of the medium. A number of students and teachers have an initially unfavorable attitude toward instructional television, although the incidence of unfavorable attitudes tends to diminish as institutions gain experience with the medium. After such experience a majority of students have neutral attitudes toward instructional television.[2]

While these findings of equal effectiveness disappointed those hoping for significant improvement in the quality of instruction, they had at least two important implications. First, the finding of equal effectiveness leaves open the possibility of reducing costs, which may be particularly important if there is a substantial unfulfilled demand for education. Second, because the media are effective, their availability makes possible the provision of instruction in areas of curriculum considered important, but in which existing teachers are untrained. Perhaps this has been used most successfully in language instruction; examples include using radio to teach English in Thailand, the Philippines, and the Peoples Republic of China, and using television to teach French in the Ivory Coast. Other areas in which existing teachers may be poorly trained include natural sciences, mathematics, agricultural practices, and hygiene and public health.

Despite the general finding of no significant differences, there are some examples of projects in which the media have outperformed traditional instructional practices. An early evaluation of the Nicaragua Radio Mathematics Project suggests that classes using the radio lessons had lower repetition rates and greater achievement gains than the traditional classes. The Mexican *Telesecundaria* is of interest because it provides access to school for a hitherto excluded rural group, but evaluation also suggests that it has improved quality and is potentially less costly than the extension of traditional secondary schools into rural areas.

Part of the reason that so many comparisons of media with traditional instruction found equal effectiveness may result from the notions of scientific adequacy held by some researchers. They seemed to feel that in order to be scientifically adequate, a comparison of television with traditional instruction should hold everything constant except the medium. One should have the same lecturer (on TV and off) lecturing in the same way to the same sorts of students in the same environment. The results tended to show no difference in outcome. But as more and more projects begin to fully explore the potential of the media, we predict an increasing number of findings of quality improvement.

Another important aspect of improving quality is to decrease repetition and dropout rates. Several instructional technology projects seem to have had such an effect, although the evidence on repetition is often ambiguous because the standards for passing from one grade to another may have changed at the same time that the instructional medium was introduced. The Niger Instructional Television (ITV) project reported a dropout rate of practically zero in its television classes, although dropout rates in primary schools in Niger were traditionally quite high.[3]

Reduction of Cost

The argument that media will be increasingly used to help keep costs down in the long term results from the rising real costs of traditional instruction. Experience over the last two decades has shown rapidly rising costs for both developing and developed nations. One reason for the observed increase in expenditures on education has been large enrollment expansions, especially in developing countries. However, also of great importance is the fact that in many countries it has become increasingly expensive to educate each child in the system.

The increasing costs of educating a student are probably unrelated to increases in the quality of education offered. On the contrary, it is probable that the quality of educational output is at best constant, or perhaps even declining.[4] The most plausible explanation of the increasing costs per student was formalized by Baumol[5] and stated simply by Coombs: "Education's technology, by and large, has made surprisingly little progress beyond the handicraft stage."[6] Essentially, the point is that the educational process has made little if any gains in productivity, although most other sectors of the economy have. Relatively progressive industries, using more advanced technologies, affect the salary levels that less progressive industries will have to pay to attract competent people. Educational systems generally have had to pay increasing amounts for the same quality teachers.

It was hoped that innovations in instructional technology could help the education sector increase its productivity to keep pace with the more progressive sectors of the economy. Relatively little of the potential of such technologies to increase productivity has yet been realized. It is likely, however, that the cost of traditional educational systems will increase in the near future relative to the cost of instructional technologies, thus increasing the pressure to introduce the latter, which are more physical-capital intensive. Traditional system costs will rise because of rising real teacher costs, whereas costs of alternative technologies will remain constant, or be reduced.

In the shorter term, the potential for use of technology to reduce costs per student per year is probably strongest for secondary and post-secondary or adult education. At those levels, the use of radio (and perhaps television) with written correspondence for "distance learning" has been able to reduce costs by virtually eliminating the need for teachers' salaries or classroom facilities.[7] The Open University of the United Kingdom is perhaps the best known distance learning system, but others are in operation in Botswana, the Dominican Republic, France, Germany, Japan, Kenya, Mauritius, and elsewhere.[8] In this paper we discuss the case of the Radio Escuela Santa Maria in the Dominican Republic, which provides access to elementary education for rural adults for whom schools had previously been unavailable.

Improving Access to Educational Opportunities

A final potential use for instructional technologies is to improve access to schooling for rural or urban disadvantaged groups. Soifer[9] points out that one of the educational problems in much of Latin America, outside the urban centers, is a lack of infrastructure: traditional schooling with a teacher and textbooks implies a classroom with a blackboard, electricity, and a road for transport of supervisors and many of the more educated teachers. Battery-operated radios allow schools to be created without electricity, roads, or even a school building. There are two broad approaches by which technology has been used in this way—distance learning and what might be called the "extended school".

Distance learning, as mentioned above, is much less costly than more traditional forms of secondary and post-secondary instruction. For any given budget level, more individuals can be reached with a distance learning system than with a traditional system. Perhaps more important in terms of access to schooling is the fact that distance learning systems can dissolve both barriers of distance and time. Traditionally, schools at higher levels have existed primarily in population centers because large numbers of students are required to make them economically viable. The result is that students from rural areas are either denied secondary schooling or have to bear large travel or subsistence costs. Since this is far less of a problem with distance learning systems, they can be used to break barriers to access. Since traditional schools typically meet at fixed hours during the day, attendance is also frequently a problem for the poor who must work during the day to maintain their incomes. Distance study allows shifting the time for learning to the evening. These points reflect the attractive side of distance learning, but important problems of organization, program preparation, management, accreditation, and political acceptance remain.

A second way that technologies have been used to improve access is by allowing the creation of relatively small but nonetheless self-sufficient schools in rural areas. An excellent example of this is the Mexican *Telesecundaria,* which will be discussed in the next section. Oliveira[10] describes a similar use of television in Brazil, and Spain[11] describes a more limited effort, also in Mexico, which uses radio. This is a more costly way of extending access than distance learning, but closer in structure to traditional schooling. There is enough experience now with this type of program to make it a serious option for educational planners.

Case Studies in Latin America

In this section we describe three of the more interesting projects in Latin America that use instructional radio or television within the formal education sector. One of these involves the use of instructional media within the traditional school system; in Nicaragua, the Radio Mathematics Project is using media to improve the quality of mathematics instruction at the primary level. The other two projects discussed are examples of the use of media to provide an alternative to or substitute for instruction offered within the traditional school system. The initial goal of the Mexican *Telesecundaria* was to increase access to middle level instruction, but it may also have reduced costs and increased quality compared to the traditional school system. Radio Santa Maria in the Dominican Republic also has increased access as its primary goal; in this case the students are adults who want primary level instruction. Radio Santa Maria seems to have reduced costs compared with traditional adult education.

The Nicaragua Radio Mathematics Project

Early in 1975, a group of researchers and mathematics curriculum specialists sponsored by the Agency for International Development, began working with Nicaraguan counterparts in Masaya, Nicaragua, on radio programs to teach elementary school mathematics. They produced 165 first-grade lessons. During 1976 these were revised and broadcast to approximately 1,700 first-grade students on an experimental basis. Initial versions of second grade lessons were also prepared. Current plans call for continued expansion of curriculum to cover higher grade levels, and for implementation of the radio curriculum throughout Nicaragua.[12]

The Radio Mathematics Project (RMP) assumes responsibility for all the mathematics instruction that children receive. A daily lesson consists of a thirty-minute radio presentation, followed by approximately thirty minutes of teacher-directed activities, for which instructions are contained in a teachers' guide developed by the project. No textbooks are used, and printed materials are limited to a one-page worksheet each day for each child.

Before the broadcast portion of the lesson, the teacher gives each child a worksheet, on which the child writes his name and student number, a task that most first graders can learn to do adequately. During each lesson two main characters join with one or two subordinate characters to sing, play, and talk mathematics, usually inviting the children to join in. The children are asked to respond orally, physically, and in writing, which they do up to 100 times during each thirty-minute lesson. Initially the RMP used stories to engage the children, and embedded mathematical work in a story context to maintain interest. Early test of lessons with stories, using kindergarten and first-grade children in California and first-grade children in Nicaragua, convinced the curriculum developers that frequent student response is a more valuable pedagogical technique than story support. Sometimes children handle concrete materials during the broadcast, for example, counting or grouping small objects. Dialogue between radio characters introduces new mathematical material and children are asked to respond orally. For reasons of cost, the RMP may reduce the use of printed worksheets, but frequent student response will continue either orally or by manipulating counted objects.

After the radio transmission, the teacher continues the lesson by following directions given in a teacher's guide. Children usually continue working on the worksheet during this portion of the lesson. During the lesson developmental phase of the project, worksheets were collected and returned to the project office for analysis.

The RMP uses four tools for evaluation: extensive observations made in the radio classrooms; evaluation of student worksheets; measurement of teacher attitudes by questionnaires and interviews; and an achievement testing program, carried out in two different groups of experimental schools and a group of traditional schools.

The 1975 evaluation showed that both students and teachers were enthusiastic about the radio lesson. It is important to keep in mind, however, that this evaluation was made by project staff who may not have been completely impartial, and that initial enthusiasm for an innovation often declines, as in the case of the El Salvador educational television project. Nonetheless, it was found that children were attentive to the half-hour radio lessons as long as they had an opportunity to respond frequently, and that they could keep their place on worksheets with up to thirty different items. Fifty-eight percent of the teachers said they enjoyed teaching mathematics more with radio than without, thought their students learned more than they had the year before, and 59 percent felt that their work load was reduced by using radio lessons.[13] Teachers had a wide range of suggestions for improving the radio lessons but almost all said they would recommend the lessons to other teachers.

The Spanish version of McGraw Hill's mathematics subtest of the *Test of Basic Experiences, Level K* (published by CTB/McGraw Hill) was administered as a first-grade pretest. It was given to 533 students in the sixteen experimental classrooms two weeks after school opened (early March 1975), and to 267 students in nine traditional classrooms four weeks later. In April, six additional classrooms in the Department of Granada were provided with radio lessons, but these classrooms were supervised by the school inspector for Granada and no pretests were given.

The first-grade post-test was designed by the project staff to assess performance on the objectives defined for the radio instructional program, and on additional topics taught in the traditional classroom. In November the test was given to 323 students in experimental classrooms, 195 students in traditional classrooms, and 242 students in the Granada classrooms. The results of the performance on the post-test are shown in Table 18.

TABLE 18
Nicaragua Radio Mathematics Project:
Post-test Performance—Item Scores[a]

Group	Percentage correct	
	Mean	Standard deviation
Experimental	67.3	23.8
Traditional	55.5	21.4
Granada	68.4	25.1

Note:
[a]There were four student test forms, each containing twenty-two items, so data were collected on a total of eighty-eight items.
Source: B. Searle, J. Friend, P. Suppes, and T. Tilson, *Application of Radio to Teaching Elementary Mathematics in a Developing Country* (Stanford, California: Institute for Mathematical Studies in the Social Sciences, 1976).

The difference in performance between students in the experimental group and students in the traditional group is significant, and may be even more significant if the two groups were not initially comparable. The mean scores on the twenty-eight-item pretest were 19.9 for the experimental group and 21.2 for the traditional group. It seems quite possible that the higher score for students in the traditional group results from the later testing date, but RMP staff also believe that if there is a difference between the two groups, it is in favor of the traditional group.

Information on costs of the project comes from an analysis performed early in 1976.[14] Annualized total cost (TC)[15] is considered as a linear function of two independent variables—the number of lessons presented per year (h) and the number of students enrolled in a course (N).

This cost function can be expressed as follows:

$$TC = F + V_h h + V_n N$$

where F, V_n, and V_h are cost parameters.

The first parameter, F, includes all cost components which do not change with respect to hours of programming or student usage, in other words, the central project costs:

$$F = \text{annualized starting costs}$$
$$+ \text{ project administration costs}$$
$$+ \text{ (research costs).}$$

Research costs are in parentheses because it seems doubtful that they should be included in the Nicaragua cost function. Because the research covered by these costs has results directed outside Nicaragua, they will be excluded from the total cost equation. On the other hand, the cost of formative evaluation research is included, as being directly related to program production. The value of F, when capital costs are annualized at 7.5 percent, is $91,800 per year.

The next parameter, V_h, depends on transmission costs and program production costs; it equals the annualized cost of a lesson plus the cost of transmitting it once. The annualized cost of a lesson is $160 at a 7.5 percent discount rate; the cost of transmission is $16. Thus $V_h = $176 per lesson per year, or since each lesson lasts thirty minutes, $351 per hour of programming per year.

The final cost parameter, V_n, depends only on the cost per enrolled student per year; the estimated value is $V_n = $3.83/yr.

The final cost equation (in dollars per year) is given by:

$$TC = 91,800 + 176\,h + 3.8\,N.$$

Even with 10,000 to 50,000 users, it can be computed from the above cost function that the average costs remain substantially above the marginal cost of $3.80 per student per year. And, because of high marginal costs per student and high programming costs, the costs of the RMP are substantially higher than for most other radio projects.[16]

The Mexican Telesecundaria

During the 1960s the Mexican government identified limited access to schooling beyond the sixth grade as a major problem with their educational system. In 1965 approximately 37 percent of the previous year's sixth graders were unable to enter secondary school, and the fraction was even higher in rural areas where there are few secondary schools.[17] Mexico turned to instructional television in order to make rapid changes in the availability and structure of grades seven, eight, and nine. The basic purpose of the Mexican *Telesecundaria* (hereafter TS) was to extend access to secondary education rather than to reform or replace the traditional secondary schools.

The TS system has the same pedagogical objectives, and uses the same curriculum as the traditional secondary school, but students in TS classes receive a twenty-minute television lesson as part of each hour lesson. The remaining forty minutes are divided between preparation and follow-up activities.

The TS differs structurally from the traditional secondary education (*Ensenanza Directa,* hereafter ED) in that it does not use regular school buildings or regular secondary teachers, but rather space provided by the local community, and primary teachers who have special training in coordinating the teleclasses. Instead of a hierarchical administrative system, TS has a local organization composed of parents or *patronato* to provide meeting space and learning materials. Professor Emma Lopez Perez, one of the directors of TS, credits much of the success of the TS system to the resourcefulness and cooperation of the *patronato*.[18] Other differences between the ED system and the TS system important to keep in mind during the subsequent comparison of effectiveness and cost are the following: (1) TS schools are usually much smaller than ED schools, (2) class sizes are half those of ED schools, (3) TS schools use fewer ancillary learning aids, and (4) more of them are located in rural communities. Furthermore, the two systems do not serve completely comparable groups of students. TS students come from homes where the parents have less schooling and lower status jobs than those of the ED students, TS students are generally older, and more of them are male.

The effectiveness of the Mexican TS can be viewed both in terms of its effect on enrollment and on the quality of learning by students in the system. Because of the difference in structure between the Mexican TS and ED schools, socialization effects could also be expected to differ considerably. However, it is difficult to measure the affective component of education with reliability, and we do not feel that our data allows us to draw any conclusions about differences in socialization.

Enrollment figures can provide information on the TS's ability to increase access to education. In 1965, over 180,000 of the previous year's sixth graders were unable to enter secondary school. In 1975, 36,000 students were enrolled in the TS system.[19] If it is assumed that one-third (13,000) of the TS students were in the seventh grade and that secondary schools continued to lack places for at least 180,000 graduating sixth-grade students, then the TS system was able to absorb about 7 percent of the students who otherwise would not have had access to grades seven, eight, and nine. Another way of evaluating the degree to which the TS system extended access is to consider graduates of the two systems. In 1972 there were 238,300 graduates of the ED system and 6600 graduates of the TS system, meaning that the TS system increased the total number of graduates by almost 3 percent.[20] Considering that the TS system is not nationwide, but serves only the Federal District and the seven states of Hidalgo, Mexico, Morelos, Oaxaca, Puebla, Tlaxcala, and Veracruz, the increase in number of grades is significant. Dropout and promotion rates are almost identical for both systems; dropout from the seventh grade is about 18 percent, from the eighth grade is about 12 percent and graduation from the ninth grade is about 90 percent.

The ability of the TS to extend educational opportunity is impressive, but even more impressive is that it seems to have been achieved without a drop in learning performance, and at a lower per student cost than the ED system. Achievement tests in mathematics, Spanish, and chemistry were given to samples of ED and TS students in February and June 1972. When the achievement tests were first given to both samples of students, there was very little difference between their scores. When the same tests were given five months later, the TS students scored higher in all three subjects and their gains, although small, were 1.5 to 2 times as large as those of the ED students.[21]

Furthermore, when the scores of both samples were stratified by geographic origin, an equally striking difference appeared. For both TS and ED students, greater gains in learning were recorded in samples from the Federal District and the Valley of Mexico, representing more urban areas, than in the more rural states of Hidalgo and Morelos. Family background characteristics, such as educated parents who had better jobs, were positively correlated with higher scores on achievement tests and higher aspirations for future schooling and jobs, but the relationship was stronger for ED students than for TS students. The quality of education offered by the TS seems to be equal to that offered by the ED system. The TS system seems to have allowed relatively disadvantaged students to catch up with generally more advantaged ED students in the areas of Spanish, mathematics, and chemistry. Although many outside observers of the Mexican TS consider it a second-class system, 60 percent of TS students said they would not want to change to a traditional secondary school.

The cost of establishing the TS system was added on to the cost of the entire budget for secondary education in Mexico, but for most of the individual communities served by the TS there was no need to add cost because no secondary level education had been provided.[22] The annual cost per student in 1972 was calculated to be $200 for the ED student and $151 for the TS student. Of that $151, $26 per student went for the television component of the TS system. The four major costs of traditional education: administration, teachers' salaries, facilities (classrooms and equipment), and student costs (books and uniforms), were all lower for the TS student. Teachers' salaries and facilities were less expensive in the TS system, but the differential would have been even greater except for the fact that the larger class sizes and double sessions of the ED system allowed costs to be spread among more students.

Direct student costs were lower for the TS system because the guidebooks that accompany televised lessons were cheaper than ED textbooks; but for most of the students in TS schools, the real saving was even greater because they would have incurred considerable travel expense in order to attend a traditional secondary school. However, the costs borne by the family of a TS student may be much greater than simply buying workbooks, due to their participation in the *patronato,* which often buys equipment and builds or remodels classrooms.

Also, the forgone earnings of the TS students whose families are usually poorer, probably represent a much larger fraction of the potential family income than do the foregone earnings of the ED students.

One final point should be made about the comparative cost of the two systems. Currently, Channel 5 in Mexico is donating transmission time to the Secretariat of Public Education; if this time were leased from Channel 5, the fixed costs of the TS would be increased by about $500,000 a year. However, with at least 20,000 students in the system (the 1975 figure was about 36,000 students) the per-student cost of the TS system, including full distribution cost, would still be only about $175 per student per year.

Radio Escuela Santa Maria in the Dominican Republic

In 1964 a radiophonic adult literacy program, modeled on the Colombian *Radio Sutatenza,* was initiated in the Cibao region of north central Dominican Republic. During the next six years, more than 25,000 adults received literacy certificates. But many participants considered these radiophonic schools to be remedial and inferior to traditional schools.

Radio Santa Maria then launched a much more comprehensive adult education program in 1971, partially modeled on a program in the Canary Islands. All the programs of Radio Santa Maria are designed to give educational and cultural support to the core curricula, but formal instruction at the advanced primary and intermediate level is provided by a daily one hour broadcast, accompanied by lesson sheets, and weekly sector meetings with a field teacher. Arrangements were made with five radio stations in other parts of the Dominican Republic to broadcast the daily radio lessons, so that by 1975 a primary and intermediate level education was available in virtually all rural communities in the country. Examinations at the end of grades six and eight are held in accordance with the regulations of the Secretariat of Education, allowing graduates of the radiophonic schools to receive official diplomas. A detailed description of this project is provided by White; most of this case study is based on his work.[23]

Adult education has been a well-integrated part of the conventional educational system of the Dominican Republic since 1953. The

Direcion General de Educacion de Adultos uses day school facilities in towns and cities, and offers a primary education through grade eight to the very large number of youths and adults who missed this opportunity earlier in their lives. This adult education program has provided educational opportunities for over 30,000 students from 1968 to 1975, but primarily in urban areas. However, the difficulties of recruiting teachers and finding well-lit classrooms for nighttime use in rural areas has almost completely prevented the spread of the program to rural areas.

Radio Santa Maria's adult education program encourages students to listen to the general education and cultural broadcasts as well as to the instructional programs, and assumes that they will participate in community organizations as part of their education. The academic material presented in instructional broadcasts and weekly worksheets is offered at an accelerated pace, so that adult students can complete eight years of schooling in four calendar years.

Students meet with a field teacher once a week in order to discuss the previous week's lesson and to receive worksheets for the next week. The median age of the field teachers is twenty-four, about 85 percent have some secondary education; and all have another job or are secondary school students. As was discovered in the Nicaragua Radio Mathematics Project, active participation of the adult student during the instructional broadcast is considered an important pedagogical technique. "To insure that the learning process is an active search and not just a passive listening to the broadcast, a series of small completion exercises are built into the presentation: a word to be underlined or written into the text; a small mistake which the broadcast dialogue helps the student to detect and correct, etc."[24]

In its fourth year (1974-75 school year) the radio program was expanded nationwide. There were approximately 20,000 students attending classes; about 2000 students took the eighth-grade examination with a 96 percent pass rate. "One of the most notable achievements in the program is the high retention rate of students who enroll, given the great flexibility of the system. Even if one allows for the fact that enrollment is closed at the midsemester point, that retention is approximately 70-75 percent in some of the advanced grades is remarkable compared with most radiophonic adult education programs.''[25] Retention in the first four grades is considerably lower, in part because most of the students are dropouts from the regular primary school.[26]

Two studies have compared the academic achievement of students in the radio program with that of students in conventional adult education programs. In 1973 a small study compared fifteen students from the radiophonic schools of Santa Maria with fifteen from the official adult education program in the city of La Vega. A special test instrument based on the official curriculum was used. Students tested were from the second, fourth, and sixth grades. At the second-grade level there were no significant differences in scores, but at the fourth-grade level the radio program students had a mean score of 66, while the conventional students had a mean score of 40. At the sixth-grade level, radio program students had a mean score of 69 while conventional students had a mean score of 47.[27]

In 1975 a much more extensive comparison was carried out in two different educational districts. Students at the end of the sixth and eighth grades were compared, and both groups were given the examination prepared by the district office of the National Office of Adult Education. This examination was similar to one usually given to students in the radio program but was in a different format and covered some unfamiliar material. An example of comprehensive scores for sixth-grade students in District II can be found in Table 19. The scores of radio program students in District I were relatively higher.

We differ, however, with White's conclusion that ''the data do support the hypothesis that students in the radiophonic schools have levels of achievement superior to those of students in the schools using traditional methods of instruction''.[28] Our conclusion is that students in the radio program can perform as well as students from the conventional system. Only eight of twenty-one comparisons show a difference in score of five points or more, and of these four favor the radio program students while four favor the conventional students. Evidence that the academic performance of radio program students was equal to that of conventional system students seems particularly significant when it is realized that all conventional school students were from urban communities while 78 percent of the radio program students were from rural backgrounds. As might be expected, within the radio

TABLE 19

Radio Escuela Santa Maria: Comparison of Median Examination Scores of Sixth-grade Students in Schools with Radiophonic and Conventional Classroom Methods: District II

Subject	Radiophonic students					Conventional classroom students				
	No.	% Less than 60	% 60-79	% Higher than 80	Median score	No.	% Less than 60	% 60-79	% Higher than 80	Median score
Spanish language	198	11.1	64.2	24.7	73.0	87	17.2	70.1	12.6	70.7
Spanish grammar	198	40.9	39.4	19.7	63.9	83	44.6	42.2	13.2	63.5
Mathematics	199	82.9	13.6	3.5	less than 50.0	33	72.7	24.3	3.0	50.6
Natural sciences	199	36.2	50.8	13.0	64.9	52	59.6	38.5	1.9	57.4
Dominican economy	200	74.5	24.5	1.0	less than 50.0	52	71.2	28.8		54.2
Social studies	201	62.1	33.4	4.5	54.4	60	66.7	31.7	1.7	55.8

Source: R. A. White, "The use of radio in primary and secondary formal education: the Radio Santa Maria Model in the Dominican Republic", in Peter Spain, D. Jamison, and E. MacAnay, eds., Radio for Education and Development: Case Studies (Washington, D.C.: Education Department, World Bank, 1977).

program group students from urban communities scored somewhat higher than the rural students.

The equality in performance between students of the two systems is also significant considering that per student cost of instructional radio is apparently lower than that of the conventional system. There are not enough data on the costs of the two systems to allow a complete cost analysis, but a broad-brush comparison suggests lower per student costs for radio program students. With data provided by White, who includes broadcasting and assumes more supervisory personnel per student than are currently provided, a cost equation of TC (N) = $152,000.00 + $8.7 N can be constructed. For 20,000 students, this is $16.30 per student. If the system were to enroll 40,000 students, the same number in the program run by the Secretariat of Education, the per-student cost would be $12.50. Information on the cost of the conventional system was quite general, but excluding classroom costs (these are borrowed from the day school program) and special subject adult education programs, the budget seems to have risen from $629,331 in 1970 to $1,044,788 in 1974. Since the enrollments only increased from 37,013 to 40,561 the estimated per student cost rose from $17.00 to $25.76.

Implications for Policy

There are a number of implications for policy that can be drawn from the experience with these alternative technologies. A few caveats must, however, be kept in mind. First, these are projects that rely heavily on the electronic media and therefore provide little comparative information about other approaches to educational improvement, such as increasing the quantity or quality of textbooks available, or retraining teachers. The results summarized, then, must be used in conjunction with evaluative studies of other options. Second, the ways in which media can be used in education are numerous and any particular project can shed direct light on only one; generalizations of experience must be made with care.

Finally, the project evaluations used to provide information often do not contain all the data that a careful planner would like to have. This poses the dual problems of how to use the information that is available, and how to restructure future evaluations so that they will yield more information, given the ever-present constraints of limited time and budgets, and inadequate controls on research. In particular, the evaluations summarized here generally fail to provide information on affective consequences of the projects. Information on the project's effects on dropout and repetition rates are usually inadequate, and it is not indicated whether the education provided by the technology is perceived to be less economically valuable than traditional instruction.

Nonetheless, we have learned a good deal from evaluations of these and other instructional technology projects, and this information has the following implications for educational planners:

(a) Since television seems, for most purposes, to work no better than radio and is much more expensive and complicated to implement, television should almost never be used for instruction in low income countries. Exceptions to this general conclusion might occur in relatively rare cases when the marginal cost of television is unusually low or when visual methods are absolutely essential for instruction.[29]

(b) It is probably possible to improve the quality of in-school instruction at the elementary and secondary levels using radio.

(c) Distance learning systems can reduce cost and improve access to secondary and higher education; they can also provide a means for adults to receive elementary certificates without having to leave the labor force.

The relatively hopeful tone of conclusions (b) and (c) should be tempered with a reminder that the existing research has focused only on success, and that research on radio and learning is still in its early stages. Yet research does suggest the potential for cost-effective educational reform using instructional technology.

Notes

1. There are a number of comprehensive surveys that discuss this issue. See G. C. Chu and W. Schramm, *Learning from Television: What the Research Says* (Washington, D.C.: National Association of Educational Broadcasters, 1967); Dean T. Jamison and E. G. McAnany, *Radio for Education and Development* (Beverly Hills, and London: Sage Publications, 1978); Dean T. Jamison, P. Suppes, and S. Wells, "The effectiveness of alternative instructional media: a survey", *Review of Educational Research,* vol. 44 (1974): 1-67; W. Schramm, *Big Media, Little Media* (Beverly Hills and London: Sage Publications, 1976).

2. Dean Jamison, P. Suppes, and S. Wells, "The effectiveness of alternative instructional media", op. cit., p. 56.

3. W. Schramm, *Big Media, Little Media,* p. 146.

4. M. Woodhall and M. Blaug, "Productivity trends in British secondary education, 1950-1963", *Sociology of Education,* Winter 1968.

5. W. Baumol, "Macroeconomics of unbalanced growth: the anatomy of urban crisis", *American Economic Review,* vol. 57 (1967): 415-26.

6. P. H. Coombs and J. Hallak, *Managing Educational Costs* (New York and London: Oxford University Press, 1972), p. 7.

7. A distance learning project is one that provides very little instruction by face to face contact between a teacher and a student.

8. N. Mackenzie, R. Postgate, and J. Scupham, *Open Learning* (Paris: UNESCO Press, 1975), and W. Schramm, *Big Media, Little Media.*

9. Jack Soifer, *Manual de Teleducacaõ, Volume I* (Manaus, Brasil: SUDAM/SEDUC, 1974).

10. J. B. A. Oliveira, "ETV-Maranhaõ: an effective case of endogenous growth." Proceedings of the International Conference on Evaluation and Research in Educational Television and Radio (Great Britain: The Open University, 1976).

11. Peter Spain, "The Mexican Radioprimaria Project", in Peter Spain, D. Jamison, and E. MacAnany, eds., *Radio for Education and Development: Case Studies* (Washington, D.C.: Education Department, World Bank, 1977).

12. For a more detailed description of this project, see B. Searle, P. Suppes, and J. Friend, "The Nicaragua Radio Mathematics Project", in P. Spain et. al., eds., *Radio for Education and Development;* and B. Searle, J. Friend, P. Suppes, and T. Tilson, *Application of Radio to Teaching Elementary Mathematics in a Developing Country* (Stanford, California: Institute for Mathematical Studies in the Social Sciences, 1976).

13. B. Searle et al., *Application of Radio to Teaching Elementary Mathematics,* p. 7.

14. Dean Jamison, S. Klees, and S. Wells, *The Costs of Educational Media: Guidelines for Planning and Evaluation* (Beverly Hills and London: Sage Publications, 1978).

15. Capital costs are incurred for inputs whose useful lifetime extends over many years; an *annualized* capital cost is essentially what the appropriate annual rent would be if the equipment were rented instead of purchased. Annualized costs are the sum of annualized capital costs and recurrent costs.

16. It should be noted that subsequent to this cost analysis (and in part because of it) the marginal costs of the RMP have been reduced. They appear now to be about half the value indicated here. Searle et al., *Application of Radio to Teaching Elementary Mathematics.*

17. J. K. Mayo et al., "The Mexican *Telesecundaria*", p. 193.

18. "Mexico: Ensino medico posto em debate", *Revista Basileira de Teleducacaõ* (3rd and 4th quarters, 1974), pp. 55-60.
19. Ibid., pp. 55-60.
20. J. K. Mayo et al., "The Mexican *Telesecundaria*", p. 207.
21. Ibid., pp. 212-3.
22. More complete cost data and detailed cost effectiveness analyses can be found in S. Klees, "Instructional technology and its relationship to quality and equality in education in a developing nation: a case study of instructional television in Mexico" (unpublished Ph.D. Dissertation, Stanford University, 1974); and in Dean Jamison et al., *Cost Analysis for Educational Planning and Evaluation,* Chap. XI.
23. R. A. White, "The use of radio in primary and secondary formal education: the Radio Santa Maria Model in the Dominican Republic", in P. Spain et al., eds., *Radio for Education and Development.*
24. Ibid., p. 45.
25. Ibid., p. 87.
26. When considering the number of students who benefit from a radio or television distance learning project, it is important to keep in mind the spill-over effect. It is likely that many people will not be officially enrolled, and may not be regular listeners, but will nonetheless derive educational benefit from the broadcasts.
27. H. V. Decena-Dilone, "Estudio comparativo del rendimiento de los Alumnos de las Escuelas Radiofonicas de Radio Santa Maria y de la educacion de adultos oficial" (Thesis presented to the faculty of education at the Universidad Catolica Madre y Maestra, Santiago, Dominican Republic, 1973).
28. White, "The use of radio in primary and secondary formal education", op. cit., p. 108.
29. The Mexican *Telesecundaria* is a good example of a situation where the marginal cost of TV is low—partially because TS uses the medium in a particularly inexpensive way, and partially because it is able to utilize transmission facilities at far below the average cost.

*A slightly longer version of this paper was prepared for the Inter-American Development Bank's Seminar on the Financing of Education in Latin America, which was held in Washington, D.C., 15-19 November 1976. That version of the paper appears in Spanish in the Proceedings of the conference, *Financiamento de la Educacion en America Latina,* edited by M. Brodersohn and M. E. Sanjuro (Mexico D. F.: 1978). The paper is reprinted in this volume because it is otherwise unavailable in English and because it is based in part on Mr. Jamison's presentation to the World Bank Workshop on Economics of Education at which other papers in the volume were presented. The U.S. Agency for International Development provided partial support for Ms. Leslie's contribution to this paper through EDUTEL, Inc. (Views expressed herein are those of the authors and do not necessarily reflect those of the Agency for International Development, the Inter-American Development Bank, or the World Bank.) C. L. Germanacos, S. Klees, and S. Wells provided helpful comments on an earlier draft of this paper.

CHAPTER 7

The Impact of American Educational Research on Developing Countries

ERNESTO SCHIEFELBEIN

Christopher Jencks and his colleagues' book, *Inequality,* which summarized the results of American research, has received wide commentary from the mass media. Its influence is on two audiences, the first from the academic world, able to appreciate the worth of the data and qualifications of the conclusions; the second of policymakers and the public. With regard to the first audience, there is less concern, since critics in professional journals do not usually modify public opinion. The influence on the second audience will be important if it affects appropriations for educational systems. The public has heard Jencks say that schools do not really make much difference, and the implication is that it is not worthwhile to put much money into education.

Research is fast becoming a powerful source of persuasion in the political arena. The evidence presented by Jencks may therefore alter the present equilibrium of the American educational system with respect to multiple moral, political, and economic commitments. Any change in the educational policies of the United States, however, will be the result of a careful assessment of many points of view. Developed countries have built-in forces that help avoid weakly supported decisions. For example, at least two books are circulating about the influence of schools on student performance.[1]

Unfortunately, there is no similar defense mechanism in the developing world. For that reason I would like to explore some implications of Jencks' work for such countries.

Shortcomings of Jencks' Analytical Model

It is well known that cross-sectional analysis performed on data gathered at one point in time may prove misleading. The ideal—longitudinal experimentation—is, however, practically nonexistent in education.[2] In addition to the weaknesses attributable to the cross-sectional analysis used by Jencks, it is necessary to mention that no more than one-third of the variance in educational achievement can be explained by the variables measured in the data used in the study. This fact may be interpreted as low reliability in measurements or exclusion of relevant variables. Previous research suggests that the ability of teachers is difficult to measure. Further, "the shadow curriculum" has yet to be illuminated. The unexplained variance shows that more relevant variables have to be measured in future studies.

In spite of these remarks, the data and the statistical methods used in the Jencks report seem to be the best model currently available. New techniques are being tested, but it will be some time before benefits will come from their development. Accepting the method used as the only valid alternative, my comments will therefore deal with some of the research results presented by Jencks. My main interest will be with the educational production function, because the economic effects of education have been widely studied by other economists.[3]

Jencks' analysis is based on a very special definition of success: getting a job that pays as much as others. It is not enough for him to observe that education has an effect on occupation or production, because he is interested in equality. His definition, however, seems of little relevance in cases where the main goal is to reach certain minimal levels of life. The question in developing countries should be: Does education help to surmount the initial barriers of development? The conclusions so forcefully presented by Jencks, even if they were valid for developed countries, may prove to be misleading when discussing educational development in the developing world. There is a real danger involved because: first, in developing countries an important percentage of the children have no schooling at all; and, second, some research shows that some school variables do affect educational achievement.

Developing countries are almost dual societies, with one group living in a modern sector and the other living in almost primitive conditions. Education is one of the means available for overcoming barriers to entry into the small modern group. The minimum level of education necessary to abandon the primitive group is not known, but it is substantially less than the lowest level of educational attainment considered in Jencks' studies. Jencks' conclusions should be examined in that context. In the United States, secondary education may be a threshold beyond which a whole array of entry occupations opens up, but in some developing countries those reaching the secondary level are members of an exclusive elite. Differences in levels of college education, therefore, may have little to do with American occupational differentials, because college is beyond the threshold. But in the developing countries, where the threshold is much lower, basic education may be a key factor in gaining a subsistence salary. Furthermore, the effect of schooling on the acquisition of basic skills is beyond doubt.

Research carried out in Brazil, Colombia, Chile, Puerto Rico, and Venezuela shows that school variables explain a large part of the total variance in educational achievement.[4] The amount of resources available and facilities per student differ markedly, however, from school to school. This is not the case in the situation studied by Coleman and Jencks. Compared to the developing countries, schools in the United States exhibit minimal differences in terms of facilities available to students from different socioeconomic classes. In fact, in some cases, lower economic status students had better input per pupil.[5] Moynihan and Mosteller had already suggested that below a threshold point schools may have significant effect when they wrote: "It is tempting to state that the conventional wisdom proved wrong on both counts (that schools are very different and that these differences influenced achievement) but this would not be quite fair. *Had* there been the *large* differences in the school facilities of the races that had been assumed, such differences *might* have proved of great consequence.[6]

The possible existence of input thresholds in the educational production function has also received some support from the three volumes of the "International Studies in Evaluation" completed by the International Association for the Evaluation of Educational Achievement (IEA). Analyses of these reports done by Coleman, Platt, Thorndike, and Vaizey call attention to systematic differences between developed

and developing countries.[7] Thorndike suggests several alternative or
complementary explanations for the differences: "A third explanation,
which does not exclude the previous one as a contributory factor, is
that the same indicator may have genuinely different significance in
different cultures."[8] It is possible that people in different cultures
may learn in different ways or that the interaction of variables is
different. In any case research should be done concerning cross-cultural
patterns of learning. Data have only recently been available to furnish
some relevant comparisons.

Variables Omitted in Jencks' Study

As Selowsky discusses earlier in this book, available research shows
that early malnutrition may cause serious brain damage.[9] Problems
of malnutrition in developing countries may affect up to 20 or 30
percent of the population. In extreme cases, individuals with a low
IQ may not be able to participate in the labor force; in most cases
malnutrition means early drop-out from the educational system.
Jencks, however, did not study the problem of malnutrition.

Other important variables influencing student achievement in
developing countries were also omitted in the Jencks study.[10] Transportation to school, absenteeism, health problems (apart from malnutrition), heating, languages or dialects, costs absorbed by the family,
changes in teacher quality from class to class and school to school,
and teachers' attitudes are a few examples of relevant variables that
may invalidate conclusions obtained through research in developed
countries. In other cases, Jencks measured the "quality of textbooks"
by their cost rather than by their availability, because every student in
the United States has at least a minimum number of textbooks.

The third problem that might arise from misinterpretations of
Inequality concerns future trends in the developing countries. Many
intellectuals, supporting Illich's proposal of deschooling, might inter-
pret Jencks' results as a further demonstration of Illich's thesis. Most
are committed to shaping a better world.[11] The developing countries,
to some observers, offer a laboratory to test controversial experiments
which are almost impossible to mount in the developed countries.[12]
It is always possible to obtain financial resources to convince private

or public officials in developing countries that it is good to try new ideas. A distorted use of Jencks' conclusions may help foreign experts, attempting to design a new project, to prepare a convincing proposal.

Economic and Educational Implications

If the existence of a threshold point, or minimum level for effectiveness of each of the main inputs into the educational system, is accepted, resources should be used not to increase facilities beyond that point, but to expand the number of students served by the existing system. The productivity of resources used in the educational system can thus be raised.

The policy design for certain inputs should not present many uncertainties.[13] For example, the number of students in a class may be substantially increased with no influence at all on student achievement, although it will provoke the resistance of teachers' unions. Results of research on class size are consistent with the IEA report and with studies done in Brazil, Chile, Puerto Rico, and Venezuela. Increasing classes from thirty-five to forty-five students means that total enrollment may be increased by a third at little cost. In many countries, this simple measure would mean that no students willing to study would remain out of the system. Classes may be increased by up to sixty students with the provision of minimal facilities.

According to research in Chile and Venezuela, the time of the day spent in the school (morning, afternoon, or the whole day) or the number of hours (beyond six) does not make a significant difference in student achievement.[14] These facts are consistent with the idea of a threshold point and with Jencks' claim that slight changes in American educational standards do not affect outcomes, since standards are generally high. But for developing countries, these findings mean that where there is a shortage of places double shifts may be used.[15] This may be complemented with a policy favoring student effort in science homework.[16]

Available research in Chile and Brazil shows that textbooks have a considerable influence on the quality of education. These results, however, are the opposite of those presented by Jencks. The explanation may be that effects of textbooks diminish once each student has easy access to texts in the key subjects of the curriculum. Given the fact that few students have textbooks in developing countries, a cheap way to increase standards might be to provide textbooks and to motivate teachers to use them.

Resources to fund the cost of textbooks could come from changes in policies regarding teacher salaries. Salaries are usually related to a teacher's degrees and experience. According to research, however, beyond a threshold point, these seem to have little influence on student achievement.

These are a few examples of policies that could be thoroughly examined for developing countries. The above suggestions are supported by actual research in developing countries, and by Jencks when he states that developed countries could improve the efficiency of their educational systems. "If schools use their resources differently, however, additional resources might conceivably have larger payoffs."[17] In his appraisal of the IEA study, Vaizey also states that there is room for more efficient and productive use of resources.[18]

Implications for Research Priorities

Educational research in developing countries is scarce. But there is no way of testing proposed policies except by experimentation. In each case some extreme alternatives may be tried out and evaluated.

The fact that attending five rather than six hours daily (in a five-day week) does not make much difference in student achievement may lead to discovery of a lower threshold point. It may also be useful to explore the possibility of a five hours, four-times-a-week schedule (in a six-day-a-week schedule for the school) in order to serve a third group of 50 percent more students with the same physical and training facilities. This would require a 20 percent increase in teaching salaries for the addition of a sixth working day.

If the threshold point is five hours a day, three times a week (in a six-day school schedule), the system could serve twice as many students with similar resources. Even if a slight reduction in quality results from this alternative, it might be worthwhile to absorb practically all the existing demand for school places in most developing countries.

Other educational means should be explored at the same time. The success noted among children from low economic status families who watched "Sesame Street" is an index of what can be achieved through educational television. Two or three current evaluation projects on the effects of "Plaza Sesamo" (the Spanish version of "Sesame Street") may provide some guidelines in the future.

A detailed comparison of results obtained for the United States by Jencks with data from Chile or Venezuela would be worthwhile. It would be interesting to make a comparison of the different weights of identical variables in explaining educational achievement in countries with such a gap in development. This comparison would help to begin to understand systematic differences in the educational development of countries with different initial situations. Furthermore, it would be possible in the future to avoid misleading influences on educational policy decisions.

Jencks' conclusions may be excellent in themselves, but my concern is with the tendency to use them uncritically and to apply them in situations for which they are not valid. I have therefore tried not to discuss the results themselves, but rather to examine their implications in the context of developing countries where the results might be misapplied.

Notes

1. American Association of School Administrators, "Christopher Jencks in Perspective" (Washington, D.C.: 1973); and Fred Mosteller and Daniel Moynihan, eds., *On Equality of Educational Opportunity* (New York: Random House, 1972).
2. David Cohen, "Social experiments with schools: what has been learned", paper prepared for a conference sponsored by the Brookings Institution, Harvard University, August 1973.
3. Jencks is interested in the effects at the individual level, while my interest is in the design of national educational policies that may improve both the per capita income and equality levels. Variables that may prove to be significant at the aggregate level may be irrelevant at the individual level and vice versa.
4. Laurence Wolff, "The use of information for improvement of educational planning in Rio Grande do Sul, Brazil" (Ph.D. thesis, Harvard University, 1971); Robert Drysdale, "Factores determinantes de la desercion escolar en Colombia", *Revista del Centro de Estudios Educativos,* vol. 2, no. 3 (1972): 11-36; L. Schiefelbein and T. R. Farrell, "Las relaciones entre los factores y los resultados del proceso educativo" (Santiago de Chile: Ministerio de Educacion, 1973); Martin Carnoy, "Un enfque de sistemas para evaluar la educacion, ilustrado con datos de Puerto Rico", *Rivista del Centro de Estudios Educativos,* vol. 1, no. 3 (1971): 9-46; and Carmen Cargia, Eduardo Castaneda, Lilian de Leon, and Ernesto Schiefelbein, "Television y Rendimiento Escolar", mimeograph (Caracas, Venezuela: Ministerio de Educacion de Venezuela, 1973).

5. Research carried out in Chile, at the end of secondary education (which most students of the lowest class do not reach), is consistent with the data of the Coleman Report, "Effects of school on learning: the IEA findings", paper presented at a conference sponsored by the Brookings Institution, Harvard, August 1973. Robert Thorndike, in "The relation of school achievements to differences in the backgrounds of children", paper presented at a conference sponsored by the Brookings Institution, also reported similar differences in the International Association for the Evaluation of Educational Achievement study, and called attention to the fact that "the dynamics of prediction across countries is rather different from the dynamics across individuals".

6. Fred Mosteller and Daniel Moynihan, eds., *On Equality of Educational Opportunity* (New York: Random House, 1972).

7. James Coleman, "Effects of school on learning"; William Platt, "Policymaking and international studies in educational evaluation", paper presented at the Harvard-IEA Conference, November 1973; Robert Thorndike, "The relations of school achievements to differences in the backgrounds of children"; and John Vaizey, "The implications of the IEA studies for educational planning with respect to organization and resource", paper presented at the Harvard-IEA Conference, November 1973.

8. Robert Thorndike, "The relations of school achievements to differences in the backgrounds of children".

9. Fernando Monckeberg, "La desnutricion en el nino y sus conseduencias", *Rivista del Centro de Estudios Educativos,* vol. 3, no. 1 (1973): 67-91.

10. Variables in developing countries may be constants in the United States. For example, most schoolchildren in the United States have textbooks and transport to schools.

11. Alice Rivlin, in "Forensic social science", *Harvard Educational Review,* vol. 43, no. 1 (February 1973): 61-75, examined the attempts to use research findings to support a given position and to ignore the counter evidence. She suggests that this "committed" position (posture) may be open to discussion by the advocates of the other side. Unfortunately, this may be difficult to carry out in developing countries.

12. David Cohen, "Social experiments in schools".

13. This is true if the validity of cross-sectional data used in the production function studies is accepted.

14. L. Schiefelbein and T. R. Farrell, "Expanding the scope of educational planning: the experience of Chile", *Interchange,* vol. 5, no. 2 (1974) and "Conocimientos generales de los educandos. Primera Parte: la evaluacion metodologica para la medicion del rendimiento del sistema educativo" (Caracas, Venezuela: Ministerio de Educacion, 1970).

15. The year-round use of schools has already been implemented in several countries. The experience in Bahia, Brazil, is positive. Martin Carnoy, in "Un enfque de sistemas para evaluar la educacion", has used as a variable the actual number of hours per day that a student attends classes in a month, and found significant correlations in 20 percent of the regressions, although some were negative.

16. William Platt, "Policymaking and international studies in educational evaluation".

17. Christopher Jencks, *Inequality, A Reassessment of the Effect of Family and Schooling in America* (New York: Basic Books, 1972), p. 97.

18. John Vaizey, "The implications of the IEA studies for educational planning".

The Impact of Education on Employment, Migration and Fertility

CHAPTER 8

Common Assumptions about Education and Employment*

MARK BLAUG

If the employment problem is considered in terms of the poverty of the general population, it is difficult to see what a ministry of education can do about it in practical terms. Education may well be a kind of investment in future productive capacity, but in the foreseeable future the benefits largely accrue to those who receive the education. The spillover effects on the rest of the population—the raising of general living standards as the number of educated people reaches a minimum threshold—take generations to be felt. Educational policy as a device for curing poverty seems to lead to a single dictum: educate as many people as possible! But the cure will come twenty to thirty years later; meanwhile, the funds devoted to educational expansion preempt resources that might have been devoted to creating productive capacity elsewhere and possibly to creating jobs now as well as in the future. It seems, therefore, that a policy of not expanding education may at times be a more effective way to eradicate poverty. Thus, educational planning directed towards alleviating the "employment problem" in the widest sense of that term cannot avoid questions about the appropriate scale of the educational system. These questions loom even larger when a narrower view of the "employment problem" is taken. And in either case, the content and quality of education are at least as important as matters of scale.

---

*An earlier version of this chapter appeared in *Education and the Employment Problem in Developing Countries* (Geneva: ILO, 1973), pp. 79-89.

Seven Common Assumptions

I will review seven widely held assumptions about the role of education in the "employment problem", assumptions which are heard in every country whenever people sit down around conference tables to discuss the problems of developing nations.

1. Education Increases the Volume of Employment

It is certainly true that education increases the volume of employment in the short run, in the sense that education itself is a labor-intensive industry, and it may be true in the long run if education is seen as a type of social investment which makes people more productive. But in what way does it increase productivity? One could argue that it provides children with manual or mechanical skills that they could not have acquired elsewhere. Although true for certain professions, this is surely not true in general. Can and do schools impart "developmental" values and attitudes? Unless the answer to this question is known, it is unclear whether more education would impart more of these appropriate values. If schools only sort out children in terms of their native drives and aptitudes, there might be better and cheaper sorting machines than the educational system. In other words, this assumption is likely to be misleading unless the time period (short or long term) is specified, and the sense in which education is said to be an "investment" is explained.

Another interpretation of this assumption is that educated people save more and spend less, and tend to consume labor-intensive goods and services. Theoretically, additional savings are invested, which creates more jobs. There may well be a relationship between education and individual saving behavior. However, it is not inadequate savings that explains the poverty of poor countries, but rather the types of investments into which the savings are transferred. And it has yet to be empirically demonstrated that factor intensity resulting from the pattern of consumption spending is a function of the educational attainment of the consumer.

2. Education Works to Eliminate Poverty

In the long run, the assumption that education works to eliminate poverty merely restates the first assumption. It is true in the sense that education reduces the birth rate, directly through the education of women and indirectly by increasing the period in which children are dependent on their parents. The lower the rate of population growth, the higher the level of per capita income. Furthermore, education is a necessary complement to sanitation and nutrition programs, and these work directly to eliminate the consequences of poverty. But these arguments do not lead anywhere. Even if it were established that education is causally related to smaller family size, the magnitude of that relationship must be determined if choices are to be made between more education and other ways to restrict population growth.

Still another interpretation of the proposition before us is that education is necessary to fill manpower shortages which inhibit the economic growth of the country. But there are no longer enough examples of this situation in the world to support such a simplistic reason for expanding education. Even some of the remaining examples are spurious. If a shortage of plumbers is holding back the construction industry, it is usually because the scarcity of plumbers has not been allowed to raise the wages of plumbers. Because one can become a plumber only by serving a five-year apprenticeship, or because labor-saving plumbing equipment cannot be imported due to foreign exchange control, or perhaps because the shortage is not of plumbers per se but only of good plumbers, this is a problem which cannot be solved simply by training more plumbers.

3. Education Causes Unemployment

Taken at face value, the assumption that education causes unemployment is clearly incorrect. What is meant, however, is that education makes people unemployable; it raises their aspirations beyond all hope of satisfying them; it gives them the wrong skills or the wrong attitudes. There is clearly something in this argument, but the point about aspirations is really true of the entire development process. Suppose there was no educational system: surely the complaint would then be that "these countries are poor because they do not want to better themselves". Is there an educational system anywhere that raises career expectations just enough to produce ambitious graduates, but not more than can be satisfied by prospective job opportunities?

If the skills and attitudes now fostered by educational system are inappropriate, what should be substituted? Of course, the emphasis should be on vocational skills and attitudes of self-reliance. But what is a vocational skill? If it is something which can be turned directly into marketable skill, it is surely better learned on the job. Is it instead a foundation which expedites on-the-job learning? If so, that is what schools intend to provide. As for self-reliance, no one has yet discovered a way to instill it, although traditional education admittedly does a poor job.

4. Education Converts Underemployment into Open Unemployment

Traditional rural societies share work among members of the family, each member with perhaps less work than he or she would like. Education motivates people to leave their communities and move into the modern urban sector, where the same amount of work will be done by fewer workers, with the rest left unemployed. In this sense, the more highly educated a poor society is, the greater the amount of open unemployment that will be observed in it.

True—and yet too general. Education indeed stimulates the "flight from farming", because the same impetus which drives parents to send their children to school sends the children to seek employment in towns. Education gives awareness of greater earnings in towns and even greater oppportunities for part-time employment while continuing the search for a full-time job. Towns in Africa and Asia are inaccurately described as belonging to the modern sector; the intermediate urban sector is not unaccustomed to work-sharing and provides ample opportunities for apprenticeship training. Furthermore, it is not just education that converts underemployment into unemployment, but the entire development process. The real problem is that education absorbs resources that might have been devoted to creating employment opportunities. Thus educated unemployment represents a more serious economic problem than open employment as such.

5. Education is Simply Part of the Scramble for a Limited Supply of Top Jobs

Employers prefer the more highly educated person for the job, whether or not the higher qualifications are necessary for efficient job performance. Hence students are motivated to acquire extra education in order to compete better in the rat race, but since their education does not make them more productive, it has no ultimate influence on total output or total employment.

If education by its irrelevant content renders people unemployable, why are employers "conspicuous consumers" of more highly educated people? Perhaps it is the government which is the irrational employer in question. Is education relevant to the clerical needs of the civil service but not to the profit-maximizing needs of industry? Why then is industry reluctant to convert these poorly educated workers by means of labor training? And if it already does so, why does it prefer educated people as trainees instead of simply hiring able people, as revealed by aptitude tests, whatever their educational qualifications? But enough said. Assumption 5 is too extreme to merit a full discussion.

6. Public Subsidies to Promote Education Always Result in Excess Demand for Education and Hence in an Excess Supply of Educated Manpower

The argument simply states that because it is the educated individual himself (or herself) who receives the benefits of education, in the form of higher salaries, while the costs of education are largely borne by society as a whole, further education continues to be a privately profitable investment far beyond the point at which it has ceased to be socially profitable. Moreover, the much greater visibility of the earnings of those who are employed, as opposed to the lack of earnings of those who are not, exaggerates the profitability of more education to individuals, and so encourages the demand for education. By implication, the remedy is to shift more of the costs of education to students and parents and to publicize the evidence on educated unemployment.

This is certainly true, but it does not present the whole story. If the labor market ran smoothly and more or less instantly, it would have adjusted long ago to the excessive demand for education by eliminating the earnings differentials between more educated and less educated people. If the labor market does not run smoothly, there may be unemployment of the educated even though education is heavily subsidized, as in the case of the Philippines. Thus, unemployment of the educated must be attacked both through educational finance and labor market policies.

7. Excessive Salary Differentials in the Interests of the Ruling Elite are Responsible for Educated Unemployment

Earnings differentials in developing countries are excessive by international standards. In the United States a doctor earns five times the average income per earner; in India he earns twenty times as much. These differentials were often created at the time of the countries' independence, in an effort to attract expatriate personnel, and they have been maintained by highly educated political elites through their control of the public sector and their influence on private firms. This creates an insatiable demand for higher education, and unemployment of the educated results when the public sector proves incapable of absorbing more graduates.

This argument is clearly modelled on the former British colonies of tropical Africa but, if suitably amended, has some relevance to Asia as well. It depends heavily on what is meant by excessive salary differentials. International comparisons prove nothing except that, as economic theory predicts, a scarcer factor commands a relatively higher price; after all, educated people are more scarce in India than in the United States. Nevertheless, earnings differentials associated with education *are* excessive in developing countries; the existence of unemployment of the educated indicates that there are more job seekers at going wage rates than there are vacancies. But the maxim "Reduce differentials!" is not by itself very helpful. What keeps the differentials artificially high? Is it government policy? Surely this is not true in all countries, for in many of them salaries are dictated by private firms. More needs to be known about the hiring practices of both the private and the public sector in developing countries.

Research and Experimentation

There are many proposals for reforming the educational system, but little evidence to support them. Some of the proposals, yet to be tested, include: making the curriculum responsive to vocational and rural needs; abolishing examinations; selecting students by geographical and social quotas; adopting the principle of "working gaps" in post-compulsory education; concentrating resources on nonformal rather than formal education; reducing earnings differentials by fiat; recruiting civil servants in total ignorance of their paper qualifications, or at any rate promoting them on merit instead of age and educational attainment; raising fees to cover the total costs of instruction and gearing scholarships strictly to parental income; and replacing all grants and scholarships by loans at the higher education stage. There is some evidence around the world that would be relevant to the effects of implementing these proposals, such as vocationalized curricula or out-of-school programs. But for most of these proposals there is no evidence whatsoever, because so far they have not been put into practice.

It follows that experiments are needed. The educational authorities of developing countries must be persuaded that a suitable method for making education "relevant" to employment opportunities will not be discovered until controlled field experiments are conducted. Alas, pilot schemes are fraught with difficulties! To select a school or a group of students for an educational experiment invites criticism on the grounds of discrimination or on the grounds of special treatment. Further, the impossibility of holding other factors constant makes it difficult to evaluate pilot schemes. Nevertheless, without experiments, educational reform turns into a hit-or-miss affair.

Conclusion

At present, unemployment rates in the developing countries are highest among the young, and even for them the period of greatest unemployment occurs early in their working lives. Is this an invariable pattern or, in the future, will high unemployment rates be characteristic of older as well as younger age groups? In other words, do the young who suffer the greatest unemployment do so because, in a rapidly expanding educational system, they receive most of the additional education? Or, will unemployment gradually filter throughout all age groups and levels of education?

The answer to these questions might be that if developing countries maintain their present growth rates, unemployment will continue to be heavily concentrated among the fifteen- to twenty-five-year-olds, at least for the foreseeable future. Unfortunately, there is no easy remedy in sight for unemployment among the young or the educated. Somehow, the tendency of educational systems to grow more quickly at the top than at the bottom of the educational ladder must be reversed, and this can probably be achieved only by a restructured pattern of educational finance combined with deliberate intervention in labor markets. But to reverse these trends means that the problem of unemployment of the educated will be solved only to create or to aggravate the "school-leaver problem". The remedy for the school-leaver problem, at least in the short run, lies in the provision of out-of-school education. In the long run, it lies in the slow and patient reform of primary education from within by curriculum reform, examination reform, and the improvement of teacher training. It may not be a very exciting prospect to those who desire quick results, convinced that somewhere there is a clever idea never previously considered which will solve all difficulties overnight. But here, as elsewhere, "piecemeal social engineering" may prove to be the eventual solution.

CHAPTER 9

Can Education Alone Solve the Problem of Unemployment?

MARTIN CARNOY

In the 1950s, economists in the industrial nations worried that major bottlenecks to economic growth would occur in the developing countries because they lacked high and mid-level manpower. Manpower planning was instituted as a partial solution to the anticipated problem. But now, only twenty years later, many developing countries face an apparent excess of highly educated labor; the average level of education in the labor force has increased, but so too has the average level of education among the unemployed. Furthermore, unemployment shows no sign of diminishing, even though the unemployed are in theory more adequately prepared than formerly to participate in the growth of the economy.

One example of this problem is provided by the data in Table 20, which shows the growing open unemployment—that part of the labor force actively seeking but unable to obtain work—in Latin America. The rate of unemployment almost doubled in fifteen years, from 5.6 percent to 11.1 percent.

While the Organization of American States has described the situation in Latin America as an "employment crisis,"[1] in Asia development plans "have not made any sizeable impact on the overall employment situation and employment opportunities have lagged far behind the growth in the labor force".[2]

In West Africa, even in the early 1960s, unemployment among primary school leavers was very high.[3] After independence, with increased expansion of the educational system, unemployment began to be observed in the secondary and university educated labor force in East Africa, despite the elite nature of these schools.[4] Nonindus-

TABLE 20

Population, Labor Force, and Employment in Latin America, 1950-65

Category	1950	1955	1960	1965
Total population (thousands)	151,116	173,104	199,307	229,691
Rate of participation (percent of total population)	34.85	34.80	34.70	34.60
Labor force (thousands)	52,664	60,240	69,160	79,473
Persons employed (thousands)	49,739	56,077	62,866	70,651
Persons unemployed (thousands)	2925	4163	6294	8822
Rate of unemployment (percent of labor force)	5.60	6.90	9.10	11.10

Source: Secretariat of the Organization of American States, General Secretariat, *Employment and Growth in the Strategy of Latin American Development: Implications for the Seventies,* Proceedings of the VIIth Annual Meeting of the Inter-American Economic and Social Council (CIES), 10-20 September 1971, Panama, p. 2.

trialized economies—especially small, African economies—cannot expand nonagricultural employment quickly enough to absorb the output of schools. At the same time, the educated are loath to work in manual, especially agricultural, jobs.[5]

Unemployment: More Efficient Mechanisms or Structural Change?

Is large-scale unemployment an inherent and necessary part of the capitalist development or does such unemployment result from inefficiencies in capitalist development? Unless this question can be answered, solutions to the problems of unemployment—such as expanded educational systems—cannot be found.

There are several persuasive arguments that unemployment is inherent to capitalist development, particularly in dependent economies in the process of industrialization. The owners and managers of physical capital are the ones who make the investment decisions. They prefer to use less labor than more, simply because of the production problems which accompany human relations. Machines do not arrive late to work; they do not strike or argue about working conditions. Rather than deal with an aggressive labor force, employers quite reasonably would prefer to eliminate entirely the use of labor.[6]

As long as investment decisions (decisions concerning the adoption of technology, the choice of production, working laws, working conditions, and methods of production on the factory floor) are made by the owners of physical capital, there will be a tendency to employ less labor than would be possible with the technology available, the given product mix, and the prevailing "market" price of labor. More important, less labor will be employed than would be with an alternative mix of goods to be produced, based on a set of societal needs defined by the lower income levels rather than by the higher. Furthermore, a reserve army of unemployed individuals exerts downward pressure on the wages of those with jobs by allowing the employer to remind his workers that others would be glad to work for minimal pay: thus a reserve army serves the employer's interest.

Developing countries which have achieved very rapid growth rates in gross national product (GNP), such as Puerto Rico and Mexico, have done so with consistently high unemployment rates. In Puerto Rico, open unemployment remained at 12 percent from 1940 to 1960 despite massive emigration of rural population to the United States. Under such conditions of dependent capitalist development, the prospects for solving the unemployment problem by increasing the economic growth rate are not very promising. The increase in growth rates in such economies probably implies the use of advanced, capital-intensive technology by foreign capital, which exacerbates the unemployment problem.

Unemployment as a Function of Class Status

Although unemployment rates tend to remain high in developing capitalist countries, even in the face of rapid growth rates, and although this unemployment continues to include the highly educated, most evidence indicates that unemployment rates will drop more substantially for the college educated than for those with primary or high school education.[7] Apparently, the demand for highly educated labor grows more rapidly than the demand for less educated labor; employers substitute better educated for more poorly educated workers as the labor-capital ratio falls.[8] Thus, the preference for capital by owners and managers is not limited to physical capital; it includes hiring those with more rather than less education. The poor, who tend to receive less education than the rich, are hit harder by unemployment; eliminating unemployment would have profound income distributional consequences.

Unemployment rates, furthermore, vary for individuals who have the same amount of education but come from different social classes. Although they may have been in school the same number of years, those from lower social classes are more likely to be unemployed than those from higher social classes.[9] This is partly due to the kinds of schools available to the various social classes: children from wealthier families attend private schools or better (high cost urban or suburban) public schools and universities, while poorer children attend rural or provincial schools. Given the choice, employers seem to prefer the former to the latter.[10] This is also partly due to less well-developed labor market connections among poor families. Both of these situations produce similar effects on average income.

So far, I have only been discussing open unemployment, not the intensity of employment by those who have jobs. Richard Eckhaus argues that in the United States a large percentage of income differences among individuals (with different levels of schooling) can be explained by the fact that the better educated usually work more hours annually.[11] They have access to jobs which require (or allow) them to work longer hours and pay more per hour of work. Thus the more highly educated not only have a better chance of finding work, they also have access to jobs with higher income potential.

I have discussed the structure of unemployment in order to emphasize the class basis of the problem.[12] Capitalists and managers of capital prefer physical capital to labor, and higher to lower social class labor. Expanding the educational system without effecting class changes in society will not solve unemployment; it will only perpetuate existing inequalities.

Can Education Solve Unemployment?

Solutions to the problem of unemployment, as they are now being discussed by planners, do not seem to take these issues into account. They advise the production of goods which use more labor and argue that alternative forms of technology can be employed which are more consistent with the availability of cheap labor in the developing countries. This proposition fails to acknowledge the capitalist hierarchy of investment decisionmaking. Planners assume that technological decisions have been a matter of fortuitous circumstance; in other words, they assume that the capitalist system could achieve full employment, if only it would operate more efficiently. They fail to realize that capitalist decisionmakers would not choose to implement capital-saving technology, for the reasons above.

In this same context, planners and politicians are proposing that urban school curricula be made more relevant, more vocational, under the assumption that people are unemployed because the schools are not preparing them for jobs available in the urban sector. Attempts are also being made, through curriculum changes, to orient rural schools toward rural life and work.

But again, unless unemployment is a result of inefficiencies in an otherwise sound system, rather than an unalterable part of the system itself, major changes in school curricula will not solve the problem of educated unemployment. This proposition incorrectly assumes that the problem is on the supply side alone—that there is a fundamental mismatch between skills provided by schools and jobs available on the market. It also assumes that schools can convince people to want certain jobs by training them for those jobs. Neither assumption is supported empirically, and both demonstrate a naïve view of capitalist labor markets.

The problem is as much of demand as of supply. Unemployment of the educated is high in developing countries because, at the going wages, and given the kinds of technology used by capitalists, there are fewer jobs than people capable of filling them. Producing an educated supply of labor will not solve unemployment unless, concomitantly, the demand for labor is increased. Philip Foster has noted that:

> . . . curriculum reform will not alter the current situation, since the causes of under-utilization of manpower have very little to do with what is taught in the schools. Moreover, lower level schooling can nowhere prepare individuals for specific occupations. Indeed, the attempt to do so would vastly increase educational costs and, if anything, reduce the existing flexibility of the system.

To my mind, there are more viable strategies that can be pursued, and these hinge on examining what goes on outside the schools rather than what goes on inside them.[13]

As for the second assumption—that schools can convince people to want certain jobs by training them for these jobs—student motivation is strongly influenced by perceptions of subsequent job opportunities. These perceptions are derived from the realities of the socioeconomic environment. British attempts to use formal education to impose agricultural occupations on Africans during the mid nineteenth century and colonial rule were unpersuasive because Africans saw the highest rewards in European-type work, not in agriculture. Schools cannot make people want certain kinds of jobs if these jobs are less lucrative and prestigious than others.

Today, the nationalist bourgeoisie is the highest status class in capitalist countries. The kind of education its children receive is widely aspired to by other social classes.

> Those who criticize the "traditional" nature of . . . demand for "academic" as opposed to "vocational" education fail to recognize that the strength of academic education has lain precisely in the fact that it is preeminently a *vocational* education providing access to those occupations with the most prestige and, most important, the highest pay. . . .[14]

My argument is simple: unemployment is not a function of the amount of schooling or type of schooling of the labor force. While some marginal improvements may be made with changes in curriculum or attempts to channel people into professions for which there appears to be some excess demand, that demand is soon filled and the field soon becomes oversupplied; the problem of unemployment remains. If capitalist decisionmakers will employ only a certain number of workers, that number will not be raised by making education more relevant.

Supply and Demand: The Total Picture

In order to solve the problem of unemployment, the aggregate demand for and the supply of labor must be examined. The demand for labor in a capitalist economy is based on the number of workers that capitalists want to employ. This is theoretically a function of the price of labor and the technology used. However, I have argued that owners of capital prefer technologies which employ less labor than is implied by labor/capital price ratios. Also, the choice of products to be produced is not determined purely or even predominantly by sovereign consumer demand. Owners of physical capital are oriented towards goods which use more physical capital in their production. Thus, in order to increase the demand for labor associated with a growth in output, the decisionmaking hierarchy (and therefore the social structure) of the economy must be confronted.[15]

On the supply side, rates of population growth may be considered important. As long as population growth continues unabated, educating and employing an ever-increasing number of people will strain the capacities of most countries. Lowering population growth rates will certainly aid on both counts, although even major declines in population growth such as in the United States by no means assure the solution of unemployment problems. The labor shortages in some Western European economies have resulted from decades of low population growth, following genocidal wars, in combination with politically powerful labor union organizations pushing for full employment policies.

For most countries, demand conditions and the weakness of organized labor are such that even low population growth rates and rapid increases in the education of the labor force and GNP will not reduce the current unemployment rates. Again, Puerto Rico, despite its peculiar situation as a colony of the United States, serves as an interesting example. The island's net population growth rate between 1940 and 1960, because of emigration of the rural poor, was only 1.5 percent annually. Unemployment did not decrease, although it was probably far below what it would have been without emigration. Rises in wages, the product mix, and imported capital-intensive technology effectively reduced the absorption of the slowly-growing island labor force into the industrial and service sectors.[16]

In summary, I am convinced that research on unemployment should be concentrated on full employment of the labor force. There is no logic or empirical evidence to support the argument that having more educated workers in the labor force will create more employment, unless production and investment decisions are turned over to the workers themselves. In that case, a more highly educated and politically aware labor force might be able to invent labor intensive techniques so that they can hire more workers. But the evidence is mixed.

Instead of trying to use education to increase employment, it might be better to develop an accurate picture of production functions for various goods, of the alternate technologies for producing these goods, and of alternate kinds of goods that would satisfy general consumer demand. For example, transport demand might be met in a number of ways. Each way implies alternative technologies of production, and within each technology are various combinations of labor and capital that can produce the goods. Since at each of these three levels subsidies can alter the capital to labor price ratio (and usually do, in favor of more intensive use of capital), the price ratio is not necessarily exogenously determined.

But technical alternatives to increased employment have implications for the distribution of output, just as employment rates themselves have implications for distribution. If product mixes and technical methods that increase labor use without average salary reduction are chosen, labor will receive an increased share of output at the expense of capital's share. These distributional consequences must be taken into account in order to understand how the volume of employment can be increased.

The Effect of Unemployment on the Demand for Education

Education has little effect on unemployment, but unemployment may have a significant effect on the demand for more education. Paradoxically, a decreased unemployment rate could reduce the demand for education, because when unemployment decreases, income foregone by remaining in school increases.

Lower rates of unemployment probably decrease the gap in income between the less and more educated individuals, and therefore may reduce the absolute income benefits of going to school, since unemployment is presently greater amongst those with less schooling. The combination of increased income foregone, and lower or constant benefits of more education, reduce the private rate of return. If students and their families respond to changing rates of return to private investment in education, they might reduce the number of years they spend in school.

Thus, reducing unemployment may reduce demand for education; increased demand is usually related to diminished job opportunities for the young and relatively uneducated. In the United States, for example, school applications and even enrollments increase during slumps (higher unemployment) and decrease during booms (lower unemployment).

The fact that unemployment has been relatively high in almost all low income capitalist countries (see Table 20 above) since World War II has contributed to an education "explosion", which seems to affect higher and higher levels of education as each successive "exploded" level produces unemployed graduates. In the current period, increasing unemployment of secondary school graduates is helping increase the pressure on the part of young people and their families to expand the college/university system.

But even assuming that reducing the demand for education through increased employment has a certain appeal, we must ask whether that appeal is great enough to overcome the value of a reserve army of unemployed, especially an educated reserve army, to the capitalists and managers. Because unemployment controls labor so effectively, a full employment policy may not be politically feasible in economies where labor organizations do not exercise pro-labor political power.[17] I would argue that the consequences for production and social class relations of full employment are so great and immediate that most capitalist governments will choose to continue rapid school expansion.

Notes

1. "The general employment situation in Latin America as a whole is one of disequilibrium between the population in the mass and the economic structures of the hemisphere. The quickening growth of population in the region, its rapid urbanization, and the high growth rate of the labor force are part of the complex socioeconomic situation that may be summarily described as an employment crisis, manifested partly by a relatively high rate of open unemployment—particularly in urban areas—but also by extensive underemployment and a low rate of participation." Secretariat of the Organization of American States, General Secretariat,

Employment and Growth in the Strategy of Latin American Development: Implications for the Seventies, Proceedings of the VIIth Annual Meeting of the Inter-American Economic and Social Council (CIES), September 10-20, 1971, Panama, p. 1.

2. "In some countries, like India, Pakistan, and Ceylon, the backlog of unemployed and underemployed at the end of the plan period appeared to be far larger than at the beginning of the plan period—indicating that the new employment opportunities have not kept pace with the growth in the labor force. Such data as are readily available do suggest that the situation on the employment front is assuming quite serious proportions. In the Republic of Korea, despite all efforts at industrialization, the number of unemployed and underemployed persons has increased in 1963 to 703,000 and 2,220,000 respectively. . . . In other countries like Indonesia, Burma, or the Republic of Vietnam where the development plans remained practically inoperative either due to economic and political instability or serious shortage of external and internal resources, the impact of development planning on employment was even less significant." M. Mehta, *Industrialization and Employment with Special Reference to Countries of the ECAFE Region* (Bangkok: Asian Institute for Economic Development and Planning, 1968), pp. 24-25.

3. Archibald Callaway, "School leavers in Nigeria", *West Africa* (March 25, April 1, April 8, April 15, 1961), pp. 325, 353, 371-2, and 409, respectively.

4. Hans Thias and Martin Carnoy, *Cost-Benefit Analysis in Education: A Case Study of Kenya* (Baltimore: Johns-Hopkins/IBRD, 1972).

5. Lewis Brownstein provides some contrary data based on a survey in rural Kenya. In his small sample, the primary school leavers were not so universally opposed to a career in agriculture as migration patterns would have us believe. See Lewis Brownstein, *Education and Development in Rural Kenya* (New York: Praeger, 1972).

6. Steve Marglin, "What do bosses do?", *Review of Radical Political Economics,* vol. 6, no. 2, Summer 1974.

7. See, for example, Mark Blaug, et al., *The Causes of Graduate Unemployment in India* (London: Penguin Press, 1969).

8. Martin Carnoy and Dieter Marenbach, "The return to schooling in the United States, 1939-69", *Journal of Human Resources* (Summer 1975). We show that the rate of return to primary schooling in the U.S. fell despite a decrease in the absolute number of people with primary school education in the labor force, while the rate of return to taking college education remained stable and the rate of return to graduate school education rose (we only have data on graduate school incomes for the period 1959-69) despite rapid increases in the number of people with that level of schooling in the labor force.

9. M. Carnoy, R. Sack, and H. Thias, "Middle level manpower in Tunisia: the links between socio-economic origin, schooling and job history", in Russell Stone and John Simmons, eds., *Change in Tunisia* (Albany: State University of New York Press, 1976).

10. Martin Carnoy, "The return to university education in Peru", mimeograph, CONUP (Peru) and Stanford University, 1975.

11. Richard Eckhaus, *Estimating the Returns to Education: A Disaggregated Approach* (Berkeley, California: Carnegie Commission, 1973).

12. For more detail on the issue, see David Gordon, *Theories of Poverty and Underemployment* (Lexington, Mass.: D. C. Health, 1973).

13. Philip Foster, in Lewis Brownstein, *Education and Development in Rural Kenya* (New York: Praeger, 1972), pp. x-xi.
14. Philip Foster, "The vocational school fallacy in development planning", in C. A. Anderson and M. J. Bowman (eds.), *Education and Economic Development* (Chicago: Aldine Publishing, 1965), pp. 145-6.
15. For an attempt to do this, see Carl H. Gotsch, "Technical change and the distribution of income in rural areas", *American Journal of Agricultural Economics,* vol. 54, no. 2 (May 1972).
16. We also have to consider that the absorption of labor into the industrial and service sector will have to come from rural areas, and this may decrease domestic food production and agricultural surplus. Much of the increased urban production may have to be used for exports in order to import food. The choice of goods (urban vs. agricultural) to be produced again enters into the picture.
17. For further development of this concept, see Martin Carnoy, *Education and Employment* (Paris: International Institute of Educational Planning, 1976).

CHAPTER 10

Education and Employment after Independence

REMI CLIGNET

Before assuming office, many political leaders in developing countries claimed that limitations imposed on educational development by the colonial authorities were responsible for poor economic growth. As a result, the first decades of independence have been almost uniformly characterized by heavy investments in formal education.

These investments were based on three main assumptions formulated by political leaders and social scientists. First, they believed that economic stagnation resulted from a shortage of qualified technical and managerial cadres. In other words, the emergence of a class of highly skilled individuals would surely stimulate economic growth and employment. This meant that school enrollments, particularly enrollments of post-primary institutions, had to be increased. A second explanation for economic stagnation was the scarcity of appropriate behavioral orientations, specifically the persistence of a traditional, particularistic, and ascription-based system of values which is oriented towards individuals in terms of what they *are* rather than what they *do* and which discourages individual entrepreneurship. It was believed that economic growth required both the eradication of this system and the socialization of individuals toward achievement motivations. In turn, it was held that this socialization could be accomplished most effectively by the schools. Finally, economic stagnation was seen to result from the "scarcity of equality" and from the perpetuation of political and economic inequalities among ethnic and social groups. Since the main function of formal schooling was to ensure upward mobility, it was assumed that this could minimize the impact of these inequalities.

Twenty years and more have passed. Experience suggests that previously perceived interactions between educational and economic activities are not necessarily accurate. This chapter will examine each of the assumptions summarized in the previous paragraphs and assess the extent to which the assumed interaction appears to be valid.

Education and Access to the Labor Market: The Assumptions

The first assumption mentioned above is that formal schooling stimulates employment and access to the most rewarding slots in the modern sectors of developing countries. For a long time social scientists studying African countries were eager to understand the psychological and noneconomic motivations underlying individual geographic mobility. More recent studies, however, suggest that education influences both the final destination of migrants and the procedures they use to enter the labor force. Additional years of schooling increase the distance individuals are willing to travel, and result in more diversified geographic options. In turn, these give the educated individual a better chance to find a job.

In addition, formal education gives the individual greater access to information about local job opportunities. Illiterate adults, or adults with a minimum of education, rely only on ethnic peers, relatives, or former employees, while their more educated counterparts are likely to use the services made available by the mass media or by public employment agencies.

Since education enhances geographic mobility and leads to a more rational use of the various channels facilitating access to labor markets, it should become easier for employers to find the most qualified workers, and for individual job-seekers to find the most rewarding jobs in the labor market. Although political leaders, students, and employers have often seen education in this positive light, the actual picture is less rosy. In the following discussion, I will analyze two factors—the differential effect of unemployment, and differences between manual and nonmanual workers—which prevent education from exerting a uniformly positive influence on economic growth and on employment opportunities.

Unemployment Among the Better and Less Educated

Because formal education facilitates urban migration, it leads to a concentration of job seekers in the larger cities. This concentration changes the definition of relevant social problems. Indeed, while rural populations are often characterized as underemployed, their urban counterparts face more serious difficulties. This is because an urban economy does not allow further differentation of existing jobs, for example, the allocation of part-time positions. For those looking for jobs under such conditions, the extent to which urban job-seekers may gain access to modern occupational roles depends either upon the extension of existing investment (and hence upon a problematic development of the markets for the products manufactured, or the services rendered by the relevant enterprises) or upon the creation of new activities or enterprises. In brief, while the concentration of educated individuals in urban centers allows employers to obtain the qualified manpower they need to increase the productivity and profits of their enterprises, it exacerbates the variety of tensions which result from disparities existing between the relative growth rate of educational enrollments and of economic opportunities. Such tensions are also reinforced by the segmentation of urban labor markets, both by types of jobs and types of employers. Because of such a segmentation, the economic value of formal schooling is not constant across economic sectors or over time.

The fact that schooling has no constant economic value leads to the emergence of two types of jobless populations. In the Cameroon, for example, it is possible to distinguish between the "de-employed" individuals who have been pushed out of the labor market because their educational qualifications are lower than those of the newer cohorts of job-seekers, and the unemployed individuals who have not yet been able or willing to join the urban labor force. The former, who are generally older, are out of the labor market because of educational shortcomings. The latter, who are younger, remain without a job despite their higher educational attainments because of the discrepancies between their occupational aspirations and the opportunities offered them by the labor market. The two types of jobless populations also typically have different periods of unemployment.

Those who have lost their jobs either return to their villages and leave the urban labor market for good and/or accept an inferior position, while their better educated counterparts often stay in towns and remain jobless for over one year.

Time lags between educational and economic development and the ensuing emergence of the types of jobless populations in urban centers must therefore create tensions between generations. While the less educated individuals are likely to claim that access to jobs and to the corresponding sets of rewards should depend primarily upon seniority, their more educated and younger counterparts who have already entered the labor market would argue that the definition of existing jobs and relevant salaries or wages should rely more on the level of educational attainment. The younger job-seekers are themselves confronted with serious dilemmas. It is difficult for them to identify the point at which their occupational aspirations cease to be realistic and the point at which the acceptance of an unskilled occupational role may limit subsequent chances of upward mobility, and hence of gaining access to the kind of job to which they aspire.

While disparities between the growth rates of educational enrollment and occupational opportunities are likely to be associated with an increase in the number of individuals unable or unwilling to enter the formal and modern labor market, the size and characteristics of the corresponding unemployed population vary with the types of institution attended. At the same time, individuals graduating or dropping out of vocational schools are often less easily hired and remain jobless for longer periods of time than those with the same number of years of an academic—and hence more general—background. In societies where occupational roles are few in number and entail the performance of diffuse activities which often change over time, students who have acquired a general rather than specific training have less definite expectations of the types of jobs they are willing to accept. In addition, they are also preferred by employers who deem them able to adapt more easily to the discipline of modern industrial or commercial operations.

On the other hand, there are also contrasts in the types of access to the labor market for students enrolled in public, as opposed to private, institutions or for those attending centralized, as opposed to decentralized, educational systems. Thus, the administrators of public and centralized school systems can manipulate the difficulties of examinations or the standards required for moving upward on the educational ladder in order to obtain a better fit between the supply of school leavers and the demands of the labor market. Conversely, if the administrators of private and decentralized school systems have a less precise image of what goes on in the labor market at large, they often have a greater sense of commitment to the occupational fate of their graduates or alumni. This leads them to use more formal and informal strategies (such as newsletters and alumni associations) to help their students find jobs.

Educational Background to Manual and Nonmanual Workers

Disparities between the growth rates of educational enrollments and occupational opportunities do not necessarily have the same effects on different parts of the labor market. Indeed I have shown, in the *Africanization of the Labor Market,* not only how the relative influence of educational attainment on occupational success varies both between job categories and across type of enterprises, but also how the relevant differences change over time.

Among the oldest workers in the Cameroon, there is a sharp contrast in the educational background of manual and nonmanual wage earners of modern private enterprises. The former are often illiterate, but a large number of older nonmanual workers have at least completed a primary education. Conversely, marked increases in the educational enrollments of the Cameroon enable employers to be more choosy when they hire manual workers and, correspondingly, differences in the educational qualifications of newcomers in blue collar, as opposed to white collar, activities have sharply declined. While education used to be the key determinant of the access of job-seekers to these two categories of jobs, the hierarchy of occupational roles both *within* and *between* such categories is less likely to depend exclusively upon educational criteria.

Further, the sharp increase in educational enrollments, and hence the increased supply of job-seekers, has been accompanied by parallel changes in the educational policies adopted by local employers concerning the white and blue collar labor force. Among the older cohorts of manual workers, on-the-job training programs were primarily offered to those with minimal educational qualifications. In other words, employers were obliged to perform some of the functions that local schools had been unable to discharge, while the same employers felt that the majority of older nonmanual job-seekers had sufficient educational attainment to execute the tasks demanded of them, without further training. The higher educational level of entrants in the blue and white collar sectors enables employers to change the functions of on-the-job training programs. Indeed, such programs are currently geared toward providing the most educated segment of the population, seeking access to manual as well as nonmanual jobs, with the specific skills required to operate increasingly complex machinery. While on-the-job training programs initially *compensated* for deficiencies of the local school system, the functions of such programs are increasingly *complementary* to those performed by local educational institutions, for all categories of jobs.

The decline in contrasts between blue and white collar labor markets has a number of implications. Among older cohorts, variations in educational attainment are a more significant predictor of the skill level and of the salaries of nonmanual than of manual workers. Among younger generations, however, the general rise in the educational level of the entire population implies an increased homogeneity in the educational qualifications of the white collar workers, but an increased heterogeneity in the qualifications of their blue collar counterparts. As a result, variations in educational qualifications are currently a better predictor of achievement for manual than for nonmanual workers. In the same vein, during earlier stages of economic development, occupational mobility of nonmanual workers was primarily a function of their level of education and was associated almost invariably with access to more rewarding jobs, while the change of jobs or employers for manual workers was markedly related to educational qualifications, and did not automatically imply upward mobility. In contrast, among the newest cohorts of wage earners, changes of jobs and/or employers are more frequent for blue collar workers, more closely related to their educational qualifications, and provide them easier access to additional occupational rewards. In short, disparities between the growth rates of enrollments and occupational opportunities lead the nonmanual labor market to be "saturated" with educated job-seekers, whereas this is not yet true for the manual labor market. Correspondingly, the rewards resulting from educational qualifications have declined in the first instance but increased in the second.

Finally, because of the segmentation of the labor market, hiring practices differ among enterprises located in the primary, secondary, or tertiary sector, and hence according to branch activity. Practices differ between firms that are incorporated and those that are not. There are also differences between firms which have headquarters in the Cameroon, and those whose headquarters are outside the country. These relevant contrasts have not remained stable over time.

During earlier stages of development, large-scale international companies were more likely to attract nonmanual job-seekers with top educational qualifications than were small-scale, locally based enterprises. In contrast, the average educational qualification of the manual labor force did not vary much according to the type of economic organization. At present, because of the rate of educational development, different types of firms are no longer obliged to compete with one another to attract the most highly educated segments of the nonmanual population. This is because the number of highly qualified candidates far exceeds the number of positions offered. At the same time, the increased technological differentiation of enterprises operating in the Cameroon is such that there are increased differences in the average educational qualifications of their manual labor force. Indeed such qualifications are greater in the case of international large mechanical industries than in the case of locally based and small food processing enterprises.

In summary, it can no longer be safely assumed that increase in the output of educational institutions uniformly and jointly stimulates economic growth and facilitates individual access to modern jobs. If the relationship between education and employment patterns depends upon the evolving processes of segmentation operating in the labor market of a single country, there are also international variations in that relationship. As suggested by Mark Blaug in *Educational and Employment Problem in Developing Countries,* the association between these two variables is positive for certain countries, while in others this association is negative, and in a third group follows a curvilinear pattern, secondary school graduates having more difficulty finding a job than those with less or more education.

Research Implications

Because the correlation between education and occupational placement varies cross-culturally, it is necessary to determine whether such variations reflect different rates of educational development as well as disparities between rates of economic and educational growth. It is also necessary to know if such variations result from differences in the structure of local labor markets and, more specifically, from differences in the relative size of primary, secondary, and tertiary sectors of economic activity.

Indeed, the correlation between occupational aspirations and opportunities should not be the same in cultures where the job-seeking population is concentrated in one particular sector of the modern labor market and in those where it is more evenly distributed. Nor should the correlation be the same in countries where economic organizations have differing technological and ownership structures. Finally, the influence of educational attainment on occupational placement varies with the mechanisms linking the educational institutions to the economic world. There should be contrasts along these lines between centralized and decentralized educational systems.

The Socializing Effects of Educational Institutions: Implications for the Labor Market

The persistence of urban unemployment requires the perpetuation of ethnic and family solidarities. Because formal schooling supposedly stimulates the adoption of individualistic Western orientations, there should be a decline in the strength of urban traditional family groups which enable the young to remain unemployed for long periods of time. This second main assumption, however, also turns out to be incorrect. In Africa, educational attainment is often associated with continued polygamy (more than one wife), residential familism (concentration of relatives), and large families.

It is often in the least educated segment of an urban population that one finds the smallest percentage of males with more than one wife and the smallest percentage of households sheltering adult relatives and many children. It is clear that planners were mistaken when they thought that formal schooling would stimulate the adoption of familial behaviors compatible with the requirements of industrialization and economic development. If educational attainment enhances the *means* available to familial groups, it does not necessarily "westernize" the *ends* to which such groups aspire.

Thus, formal education has not had the effect on family groups—and indirectly on the labor market—that planners had expected. This is because schools are not necessarily more powerful socializing agents than traditional groups. In fact, successful Africans tend to see familism and mobility acquired through education as complementary rather than mutually exclusive. This is also because the two sexes do not receive the same exposure to the educational environment. In Douala, for example, the educational attainment of married women is inversely associated with the number of children borne, while the educational level of married men has the opposite effect.

While educated men take advantage of their educational status to marry more wives and have more children, the few women who attend school use their educational experience to acquire more autonomy and to enter or stay in monogamous households. Similarly, regardless of type of marriage, educated men view their education as a means of raising large families. In contrast, their female counterparts view their academic experience as a means to implement new ends. It is therefore evident that differences in the numbers of males and females attending schools are associated with parallel contrasts in the influence that educational experiences exert on their familial aspirations and behaviors.

Educational and Individual Entrepreneurship

Although planners had anticipated that education would stimulate entrepreneurship, many studies conducted in Africa show that the more educated the individual, the greater the emphasis placed on job security. Educated individuals would rather be employed by large firms than start their own ventures. Similarly, they accord a higher value to stable jobs than to occupations with high risks and potentially commensurate rewards.

Planners erred in basing their suggestions on the assumption that formal education stimulated entrepreneurship in European countries of the nineteenth century. Should the patterns of development for those countries be duplicated by the developing world? After all, international loans and programs of assistance are more likely to be extended to bureaucratic organizations than to individual entrepreneurs.

Many planners also expected educational experiences to help individuals adapt to particular jobs. These expectations, too, have turned out to be incorrect. The student's own assessment of the job market is more likely to affect choice of occupation than any socializing influence at school. For example, because such jobs as teaching or farming are not considered prestigious or remunerative, students in teaching or agricultural colleges are likely to move out of these fields as soon as possible.

But while educational attainment favors both the perpetuation of polygamy and large families in the main cities of East Cameroon, these two variables appear to be negatively related in the West Cameroon, formerly subject to British influence. Because the eastern part of Cameroon was following a centralized pattern of political and educational organization, it may be that centralization does not promote the acquisition of such skills as self-reliance, which theoretically underlie entrepreneurship and thus contribute to economic development.

Favoring both a commitment to traditional ideals and dependence on the government, centralization may also prevent the individual from being committed to improving his residential and occupational environment. If such assumptions are correct, then—before the intervention of any external agency—operations of self-help and of indigenous community development will be less effective in centralized countries. Differences observed between centralized and decentralized countries should lead in turn to the differentiation of appropriate strategies recommended by planners.

To summarize, two types of research on the effects of the socialization function of the schools on the operation of the labor market are needed. First, the effectiveness of the schools in promoting certain values and norms may vary as a result of contrasts with value systems in traditional family groups, and such variations are likely to be ethnically specific. Second, the effectiveness of schools in this regard may also depend on whether they are centralized or decentralized, and hence upon the historical legacies that many developing countries inherit from their colonial past.

Education and Social Inequalities

Let us turn now to the third main assumption mentioned at the outset: the relationship between education and social inequalities. Initially, traditional elites were hostile to the education of their children, because they viewed the system of values extolled in European schools as one at odds with their own. Because they were obliged by colonial administrators to send the children of their communities to school, they often preferred to first send the children from poor or politically marginal families. As a result, in the early days of colonization, access to Ghanaian, Ivory Coast, or Nigerian schools was open and these schools attracted the offspring of a relatively wide range of social classes.

More recently, however, many systems have become constricted. The first to suffer the consequences of an increased demand for education are not the children of urban elites or of farmers, but the offspring of unskilled and semi-skilled manual workers living in urban areas. In this sense, the educational consequences of the stratification emerging in new countries does not necessarily pit urban and rural groups against one another, but rather various segments of the urban population.

With the growing disparities between educational enrollments and occupational opportunities, it is clear that benefits derived from a given level of education have declined and may, in fact, have declined differentially for various social, cultural, and ethnic groups. Because of this differential decline, there may be increased differences in the demand of these various groups for further education, and in the patterns of selection underlying their access to educational institutions. If this is true, formal education will no longer facilitate upward mobility and mediate a redistribution of wealth, but confirm the advantages of the most modernized ethnic groups, as well as the privileges of emerging middle and upper classes. In this sense, schools will perpetuate existing inequities.

The educational consequences of the emerging systems of social and ethnic stratification may certainly be reinforced by differences in the rewards assigned to particular levels of education. In the Cameroon, for instance, there are sharp contrasts in the skill and income levels of individuals with the same amount of formal training, but with different ethnic origins. The *Pahouins* do not gain the same returns from the educational investments as their counterparts from more modernized coastal ethnic groups. This reflects not only their late entry into the modern labor market but also the stereotypes by which their co-workers view them, and which in turn make them less attractive to potential employers. In brief, the system of social stratification and the frictions operating in the labor market prevent not only equal access to education, but also the equalizing impact that access to education might potentially have.

Summary and Conclusions

The expansion of educational systems in the developing countries has been based upon three postulates. First, a substantial increase in the number of graduates from post-primary institutions should accelerate economic growth. But although economic stagnation may result from a shortage of qualified workers, it does not necessarily follow that their presence will stimulate economic development or employment. The relationship between education and occupation is not the same when considering the market as a whole as when considering its components. In fact, the relationship between education and employment is greatly influenced both by variations in the rate of educational development and by variations in the institutional arrangements of the educational and economic systems.

The second postulate is that schools should facilitate economic growth by socializing students to certain norms and values. Yet while formal education enables individuals to acquire specific skills, it does not enable them to acquire some of the expected sets of values and orientations. As a matter of fact, the direct and indirect effects of socialization on the labor market are more moderate than had been hoped.

Finally, available evidence suggests that although formal education initially helped to change patterns of social stratification, this is no longer the case. Educational systems are more likely to reproduce patterns of inequality in the society than to alter them.

In view of these skeptical comments, is it possible to suggest remedies to alleviate the problems of unemployment plaguing developing countries? Since these problems are often described as transitory, it could be suggested that countries either limit the pattern of mobility resulting from formal education or that they accelerate the emerging processes and facilitate the patterns of mobility acquired through schooling. In other words, one posits that the problems of unemployment are primarily political and that the major difficulty results from the presence of a large number of educated individuals among jobless populations. Correspondingly, either one reduces educational opportunities to existing job opportunities, or drastically deflates educational currency by offering universal schooling.

The first perspective acknowledges that different parts of the educational system grow at different rates and more specifically that the post-primary institutions are overgrown. Since this results in urban migration and accentuates urban-rural disparities in life style, the task is to reduce the gap between the resources and life styles of the two populations. This implies not only increases in the size of rural primary school systems and changes in their curriculum, but also the development of programs of adult education closely connected with economic activities. The success of such operations depends on the extent to which individuals perceive educational experiences as influencing the rewards resulting from their current occupation. It also depends on the planning going into the program. Frequently, these programs fail because they are launched in the least economically successful parts of the country. This may be where they are most needed, but also where chances of obtaining visible success are minimal. Insofar as the logic underlying the need for such programs is not necessarily the same as that underlying their diffusion across differing zones, the tensions which oppose them to one another are difficult to mediate.

To sum up, the strategies associated with the first perspective aim at lowering the political dangers resulting from the concentration of educated jobless individuals in large urban centers. In most cases, these strategies induce a shift from the systematic unemployment observable in cities to a more spatially diffuse underemployment across the entire nation.

The second perspective requires recognition of the fact that political and economic boundaries do not necessarily coincide. In countries such as Senegal, Mali, Algeria, and Tunisia, it seems clearly impossible to adjust rates of economic and educational development. At the same time it is obvious that a large part of the labor force of such countries is attracted to the markets of highly industrialized countries. Under such conditions, the solution requires the recognition that local labor markets extend beyond existing political boundaries. The function of education could then be to accelerate the adaptation of migrants to the demands of industrial settings, and thus to enhance the returns obtained from migration.

Clearly, however, these strategies cannot be universal. To paraphrase Mark Blaug, "there is no panacea for the time being but a series of piecemeal social engineering", the validity of which remains culturally relative. Blaug's comment, far from being an ad hoc rationalization of ignorance, recognizes the influence of history on the problems of unemployment. Social scientists too often treat the relationship between education and employment in a timeless perspective. In addition, the comment follows the lessons of Franz Fanon, who argued so cogently in *The Wretched of the Earth* that the most revolutionary forms of planned social change are successful only when they are historically and spatially circumscribed.

CHAPTER 11

The Influence of Education on Migration and Fertility

MICHAEL P. TODARO

Education appears to exert an important influence on two major components of demographic change in developing countries, rural-urban migration and levels of fertility. The relationship between education and migration is, however, much stronger than that between education and fertility. Moreover, existing empirical evidence reveals that the mechanism by which education influences geographic mobility is more direct (for example, through its influence on higher-income expectations) than in the case of fertility. I have chosen to discuss these two issues together in this chapter, although there is no direct connection between them.[1]

Numerous studies of migration in the developing countries have documented the positive relationship between the educational attainment of an individual and his or her propensity to migrate from rural to urban areas. Essentially, this is because individuals with more education face wider urban-rural income differentials and higher probabilities of obtaining modern sector jobs than those with less education. In particular, it is the greater probability of finding a good urban job which explains the continual influx of educated rural migrants, in the face of rising urban unemployment.

With regard to the relationship between education and fertility, however, the evidence is less clear. While most studies in developed countries reveal an inverse relationship between a woman's education and her fertility, particularly for those with less education, the mechanism by which education influences decisions on the size of the family in developing countries is—as has been noted in the preceding chapter—still subject to considerable speculation.

Policy Implications

Assuming that lower levels of urban unemployment (especially among the educated) and lower levels of fertility are two important policy objectives for both the developing countries and international assistance agencies, the basic issue is whether or not the continued linear expansion of the formal educational system (and the resource allocations implicit therein) will ameliorate or exacerbate the problems of rising urban employment and rapid population growth. It is my contention that, given limited government and donor agency resources, the further rapid expansion of school places beyond provision of a basic education is both undesirable and unwise for the following two reasons:

First, any rapid expansion of the primary educational system creates inexorable pressures to expand secondary and tertiary school enrollment. This is due to the increasingly greater private returns to post-primary education resulting from the tendency for scarce, highly paid modern sector jobs to be rationed on the basis of progressively higher educational certification, and the political dimensions of educational investment decisions, in which the supply of school places tends to be determined more by political pressures than by economic feasibility.[2] The net result is the widespread phenomenon of over-expanded school enrollments given the substantial resource constraints of most developing countries, and the concomitant dilemma of rising urban unemployment among a cadre of increasingly more educated and more politically vocal migrants.

Second, many have argued that a woman's education influences her childbearing decisions by raising the opportunity cost of her time in child-rearing activities. In other words, the more education a woman has the more she stands to lose, in terms of income foregone, by raising children. If so, it follows that unless sufficient employment opportunities for women (as well as men) can be created, the reliance on educational expansion as a means to lower fertility will be weak, if not totally disappointing.

Education and Migration

The accelerated movement of rural migrants into urban centers is a phenomenon common to almost every developing nation. The extraordinary growth of urban populations during the past decade can be attributed primarily to the growing pace of rural-urban migration. Many factors influence the decision to migrate, but almost all informed observers agree that economic considerations predominate. Sample surveys in Africa, Asia, and Latin America invariably reveal that the overwhelming reason for migration to urban centers is that they provide a wider range of higher paying jobs.[3] In fact, individual country surveys consistently indicate a positive correlation between an individual's level of education and his or her propensity to migrate.[4]

In a series of articles, I have attempted to provide a theoretical framework for understanding the phenomenon of high, and in some cases accelerating, rates of rural-urban migration in the face of rising levels of urban unemployment.[5] By focusing on "expected" income differentials, encompassing both the absolute urban-rural differential and the probability of obtaining an urban job, this framework facilitates a better and more accurate analysis of the dynamics of rural-urban migration. This is especially so when analyzing differential rates of migration by educational level. Individuals with higher levels of educational certification are more likely to migrate than those with less education because: (1) the income disparity between what they can earn in urban areas compared to their rural opportunity cost is larger, and (2) the probability of obtaining a lucrative modern sector job is higher.[6]

The reason that the more educated have a greater chance of finding higher paying urban jobs than those with less education is a result not so much of their superior training as it is of the widespread "certification" phenomenon characteristic of labor markets in the developing countries.[7] This phenomenon is exacerbated by the internal migration of those with more and more years of formal education. Faced with more applicants than openings, governments and private employers tend to select individuals on the basis of their educational certification, that is, their years of completed schooling. As the urban labor supply continues to outpace demand, two forces are set in motion. On the demand side, jobs which were formerly filled by primary school graduates now require a secondary school certificate. On the supply side, job aspirants now need extra years of further education in order to "qualify" for jobs which only a few years earlier were being filled by those with less education.

Several important consequences emerge from the interaction of these forces: the burgeoning of private demand for ever higher levels of formal education in order to meet more stringent job requirements; rising levels of unemployment among the educated; the growing proportion of educated individuals among migrant populations; and the gradual disappearance of employment opportunities for those with limited education. Finally, given the strong political pressures on governments to satisfy the aggregate demand for education (even though the social return on such investment is likely to be considerably lower than net private benefit), there is an inexorable tendency to expand formal educational facilities well beyond the point where such investments are economically justified.

In order to break this vicious cycle of accelerated rural-urban migration, which adds to the problems of rising unemployment, immediate steps must be taken by developing countries to change the current system of economic incentives that overvalue private returns to education in relation to social returns.[8] Simply restructuring the educational system to minimize the inherent urban bias and to orient the curriculum toward the real development needs of the nation (that is, rural development) will have limited success in curtailing rural-urban migration. Fundamental changes in the system of economic incentives *outside* the educational system are therefore necessary. These changes must focus on raising rural incomes, while holding down urban wage increases. Only in this way will rural education contribute to rural development, and not to urban unemployment.

Education and Fertility

Possession of an education is thought to influence many forms of behavior, including fertility behavior. On the one hand, there is a well-known direct relationship between a woman's educational attainment and her propensity to enter the labor force. On the other, there is growing evidence of an inverse relationship between a woman's education and her fertility.[9]

The empirical link between educational attainment, labor force participation, and fertility has been widely interpreted by economists to be the consequence of a causal mechanism in which education makes a woman's time more valuable by increasing her earning opportunities in the labor force.[10] It is thought that this shift in value causes the woman to reallocate her time from child-rearing activities to labor force activities. In effect, this theory uses the price of a woman's time to explain the widely observed inverse relationship between her educational attainment and the number of children she is likely to bear.

One of the most comprehensive attempts to test this education—cost of time—fertility hypothesis is contained in Yoram Ben-Porath's papers on education and fertility in Israel.[11] Using both longitudinal and cross-sectional data, Ben-Porath finds that the evidence does support the expected inverse relationship between fertility and the education of women. However, when the data is *disaggregated* by level of education (broken down to primary, secondary, and tertiary components), the inverse relationship between fertility and education turns out to be steep only at very low levels of education (one to four years) and tends to flatten—and in some cases become positive—at the top levels. Ben-Porath concludes that

> the relation among education of women, the wage rate, and labor supply indicates that at the low levels of education, where the decline in fertility is large, the differentials in labor supply are modest. While at the top educational categories, where differential fertility is modest, the differences in labor supply are large. . . . Thus, my impression is that the simple cost-of-living hypothesis, while consistent with some of the evidence, leaves some important aspects of the fertility-education relation unexplained.[12]

Clearly, there are many ways in which education might influence behavior through economic and social factors. For example, it is probable that better educated women are likely to marry later, and that they will practice birth control as a result of their ability to read and understand family planning literature. Unfortunately, an appropriate statistical methodology for untangling these lines of causation has not yet been adequately formulated and tested. Until this is accomplished, the promotion of expanded women's education simply as an effective anti-natal policy instrument should be approached with considerable caution.

There are other reasons to be wary of the use of education as a means to lower fertility, when there may be more direct measures that can be taken. Three examples may be given. First, if employment opportunities are in fact the vehicle through which education affects fertility, it might be important to understand the contribution of investment in job-creating activities for women compared to the simple expansion of educational facilities.[13] Furthermore, as Tobin has pointed out, it is one thing to find that educated women have fewer children than their less-educated contemporaries; it is another thing to expect that this difference will predict how much a nationwide increase in women's education will diminish national fertility. Clearly, the second effect will be weaker than the first.[14]

Second, the education-labor market-fertility hypothesis implies that investments in women's education may be less effective in reducing their fertility in rural areas, where few women find jobs regardless of their educational attainments. If reductions in fertility are to be viewed as an important social benefit of educating women, it is essential that more is known about how this change in behavior is influenced by education and how it interacts with other household and community forces.

Third, since educated women comprise a growing proportion of the urban migrant stream, the "filtering down" and "occupational displacement" phenomena described above will apply equally (if not more so) to them in determining their chances of finding a job in the highly competitive urban labor markets. Those with limited education (for example, those which Ben-Porath found to exhibit the sharpest fertility declines) will have little or no chance of competing successfully for scarce urban jobs.

In conclusion, it may be noted that the value and importance of a purposeful expansion of educational opportunities for women should be a significant social goal for a variety of economic and noneconomic reasons. However, the rationale for such a differential expansion from the more narrow perspective of potential fertility reductions is, in my opinion, simply not compelling, at least until better and more convincing evidence can be brought forward. This is clearly an important topic on which further research is urgently needed. In the meantime, I would put more emphasis on the provision of increased rural as well as urban job opportunities for women, both educated and uneducated, as the principal economic mechanism for raising standards of living and lowering fertility.

Notes

1. There is, however, an indirect connection to the extent that differentials exist between urban and rural levels of fertility (most evidence indicating lower urban fertility).

2. E. O. Edwards and M. P. Todaro, "Educational demand and supply in the context of growing unemployment in less developed countries", *World Development,* vols. 3-4 (1973): 107-17; and E. O. Edwards and M. P. Todaro, "Education and society in developing nations: conceptual relationships and emerging opportunities", paper prepared for a Conference on Education and Development Reconsidered, Bellagio, Italy, November 1973.

3. Derek Byerlee, "Rural-urban migration in Africa: theory, policy and implications", *International Migration Review* (1974): 543-66; M. P. Todaro, "Rural-urban migration, unemployment and job probabilities: recent theoretical and empirical research", in *Economic Factors in Population Growth,* ed. Ansley J. Coale (London: Macmillan, 1976); B. H. Herrick, "Urbanization and urban migration in Latin America: an economist's view", in *Latin American Urban Research,* ed. F. Rabinowitz and F. Trueblood, vol. 1 (Beverly Hills, California: Sage Publications, 1971); and International Bank for Reconstruction and Development, "Migration to urban areas", Economic Staff Working Paper No. 107, June 1971.

4. See, for example, T. L. Lin and H. H. Chen, "Rural labor mobility in Taiwan", mimeograph, 1973; B. H. Herrick, "Urbanization and urban migration in Latin America"; Henry Remple, "Labor migration into urban centers and urban unemployment in Kenya", unpublished Ph.D. Dissertation, University of Wisconsin; H. M. Barnum and R. H. Sabot, *Migration, Education and Urban Surplus Labour* (Paris: Organization for Economic Cooperation and Development, 1975); T. P. Schultz, "The determinants of internal migration in Venezuela", paper prepared for presentation at the Econometric Society World Congress, Toronto, 1975; and J. C. Knowles and R. Anker, "Economic determinants of demographic behaviour in Kenya", International Labour Organization, World Employment Program Population and Employment Working Paper No. 28.

5. M. P. Todaro, "The urban employment problem in less developed countries: an analysis of demand and supply", in *Yale Economic Essays* (New Haven, Conn.: Yale University Press, 1968), pp. 329-402; M. P. Todaro, "A model of labor migration and urban unemployment in less developed countries", *American Economic Review* (March 1969): 138-48; M. P. Todaro, "Income expectations, rural-urban migration and employment in Africa", *International Labour Review* (November 1971): 387-413; and John R. Harris and M. P. Todaro, "Migration, unemployment and development: a two sector analysis", *American Economic Review,* vol. 60, no. 1 (1970): 126-42.

6. For a review of the literature on the causes and consequences of internal migration, see M. P. Todaro, *Internal Migration in Developing Countries* (Geneva: International Labor Organisation).

7. E. O. Edwards and M. P. Todaro, "Educational demand and supply", op. cit.

8. E. O. Edwards and M. P. Todaro, "Education and society in developing nations", op. cit.

9. Carmen Miro and Walter Mertins, "Influences affecting fertility in urban and rural Latin America", *Milbank Memorial Fund Quarterly,* vol. 46 (1968); Yoram Ben-Porath, "Economic analysis of fertility in Israel: point and counterpoint", *Journal of Political Economy,* vol. 81, no. 2, part II (1973): S202-33; William Rich, *Smaller Families Through Social and Economic Progress* (Washington, D.C.: Overseas Development Council Monograph No. 7, 1973); and T. P. Schultz, "The determinants of internal migration in Venezuela", op. cit.

10. For a review of the empirical studies, see Susan Cochrane, "Can Education reduce Fertility?", (Washington, D.C.: World Bank, 1977).

11. Yoram Ben-Porath, "Economic analysis of fertility in Israel", op. cit., and Yoram Ben-Porath, "Fertility in Israel: A mini-survey and some new findings", in *Economic Factors in Population Growth,* ed. Ansley J. Coale, pp. 136-72.

12. Yoram Ben-Porath, "Economic analysis of fertility in Israel", op. cit., pp. S204-5.

13. E. O. Edwards and M. P. Todaro, "Education, society and employment: some main themes and suggested strategies", *World Development,* vol. 2, no. 1 (1974).

14. James Tobin, "Comment" on paper by T. Paul Schultz, *Journal of Political Economy,* vol. 81, no. 2, part II (1973): S275-8.

Allocation, Equity, and Conflict in Educational Planning

CHAPTER 12

Investment in Education in Developing Nations: Policy Responses when Private and Social Signals Conflict

EDGAR O. EDWARDS

In most developing countries, the net private benefit of higher education exceeds its net social benefit because education-related wage differentials are excessive and because the beneficiaries of higher education are publicly subsidized. The resulting political pressures favor investment in education over the creation of employment opportunities. A more balanced allocation of investment may require the revision of basic policies on wage determination, the incidence of educational costs, and the role of private education. The aim should be to narrow the gap between private and social signals and thus reduce excessive private demand for higher education.

Typically, the educational systems in developing countries have responded to the most obvious private and social signals confronting them. The private signals represent information that determines the *net private benefit* of education and hence the aggregate private demand for education. In particular, private educational benefits and costs include the benefits which students and prospective students expect to receive from subsequent employment and the costs which they (or their families) expect to bear. The social signals represent the information on which estimates of the *net social benefit* from education are based. These judgements about the full benefits and costs of education, as opposed to those counted in private calculations, may be based on crude estimates of social need, on manpower studies, or on sophisticated cost-benefit analyses. The two sets of signals seldom correspond precisely. Some social benefits—for example, the value of education in promoting national unity—may escape private detection,

189

while private perceptions may exaggerate the benefits to be obtained from later employment. The costs borne privately (including earnings sacrificed in order to attend school) are usually only a fraction of total educational costs. The problem of appropriate political response arises when the two sets of signals point to different educational policies.

Consider the experience of the last three decades: as long as private and social signals were mutually reinforcing and indicated educational expansion, substantial allocations to education were politically secure. Nations achieving independence since World War II (that is, most of the developing countries in Asia and Africa) immediately saw the need to expand education in preparation for indigenously managed growth. The aims were to replace expatriate civil servants and private sector employees, to diminish dependence on foreign training, and to meet the normal requirements of growth and replacement. These social needs were strongly reinforced by the private demand for education. Under these circumstances the rate of educational expansion, particularly at higher levels, was justifiably in excess of the rate which could be sustained by normal requirements of growth and replacement alone. Unfortunately, while the need for expatriate replacement and the substitution of domestic for foreign training subsided, many educational systems continued their rapid growth, producing too many graduates and school leavers given the social and economic requirements of normal growth.

Conflict between the Private Demand for Expansion and the Social Consequences of Unemployment

Today the obvious signals are in conflict. The dominant social signal is that there are too few jobs for those emerging from most educational systems. The implications are that a larger share of future development expenditures should be used to create jobs, and that the rate of educational expansion at secondary and higher levels should be reduced. But the aggregate private demand for secondary and higher education continues strong, reflecting (a) distortions in urban/rural and occupational income differentials, which tend to make private returns from education exceed its social value, and (b) subsidies to education, which mean that only a fraction of educational costs are borne by the private beneficiaries.[1]

The benefits of education, as measured by the increase in income which the educated person can expect after employment, will typically be discounted by him if employment is not assured.[2] But when the supply of educated people grows more rapidly than employment opportunities, those in education may exaggerate the probability of employment. Hence, as long as differentials persist at exaggerated levels, and higher education is heavily subsidized by governments, the aggregate private demand for education will exceed the social need for it. Thus, the conflict between expanding educational systems and creating employment opportunities becomes a real policy dilemma.

In this conflict, the obvious signals provide no clear-cut guide to those setting national education policies. If governments respond first to "imminent dangers", they will acquiesce to the pressures of the private demand for more education. Only when growing unemployment emerges much later as a threat to political stability will the challenge of job creation be given priority. Evidence on educational expansion over the last two decades in many developing countries is consistent with this hypothesis of political behavior.[3] But other evidence suggests that unemployment is the greater threat, and that it would be socially desirable to attend to it sooner.

The contradiction between social needs and the private demand for education raises three questions which seem to have easy, though in some cases unsatisfactory, answers. (a) To which set of signals should the educational system, and the development budget, respond? (*Answer*: Net social benefit.) (b) Which set has greatest influence on political feasibility? (*Answer*: Aggregate private demand.) (c) Which force takes precedence? (*Answer*: Aggregate private demand.) Even a summary examination of these questions will lead to others which are more complex and less easily answered.

The aggregate private demand for education, particularly for higher levels of education, is usually clearly and forcibly expressed. But social need is more ambiguous, and often lacks powerful support. One outcome of the growing conflict between the two sets of signals has been the demand for more careful analysis of educational needs, benefits, and costs. In the past, when signals were mutually reinforcing, such analysis could be treated casually, as a basis for refining but not for establishing policy. But if at that earlier stage the tools of sophisticated analysis were treated too cavalierly, perhaps too much is expected of them today.

Strengths and Limitations of Cost-Benefit Analysis

Policymakers are now turning to the use of cost-benefit analysis. But cost-benefit analysis, as applied to educational planning, is valuable not so much for its accuracy or indeed its use in investment decisions as for the kinds of information it seeks to disclose and for the hints to be gleaned from this information about an array of economic policies. Indeed, if these hints about price distortions and cost incidence are not needed, it is unlikely that investment decisions based on cost-benefit analysis can be implemented.

The value of cost-benefit analysis lies in what it tries to do; its limitations stem from the same ambitions. The ambitions to which I refer are three: (a) its attempt to embrace all benefits and costs, regardless of how widely they may be shared or to whom they may accrue; (b) its attempt to value all benefits and costs in monetary terms, and at social rather than market prices, where most of the relevant prices must be estimated for an array of future dates; and (c) its attempt to find objective means of standardizing benefits and costs for the time differentials related to their occurrence (discounting), as a means of facilitating comparison. Perhaps this stark summary makes the principal limitations of cost-benefit analysis all too apparent. To identify all the benefits and costs of education is a large task; to assign monetary values to many of them is a hazardous undertaking; to estimate social prices when they do not accord with market prices, and when they lie in the future, is certainly ambitious; and to attempt to compare values across time is a tricky task. Precision is not a feasible objective of cost-benefit analysis.

But what it can offer is a useful time perspective and an improvement in objectivity. Both should enhance the quality of investment decisions, compared to those which were based either on crude calculations of social imbalances, or on biased private perceptions of the costs and benefits of education. Obvious social imbalances, such as unemployment or mismatches between types of education and job requirements, are probably fair indications of needed policy change and can undoubtedly be improved through analysis of first differences, the rates at which such indicators are changing. But because of the long gestation period in education, decisions on future school output which are based on present imbalances may turn out to be deficient in addressing future needs.

On the other hand, aggregate private demand is probably an even more precarious basis for planning educational expansion. As already noted, private rewards for education may exceed its social value: beneficiaries of education may overestimate the probability of employment, and public subsidies to education reduce educational costs for those who succeed in entering and advancing in the system. Those who stand to benefit from higher education expect to pay only a fraction of its cost. They therefore constitute a strong and vocal group favoring continued educational expansion and the retention of subsidies.

Unfortunately, those who bear most of the cost of education through the taxes they pay cannot be expected to act as a private countervailing force to the expansion advocates. They are stillborn as a political lobby, because the taxes which finance educational subsidies are widely diffused among the population. Each individual pays only a small part of the total, and in any case specific taxes are rarely earmarked for education.[4] It is not surprising, therefore, that educational systems continue to expand, particularly at higher levels, and that costs continue to be subsidized, often to the greatest extent at the higher levels.[5]

In these circumstances, it is a distinct advantage of cost-benefit analysis that it recognizes educational costs and relates them to benefits. Information gained from this analysis could stir the conscience of policymakers and retard the expansion of higher education, in the face of growing pressure from private demand. But at this stage the scenario becomes interesting. Suppose that considerations of social benefit are fully persuasive to policymakers, and that they decide to reduce the rate of expansion in favor of creating more jobs. An apparent social triumph may yet slip away; the problems confronted both in making the decision to alter investments, and in implementing that decision may be formidable.

Problems Involved in the Switch to Creating Jobs

There are three main problems involved. First, deciding how to use the funds released from investment in education requires that policymakers confront another set of political pressures. Creating employment often means dispersing funds to rural infrastructure, small farmers, and small-scale industrial and service activities. Funds should not be indiscriminately allocated to programs designed to create unproductive places in the civil service or to large, capital-intensive industrial and agricultural enterprise.[6]

But those in a position to influence the uses to be made of the reallocated funds are likely to be those who will benefit from large-scale, urban development, who may include policymakers themselves. Although more productive, the promotion of small-scale, capital-economizing activities may falter in the face of political pressures for continuing capital concentration, which benefits the influential. While the social value of reducing the rate of educational expansion in order to create more jobs is reasonably clear, the social value of shifting funds from education to capital-intensive projects is a matter of considerable doubt.

Second, even if policymakers make the right decision on reallocating investment funds, the political pressures which inhibited that decision in the first place will continue unabated, and indeed may grow. There is nothing in the investment decision itself to modify signals determining the private demand for education, or the demand of the influential for capital-intensive projects. These continuing pressures may frustrate implementation, turn policymakers out of office, or force a reversal of the decision. Indeed, those in local and central governments who disapprove may assist in circumventing the decision, as in the early years of the Harambee school movement in Kenya.[7] In any event, as long as price signals remain distorted, the decision to reduce the rate of educational expansion will require that the more limited educational places be rationed among the many seeking entry, and favoritism and discrimination may creep into that rationing process.

Third, the decision only controls public investment, and any attempt to implement it as a national policy will require extending enforcement into the private sector. But because the benefits of secondary and higher education can be marketed for wages and salaries by the beneficiaries, they will be willing to pay for education; it follows that there are profits to be made by those in the private sector who are willing to supply educational services. Hence, private demand for education may spill over into the private sector, and enterprising entrepreneurs may find means of supplying it, as in the Philippines.[8] Thus, a decrease in public investment may lead to an increase in private investment. As long as the price signals determining demand are distorted, private and public investment in education will continue to be socially excessive.

The inescapable conclusion, for most developing countries, is that simply making the "socially correct" investment decisions will not mean that political and economic counterpressures, stemming from the distorted private demand for education, will cease. In fact, they may be aggravated. Moreover, if unpopular decisions are made in the face of such pressures, the obstacles of confronting effective implementation in both public and private sectors will seriously affect the desired outcome.[9]

Feasible Alternatives

The alternative is to look beyond the investment decision itself to policies which would cause net private benefit to accord more closely to net social benefit, thus modifying the demand for education. To the extent that the social costs and benefits of education can be internalized, that is, be included in the making of *private* decisions, private demand will reflect choices based on a more realistic appraisal of cost and benefits. This may not completely close the gap between private perceptions and social needs, but it should increase the probability that they will point toward similar rates of expansion. Policies which may narrow the gap between private and social signals fall into three categories.

(a) *Policies to adjust labor-market price signals and hiring practices so that they accord more closely with social realities, and education is not privately overvalued.*

Basing decisions on the relative scarcities of goods and services (jobs and educational places, for example) raises serious problems of implementation unless the market prices of these goods and services reflect those relative scarcities. When they do not, implementation requires nonprice control mechanisms which override the normal responses of people to the market prices they confront. Hence, to reduce educational expansion when market signals are stimulating private demand entails other forms of control of which the rationing of educational opportunities is most likely. Unfortunately, such rationing is often discriminatory when it is effective, and if it is not effective—such as when the private sector and local governments rise to meet the unsatisfied demand—the policy of limiting educational expansion fails. Adjusting market prices and hiring practices so that education is not overvalued should reduce the need for and the pressure on such control mechanisms. These policy adjustments are desirable whether education is supplied in the public or in the private sectors, or in both.

(b) *Policies to recover from the beneficiaries of higher education a greater proportion of the costs of providing it.*

To the extent that the benefits of education are vested in the beneficiary in the form of increased earning ability, he should be expected to pay the costs of his education as the increase in his income materializes or through the performance of recognized public services. Such policies should make entry into higher education less contingent on parents' ability to pay, temper the private demand for education, and recover a portion of educational cost for other public sector purposes.

(c) *Policies to encourage the supply of higher education by the private sector.*

As an alternative to (b), such policies would ensure that the full cost of some higher educational opportunities (those provided by the private sector) would influence some private decisions about education. The major disadvantage is that, unless such policies are supplemented by a public-sector loan program, the distribution of private-sector educational benefits will depend on parents' income, rather than on the prospective income of the student.

Finally, the question must be asked: "What political forces will be encountered by attempts to introduce these policies?" The first may encounter resistance from those who benefit from capital subsidies and high wages: the capital-intensive industries and the labor unions. The magnitude of resistance will depend on the form remedial efforts assume. The second will confront higher education lobbies, which include many civil servants and policymakers. The third should encounter less resistance if proper control over educational quality in private sector facilities is exercised. All of these changes can be introduced gradually, which may diminish the resistance to them. The implementation of socially responsible educational policies should be eased through these policies, because they diminish the main obstacle of inappropriate private demand. Policies such as these should not only promote better decisions for educational investment, but should also increase employment opportunities for those who emerge from every level of the educational system.

These suggested guidelines should not be interpreted as a complete guide to educational decisionmaking. Two qualifications are immediately apparent. First, nothing has been said about the cost, quality, and content of education—the internal effectiveness of educational systems. Second, to the extent that educational benefits are a public good (promoting national unity, cohesiveness, and communication, for example) and are not entertained in the private calculus, the removal of subsidies to education on the cost side raises a risk contrary to the one addressed in this paper, namely, that the aggregate private demand for education may fall below that which is socially optimal.

Notes

1. For a more extensive and rigorous discussion of the conflict between the need for jobs and the demand for education, and of the rationing dilemma this conflict raises, see E. O. Edwards and M. P. Todaro, "Educational demand and supply in the context of growing unemployment in less developed countries", *World Development* (March-April 1973).
2. Michael P. Todaro, "A model for labor migration and urban unemployment in less developed countries", *American Economic Review* (March 1969).
3. See, for example, the illuminating evidence of such behavior in the ILO report, *Matching Employment Opportunities and Expectations: A Program of Action for Ceylon* (Geneva, 1971).
4. An excellent exposition of this and related issues can be found in Jagdish Bhagwati, "Education, class structure and income equality", *World Development* (May 1973).
5. George Psacharopoulos and Gareth Williams have shown for Iran "that public expenditure on education has moved in a way very different from that suggested by

the rate of return calculations. Expenditure on higher education has grown much more rapidly and expenditure on secondary schools slightly more rapidly than that on primary education." See "Public sector earnings and educational planning", *International Labour Review* (July 1973) p. 55.

6. See the several related papers in Edgar O. Edwards, ed., *Employment in Developing Nations* (New York: Columbia University Press, 1974).
7. See the ILO report, *Employment, Incomes and Equality* (Geneva, 1972).
8. See the report of the Presidential Commission to Survey Philippine Education, *Education for National Development: New Patterns, New Directions* (Manila, 1970).
9. For a discussion of the extent to which educational decisions alone can contribute to a restructuring of society, see E. O. Edwards and M. P. Todaro, "Education, society and employment: some main themes and suggested strategies for international assistance efforts", *World Development* (January 1974).

CHAPTER 13

On Allocating Resources to Education

ARNOLD C. HARBERGER

This chapter is concerned mainly with the issue of determining the overall size of the education sector, rather than with the allocation of resources to its various subcomponents. Nonetheless, the approach implicitly contains elements of the problem of intrasectoral allocation dealing with social rates of return to investment in education, which normally involve comparisons of age-earnings profiles of different educational levels. A higher than normal rate of return to technical secondary education, for example, would be a clear signal that relatively insufficient resources were being devoted to that particular branch of education; however, it would not in itself be an indication that too few resources were being devoted to education as a whole. For my purposes, it will be convenient to assume that some sort of procedure is already being used to determine optimal resource allocations within the education sector, so that gross differences in the economic rates of return to different types and classes of education are avoided. Thus, when I speak of "the" rate of return to educational investments, I mean that this rate of return applies, at least roughly, to all the relevant margins to which incremental funds allocated to educational activities would be applied.

Some educational investments may have substantially higher social yields, but where this is the case they are assumed to be inframarginal. For example, primary education might have a high social yield of, say, 30 percent per annum because of the negligibility of foregone earnings as a relevant cost, and because the real costs of teachers, buildings, supplies, and so on are not very high at the primary level. At the same time that investments in primary education are showing a 30 percent yield, those in secondary and university education might be around 12 percent. These economic signals would seem to be loudly calling for more investments at the primary level. But once primary education is essentially universal, a 30 percent measured yield on that level of education could coexist with a 12 percent yield on investments in higher levels, without implying underinvestment at the primary stage. In such a case, the relevant margin would be an expansion at the secondary and university levels; this is where increases in budget allocations would normally be expected to go, or cuts to come from.

With this background, let me briefly review one of the major controversies in the field of educational planning. On one side of this argument is the "manpower planning approach", which in essence asks how many educated people (of each type and class) will be "needed" over a specified time period, and then plans an educational investment program to fill the needs thus identified. On the other side is the "rate of return approach", which does not focus on quantitative targets, but simply takes a high measured rate of return on educational investments, relative to that on physical investments, as a signal to expand activity on the educational side. Without getting embroiled in technicalities at this stage, it is fair to associate the manpower planning approach with an assumption that the function relating the yield on educational capital to the total stock of such capital is relatively inelastic, and to associate the rate of return approach with the idea that this same function has a rather high elasticity.

These characteristics of the two approaches are oversimplified—perhaps to the point of being caricatures rather than accurate representations—but nonetheless there is a real sense in which they are quite apt. Those who concentrate their attention on quantitative targets and do not consider measured yields on educational investments to be very important pieces of information seem to be implying that: (a) if due caution is not applied to planning, it is relatively easy to end up with significantly inappropriate quantities of educational capital, and (b) since rates of return can easily change in a relatively short period of time, those measured at one point in time are insecure guides for developing an educational plan or strategy. Both of these implicit judgments make sense if the relevant function is quite inelastic, and seem wide of the mark if the opposite is true. On the other hand, the notion of precise quantitative targets does not itself make much sense when the relevant yield function is highly elastic.

In examining the controversy between these two points of view in the explicit context of social cost-benefit analysis, I will also embroider my initial characterization of the two approaches with a few judgments about facts likely to apply in most real-life situations. The rate of return approach is clearly the more optimistic of the two, at least once it is recognized that most measurements of the rate of return to education yield estimates that are usually above the corresponding rates for physical capital investment. Where the measured rates of return are above those for physical capital, there is hardly any question that they point toward a significant expansion of educational investments, once the assumption of a highly-elastic yield function is accepted.

Where the measured rates for education are lower than those for physical capital, however, the case is not quite so clear. The problem arises of assessing the benefits of education that are not incorporated into the standard rate of return measurements, for example: (a) direct consumption benefits to the individual during the educational process itself (going to college is more fun than working); (b) the direct consumption benefits later on in life (an improved general cultural level can provide increased enjoyment); (c) increased "efficiency" as consumers (educated people are generally able to use a given budget more effectively or prudently than the uneducated); and (d) the positive external effects of education (the educated will generally be better informed citizens, will take more interest in the welfare of their communities, and will be able to absorb and process information more efficiently).

These points argue that the measured yield on educational investments at equilibrium should be somewhat below that on physical capital investments, for which the presumption of significant, positive nonmeasured external effects is less strong. How an educational planning group should respond to a situation in which the measured rate of return to education falls short of that to physical capital would depend upon the size of the shortfall and upon its judgment of the magnitude of the nonmeasured effects listed above. Yet, in fact, measured rates of return to education rarely fall far short of those to physical capital, and most people consider the nonmeasured effects to be substantial. As long as this is the case, even a shortfall in the measured rate for education should not be regarded as a "stop light" to further educational investments. Perhaps it could be viewed as a caution signal, but even this modest degree of pessimism may not be necessary if the yield curve for educational investments is indeed highly elastic. If the yield on physical capital were 15 percent and that on educational investment were 10 percent, and if the difference of 5 percentage points is considered to be compensated by nonmeasured net benefits of education, why be cautious about educational expansion, as long as one feels confident that the 10 percent yield will not fall significantly, as a consequence?

But there is a second point to be made in connection with the rate of return approach. Once the rate of return to educational capital has reached a level where it is judged (after appropriate adjustment for nonmeasured benefits) to be comparable to that to physical capital, then the appropriate attitude for the educational planner would be one of benign indifference to the pace at which educational investments are expanded. This, after all, simply reflects the meaning of a highly elastic yield curve, when the yield is comparable to that on the relevant alternatives. Under the conditions postulated here, there would be neither any outstanding extra benefits to be achieved through rapid expansion of the educational effort, nor any great costs involved in proceeding at a slower pace instead.

The situation is different under the "manpower planning" approach. Here the relative inelasticity of the yield curve means that there could be substantial costs of being on either side of the optimum. If too much investment is undertaken, some share of the incremental funds is wasted, in the sense that it would generate a social yield significantly below that which could be obtained from alternative applications of the same funds. If too little is invested, the foregone product is substantially higher than that yielded by the relevant alternative uses of funds. In this case, the inelasticity of the yield curve negates the ideal of indifference to the rate of educational expansion.

Even if the general line of reasoning that leads to the "manpower planning" position is accepted, however, there is likely to be a considerable asymmetry between too much and too little investment in education. Perhaps an analogy with investment in electric power is apt. I have seen situations in several developing countries in which a lack of adequate power stood directly in the way of economic growth, in the sense that it prevented the timely opening of new factories, or forced cutbacks of production in existing ones. It is quite possible that a true measure of the marginal social yield of additional investments in such cases could be 50 to 100 or more percent per annum, rather than the (for example) 15 percent which represents the social opportunity cost of capital in general. On the other hand, suppose that in the same economies there was a symmetrical overinvestment in power facilities. It is hard to believe that this could drive down the marginal social yield on investments to -20 or -70 percent (symmetrical, around a 15 percent norm, with the + 50 and + 100 percent figures cited above). Surely the extra power could be put to better use than this—keeping people a little cooler in summer and a little warmer in winter, for example. The demand for power investments can become quite inelastic in the 3 to 5 percent range of yields, even though it is quite inelastic in the range of yields of 20 percent and over.

I think the case is very similar with respect to educational investments. Where there is not enough, the whole process of economic growth can be impaired—not enough teachers to staff the schools, not enough doctors and nurses to keep the population healthy, not enough engineers and skilled technicians to build and run the factories. But where there is too much investment, the costs are not symmetrically large. Rates of return (as measured) never seem to be driven down into the zero-to-negative range, and surely are never dramatically negative (as many measured returns *are* dramatically positive when there are shortfalls of human capital). I believe that a relatively ample elasticity of the yield function for educational investments, as the yields become low, can be counted on. Some positive yield can always be derived from improving the skills of farmers and craftsmen, and there are always nonmeasured benefits of the types previously listed.

This asymmetry justifies a bias in educational planning toward investing too much rather than too little, just as an asymmetrical loss function calls for a corresponding bias in any problem in decision theory. This line of reasoning (with its implied judgments of the relevant facts) takes much of the heat out of the controversy to which this book is addressed. Indeed, on this view, it is the manpower planners who would in a sense become the optimists regarding educational investments, since they would want above all to avoid the high social cost of having too little and would presumably be willing to bear the moderate social cost that the asymmetric approach would assign to the possibility of having too much. In more practical terms, I think that there should be no concern about whether educational investments are too great until the measured rates of return fall into the range of, say, 5 to 10 percent, and only really serious concern when the measured rates begin to fall below 5 percent, and approach the zero-to-negative range. My guess is that the day of these danger signals will be far, far in the future for most developing countries.

CHAPTER 14

Education, Class Conflict, and Uneven Development*

SAMUEL BOWLES

As recently as the mid 1960s, educational policymakers in the poor countries projected a mood of optimism concerning the continuing expansion of educational opportunity and the contribution of schooling to social and economic development. Hoping to replicate the educational histories of the advanced capitalist countries, the governments of many new nations adopted universal primary education as a medium term or even short term objective. Expanded schooling, it was widely thought, could break "human resource bottlenecks" in the development process, and undercut entrenched privilege as well.

But by 1965 the rates of growth of enrollments had begun to fall. In the noncommunist poor countries as a whole, primary school enrollments failed to keep pace with population growth, contributing to an increase in the number of illiterates.[1] During the past decade, evidence has begun to accumulate suggesting that the structure of schooling not only inhibits economic growth, but also contributes to economic inequality.[2] Ministries of education around the world, under severe financial constraints, facing growing unemployment among schooled workers, and pressed by unabated popular demands for expanded access to education, are turning to nonformal basic education—a rural-based, vocationally oriented, terminal, and (most of all) inexpensive alternative to universal primary education.[3]

*I would like to thank Herbert Gintis, Nancy Folbre, Marjorie Mbilinyi, Carlos Diaz-Alejandro, Aylette Jenness, David Court, John Simmons, and Ahmed Issa for suggestions and criticism.

Dashed hopes breed second thoughts. An era of retrenchment invites a re-examination of the conceptual bases of the now faded optimism of the international educational establishment. Economists and other social scientists who have studied schooling in the poor capitalist countries have virtually unanimously shared with educators the conviction that educational policy can be a major instrument in promoting economic growth and, more recently, in achieving a more just distribution of economic rewards. This putative egalitarian and growth-inducing efficacy of educational policy is based on two fundamental propositions: first, that educational policy has strong direct or indirect effects on the rate of economic growth and the distribution of economic rewards; and second, that educational policy is sufficiently independent of the main economic relations of society to be considered an "exogenous policy instrument".

The presumption that educational policy is both effective and exogenous reflects the joint ascendency of the human capital school and the liberal theory of the state. An important consequence of the closely related success of these two approaches is that the issue of power in economic life has been banished to the abstract and arcane world of game theory (where, ironically, it is also unwelcome!), and to the even more distant reaches inhabited by political scientists, sociologists, and Galbraith.[4] If "every economic actor is a price taker", or if, more pointedly, as Samuelson tells us, it makes no difference whether the capitalist hired the worker or the other way around, we can safely forget about power in the competitive model.[5] The institutional structures which define the relations among the economic actors are objects neither of economic analysis nor of liberal policy.

Symptomatic of this approach is the assumption that egalitarian social and economic policy can operate primarily through a redistribution of productive resources, imposed, as it were, from "on high" by democratically elected or at least enlightened government "decision-makers".[6] The "outputs" of the school system are represented as "skills" or other capacities embodied in individuals. Egalitarian educational reform, it is said, redistributes these skills, much as an agrarian reform redistributes titles to land.[7]

The importance of schooling in the economic growth process and in the distribution of its rewards seems indisputable, though, to be sure, for quite different reasons than those proposed by the human capital school. However, even the most cursory reading of the history of capitalist societies suggests that the liberal view of the state as independent and egalitarian will not provide an adequate basis for investigating the relations between economic growth, education, and inequality.[8] Nor will it shed much light on the dynamics of educational development in the context of capitalist growth.[9]

I present here an alternate view of the state and of education in capitalist society.[10] According to this interpretation, the state serves to reproduce the social relations which define the position of the capitalist class and other dominant groups of the society. State policies, and the structure of the state itself, are severely limited by the prevailing economic structure and its class relations. The economic structure itself is influenced by the state, ordinarily in ways which increase the power and income of the politically powerful groups. The educational system, as an important influence on political life, ideology, and the development of labor power, is one of the main instruments of the state. The "output" of the schools is not only labor power as an input into the production process, but the reproduction or transformation of social relations; the distribution of "skills" embodied in individuals represents but one aspect—and not even the most important—of this process. The impact of educational structure on the social relations of production—the configurations of property and power in the labor process—represents the critical connections between schooling and the economy, and at the same time points to the structural limits of egalitarian reforms in capitalist social formations.

Both educational inequality and inequality of income reflect the class structure of capitalist societies. I conclude that the contribution of educational policies to either growth or equality is severely circumscribed by the prevailing class relations and by the role imposed on schooling by the dominant class, namely the reproduction of the class structure of the dominant mode of production.

To understand the position of education in capitalist social formations, then, requires an analysis of the dynamics of class relations. In order to illuminate the link between the social organization of work and of school and to locate both in the dynamics of the capitalist economy as a whole, I use the Marxian concept of class rather than other conceptual social aggregates based on status, income, or type of commodity produced. Two quite different types of class relation are presented: relations within a given labor process, for example capitalist—worker, and relations which span distinct labor processes, for example, peasant—worker. In the former, direct relations of control and exploitation are defined within the labor process itself. Class relations connecting groups involved in distinct labor processes which are related primarily through markets or through the state are necessarily less well defined by the structure of production. To capture the open-endedness of class relations in a social formation characterized by a multiplicity of distinct modes of production, I will consider the problem of coalition formation among classes.

The rejection of the most abstract two-class model of capitalist society and recognition of the indeterminancy introduced by the concept of class alliances suggests a heightened importance of political and ideological aspects of social change. Equally important, a multiclass analysis invites a reconsideration of the state as "a committee for managing the common affairs of the whole bourgeoisie".[11] In the formulation presented here, the state may also be an arena in which class alliances are formed. Over substantial periods of time, no single class can rely on the state consistently to serve as its political instrument. The multiplicity of class relations, the structural limits on state policy, and the attendant problematic nature of class power in the state also remind us not to assume that a given state policy reflects the conscious and successful implementation of the interests of any single class.

If any doubt remains, let me confirm that this essay is primarily theoretical, later appearances of regression equations and rate of return estimates notwithstanding. My intention is to identify fundamental dynamic structural relationships which, if I have been successful, will provide a starting point for the concrete analysis of particular social formations. In any concrete application, the definitions of class boundaries and modes of production, the international aspects of the problem, and the fact that the state can never be reduced totally to a simple expression of class interests—or even a complex expression—would demand close attention.

The Dynamics of Distributional Conflict

The salient characteristics of the capitalist growth process can be captured in a simple analysis which focuses attention on the internal organization of a capitalist and a traditional mode of production and on their interactions. While the economic actuality of different modes of production may differ—in the commodities produced, the technologies used, and other important respects—it is the social relations of production that define a mode of production. Thus the capitalist sector exhibits technological dynamism and a relatively rapid rate of expansion. But what distinguishes it as a mode of production is its social organization; the great majority of producers do not own what they need to secure their livelihood. Therefore, they do not sell their product; they sell their labor time for wages. This group, wage labor, has no claim on the product of its work; nor does it exercise any direct control over the choice of commodities to be produced, technologies to be used, or organization of work. The archetypal production units in the capitalist mode of production are the factory, the large business office, and the modern plantation.[12]

In contrast, the traditional mode of production is characterized by the insignificance of wage labor. ("The traditional mode of production" is used here merely as a general expression for a variety of possible noncapitalist modes, whose more precise elaboration can be bypassed for the purposes at hand.[13]) The traditional mode of production may produce cash crops for the world market. It may produce subsistence crops or handicrafts. Although the social relations of production may vary, the family farm, communal production, or the craft shop are archetypal production units. In this mode, the direct producers own or at least exercise significant control over the means of production. In addition, they exercise considerable discretion over their hours and methods of work, and often own a large part of the product of their labor. Property ownership in the traditional mode may support an exploiting class, often landowners who have little or no direct role in production, but expropriate the meager agricultural surplus through a system of sharecropping or rent tenancy. Where there is a landlord class, this group or a part of it may constitute what I call a traditional elite. It may have allies in other elites, such as the military, tribal chiefs, or the established religion. For simplicity I will refer to the direct producers in the traditional mode as peasants, and to the exploiting class as landlords. The subsequent analysis may readily be modified to include a land-owning independent peasantry, or independent petty commodity producers of nonagricultural goods.

Under the impact of modern health technology, and in the absence of effective state systems of redistribution and mutual support which might undermine the incentive for large families, rates of population increase are likely to be considerable in both modes, at least in the early stages of capitalist development.[14]

The expansion of the capitalist mode of production—the accumulation process—is accompanied by the recruitment of new wage workers from the traditional mode of production. The integration of new workers into the capitalist mode, as well as the technological dynamism and class relations of capitalist production, provide the impetus for educational expansion and the evolution of the structure of the school system. The associated process of accumulation and the resulting uneven development of the social formation as a whole—the counterpoint of dynamism in the capitalist mode and stagnation in the traditional—are the primary forces that generate economic inequality and impose limits to egalitarian educational reform. My task then is to outline the relationship between the accumulation process, education, and economic inequality.

To explore this complex relationship, I will develop a necessarily simplified interpretation of the interaction between the two modes of production. The most important simplifying assumptions are motivated by the open international economic setting of most of the social formations which constitute the periphery of the capitalist world system. I abstract from problems of aggregate demand and assume that relative commodity prices are externally determined.[15] The modification of external prices through transportation costs, tariffs, and other state policies presents no problem in this mode, but for the purposes at hand such an elaboration is unnecessary.

The degree of economic inequality in the social formation as a whole may be represented by three components: the degree of inequality which exists (a) within the traditional mode of production, (b) within the capitalist mode of production, and (c) between modes.[16] We will consider each in turn.

The division of the total product of the traditional mode between the consumption of the direct producers and the rents paid to landlords is represented by a fractional rent share, determined by the history of conflict between the two classes. In the traditional mode, the small surplus of production over necessary subsistence poses a relatively low limit to the degree of inequality in economic reward, particularly as compared to the capitalist mode.[17] In the capitalist mode, the division of the product between capital and labor depends upon the relative bargaining strength of workers and capitalists. This relative strength in turn depends on economic conditions in both modes of production and on political and ideological conditions in the social formation as a whole. I will concentrate here on the economic aspects. As long as wages in the capitalist mode exceed incomes of the direct producers in the traditional mode, wage workers will be in a relatively weak position. Their weakness is due to a "reserve army" of potential wage workers in the traditional mode, who can be recruited to replace anyone unwilling to work for the going wage. The size distribution of income in the capitalist mode will therefore depend upon the outcome of this struggle over the product, and on the degree of concentration of wealth.

The class income distribution of the entire society will, of course, change over time in response to changes in the distribution of labor between the two modes, the comparative productivity of the two modes, the bargaining power of capital and labor, and the rent share. The capitalist mode's technological dynamism and superior ability to reinvest output, together with the ceiling imposed on wages by the reserve army, tend to increase inequality in the capitalist mode and between the capitalist mode and the traditional mode. The resulting uneven development is a characteristic of peripheral capitalist social formations.[18]

Consider now the interests of each class in this distributional process. It is in the immediate interest of workers in the capitalist mode to promote labor scarcity, and thus to increase their bargaining power. This may be done by resisting labor-saving innovations and by imposing employment restrictions that limit the ability of the capitalist to substitute new labor from the traditional mode for those already employed in the capitalist mode. Competition from the reserve army based in the traditional mode will also be inhibited by productivity increases in the traditional sector and by a decline in the landlords' rent share, both of which increase the consumption levels of the peasants, and thus raise the minimum price at which capital can recruit labor. Rapid accumulation in the capitalist mode will likewise promote labor scarcity and enhance labor's position.

By contrast, the capitalist class will oppose restrictions on hiring in order to have free access to all potential workers, and thus to depress the wage more nearly to the low levels of consumption prevalent among the peasantry. Capital's economic interests are furthered by impoverishing the peasantry, either through increases in the rent share or a retardation of productivity increases in traditional production. The accumulation process will, of course, encroach on traditional production, bringing capitalist social relations to some forms of agricultural and other production. But as long as population growth and labor-saving technical change are sufficiently rapid to guarantee a labor reserve to the capitalist mode, there will be no need to increase productivity in the traditional mode (or to eliminate the mode so as to release workers for employment in the capitalist mode of production). Further, in the open economy the relative price of food (or other wage goods) is determined independently of the conditions of domestic agricultural (or other) production, thus giving the capitalist class no interest in raising the productivity of noncapitalist agriculture.[19] These considerations may represent a major difference between the early accumulation process in the currently advanced capitalist countries and that in the contemporary capitalist periphery.[20] We shall see that this contrast in the nature of the accumulation process is associated with a parallel contrast in the dynamics of the educational system.

The interests of the landlord class are generally opposed to those of the capitalist class; landlords, unlike capitalists, benefit from raising the productivity of traditional production. Conflict between these two classes may thus focus on the direction of research and development in new technologies as well as on the more conventional economic variables. Rapid accumulation in the capitalist mode gives the peasantry alternative sources of livelihood, and hence contributes to an enhanced bargaining power of the peasantry and a lowering of the rental share.

Both capitalists and landlords, however, share a common interest in maintaining a high rental share.

While the educational implications of this analysis remain to be discussed, it should be clear that changes in the structure, content and availability of schooling at all levels may play a crucial role in the distribution of economic rewards and in the distributional strategies of each class. Further, given the complex pattern of conflicting and congruent economic interests, educational policy may play a central political and ideological role in the formation or inhibition of class coalitions and in the development or retardation of class unity.

Contradictory Development and State Power

The simple mechanics of this analysis reveal the process by which incomes are distributed, but only hint at the drastic institutional changes and social conflicts which accompany the integration of workers into the wage labor system. The expansion of the capitalist mode of production undermines the traditional mode, and thus tends to weaken the political and ideological forces which served to perpetuate the old order. The capitalist class is thus faced with difficult problems of reproduction as well as production. The expansion and survival of the capitalist mode depends critically on both the productivity and the politics of the growing working class. Achieving high levels of labor productivity and assuring the reproduction of a set of social relationships that allows a substantial portion of the product of labor to be appropriated as profits by the capitalist class are thus the requisites of successful capitalist development. But neither objective is easily achieved and in many circumstances they may be contradictory.

Capitalist profits depend on (among other things) the average productivity of wage labor. Yet the social attitudes and technical skills necessary for a productive capitalist labor force are generally scarce in the populations of the traditional mode of production.[21] The movement of labor out of the traditional mode increases the demand for skills not easily acquired through emulation of parental roles in production. Growing up in a traditional community is no preparation for the demands of factory life, since the capitalist enterprise is a vastly different social organization, with a set of social relations quite distinct from those of the family or the precapitalist community.[22] The wage worker, whether in the factory, plantation, or office, has to learn time-consciousness, new forms of discipline, new sources of motivation, and respect for authority outside the kinship group. He or she has to adjust to detailed supervision in highly routine and fragmented tasks.[23]

Capitalist profits also depend on the power of capitalists over workers. But with the rapid expansion of the capitalist relations of production, it becomes difficult to thwart consciousness and militant political activity among workers. While the existence of a reserve army in the declining traditional mode of production weakens the position of workers in the capitalist mode, the living and working conditions of these workers strengthen their capacity to undertake collective action against capitalists. Workers are thrown together in large factories, often in large urban areas. The social isolation characteristic of peasant production, which had helped to maintain quiescence in the traditional mode, is broken down. With an increasing number of families no longer owning or attached to the land, the workers' search for a living results in large-scale labor migrations. "Transient" elements come to constitute a major segment of the population, and begin to pose seemingly insurmountable problems of assimilation, integration, and control. Inequality of wealth becomes more apparent, and is less easily justified and less readily accepted.

Integration of an increasing number of workers into the capitalist mode of production thus produces a potential antagonist to the capitalist class—the growing class of wage laborers. This class, unlike the peasantry and the landlord class, grows in number and becomes potentially more powerful with the expansion of the capitalist mode. The demands of wage laborers and their entry into political life threaten to disrupt the profit-making process and to transform the class structure. This contradiction between accumulation and the reproduction of the class structure has appeared in militant class struggle and other forms of political activity—in the growth of labor organization, mass strikes, nationalist movements, populist revolts, and the rise of socialist political parties.

It is in the interest of the preservation of the capitalist order and the expansion of capitalist profits that class conflict be confined to the isolated daily struggles of workers in the individual production unit. The ever-present contradiction between accumulation and reproduction must be repressed, or channeled into demands easily contained within the structure of capitalist society. The contradiction may be temporarily managed in a variety of ways: through ameliorative social reform, through the coercive force of the state, through heightening the racial, ethnic, tribalist, linguistic, sexual, and other distinctions upon which the divide-and-rule strategy is based, and through an ideological perspective which fosters popular disunity and otherwise serves to reproduce the capitalist order.

The School System as Recruiter and Gatekeeper

In capitalist social formations, the school system has embodied or contributed to each of the above strategies for stable capitalist expansion, and has thus been an important complement to the armed force of the state in managing, at least temporarily, the contradiction between accumulation and reproduction. In most capitalist countries, the school system serves as both recruiter and gatekeeper for the capitalist sector. I will consider the gatekeeping role shortly. As a recruiter, the school system helps to produce a labor force able and resigned to working productively in the novel social setting of the capitalist firm. Schooling can help increase the productivity of workers in two closely related ways: first, by transmitting or reinforcing the values, expectations, beliefs, types of information, and modes of behavior required both for the adequate performance on the job and for the smooth functioning of basic institutions such as the labor market, and second, by developing technical and scientific skills necessary to efficient production. Although few of the academic skills learned in school are directly transferable to the capitalist workplace, basic scientific knowledge, communication skills, and mathematical abilities are essential to competence in some occupations. More important, these capacities are a critical ingredient to become effective on the job learning of many directly productive skills.

The contribution of schooling to the expansion of the forces of production cannot easily be separated from the second main aspect of schooling as labor recruiter for the capitalist mode: the reproduction of the social relations of production. The preparation of young people for integration into the capitalist mode is facilitated when the social relations of the school system take a particular form. Students and their parents are denied control of the educational process. Success is measured by an external standard, grades and examinations, which become the main motivation for work. This structure subordinates any intrinsic interest in knowledge—the product of one's effort—or in learning—the process of production. Class, race, sexual, tribal, linguistic, and other distinctions are reflected in differential access to schooling, drop-out rates and promotion prospects. In short, the social relations of production are replicated in the schools. The central role of institutional structure—as opposed to formal content—is summarized in what Herbert Gintis and I term "the correspondence principle": the educational establishment, in response to pressures from the capitalist class and others will attempt to structure the social organization of schooling so as to correspond to the social relations of production. What educators often call the "hidden curriculum" is thus of paramount importance. Whether relationships among students are hierarchical and competitive or egalitarian and cooperative, whether relations among students, teachers, and the larger community are democratic or authoritarian are better indicators of what students actually learn in schools than texts or formal curricula. Of course human development, or, more narrowly, the formation of the labor force, does not begin or end in the school. Family structure and child-rearing practices are an important part of the early socialization process. After school, the social relations of production on the job exert a continuing influence on personality development. Some types of behavior are rewarded; others are penalized. The nature of the capitalist labor processes itself limits the range of attitudes, values, and behavior patterns which people can exhibit. But schooling does play a central role in the formation of the workforce, particularly in periods of rapid social change.

The correspondence between the social relations of schooling and the social relations of production does not mean that all children receive the same education. Capitalist production, characterized by a hierarchical division of labor, requires that a relatively small group of future technical and managerial personnel develop the capacity to calculate, decide, and rule, while a much larger group "learns" to follow instructions accurately. This stratification of the future labor force is partly accomplished by making different amounts and types of schooling available to different children. Thus, the school system incorporates a capitalist class structure. Though it will not concern us directly here, the correspondence principle has an international dimension: where the international division of labor results in a class structure dominated at the top by foreign management and technical personnel (often located in New York or Tokyo), a corresponding underdevelopment of the employment demand for indigenous college graduates may be anticipated.[24]

The capitalists' interest, I have argued, is to pattern the structure of schooling after the social relations of capitalist production. Analogously, it is in the interest of the capitalist class to regulate the quantitative growth of the school system according to the expansion of the capitalist mode of production. In part because of the widespread ideological emphasis on education as the road to success, popular demands for rapid educational expansion may often exceed the rate appropriate to the employment needs of the capitalist mode of production. This will be particularly true when the accumulation process embodies very labor-saving technology. Nonetheless, pressures for mass education, even for youth destined to work in the traditional mode, may be met if the ideological or political benefits of expansion are seen as particularly great, or if the capitalist class is unable to control the rate of educational expansion.

From the standpoint of the capitalist class, the risks of overexpansion are evident. First, education for all might facilitate productivity increases and technological progress in the traditional mode of production, a development which capitalists would oppose in the interests of maintaining a ready supply of cheap labor.[25] Second, the fiscal costs of educational overexpansion represent a tax burden on capitalists and a diversion of state fiscal resources away from projects and subsidies which may be more beneficial to profits. Third, if the entire population of a specific age group were to receive a fairly high level of education, all might anticipate employment in the capitalist mode. The result would be urban migration, massive urban unemployment, and outrage at frustrated expectations on the part of the unsuccessful.

While the resulting downward pressure on wages would be welcome to the capitalist class, there are less expensive and less dangerous methods of maintaining the reserve army. In any case, the possibility that universal education would facilitate the development of a common consciousness between peasants and wage workers may more than offset any short-term economic advantage. Thus, in addition to preparing some young people for wage work, the school system, if it is to contribute to the capitalist growth process, must also act as a gate-keeper. The use of school credentials as job requirements serves this purpose well, for credentials provide an apparently objective means for keeping a certain number of people out even when the "learning" so signified has little bearing on the jobs in question.

Class Alliances and Educational Dualism

The long-term reproduction of the capitalist order thus often favors the use of educational and employment policy to restrict the pool of potential wage workers. A necessary cost of this strategy to capitalists is a significant wage premium to workers in the capitalist mode of production over incomes in the traditional mode. This wage premium gives the small working class a basis for commitment to the capitalist system, and sets them apart by education and consciousness, as well as by material privilege, from those who work in the traditional mode.[26] Wage workers, hoping to minimize the competition for jobs, will have little immediate interest in expanding access to schooling to others than themselves and their children.

Landlords and traditional elites also have little economic interest in expanding education. Their main economic asset is the land, often farmed at a near subsistence level. Because of its limited technological development and its family or community-based social relations, traditional production does not require that its workers receive the type of training or socialization that is ordinarily undertaken in schools. In fact, school is often the means by which children escape from the traditional economy. Because the preservation of the traditional economy is of paramount importance to the traditional elite and the landlord class, they tend to oppose educational expansion.

The political interests of the landlord class and the traditional elites reinforce their opposition to mass education. While the political position of the traditional elite requires maintenance of traditional values and often the support of religious institutions, the capitalist economic life tends to weaken and circumscribe many of these values and institutions. Indeed, historically, capitalist support of the expansion of primary schooling in the advanced capitalist countries was at least partially due to its purported efficacy in developing a habit of respect for the liberal state and other forms of modern bureaucratic authority which could replace religion and obedience to traditional rulers. In the mid-nineteenth century, Marx wrote that, ". . . the modern and the traditional consciousness of the French peasantry contended for mastery. This process took the form of an incessant struggle between the school-masters and the priests."[27]

While capitalists and workers share an interest in promoting education among wage workers, these two groups share with the landlord class and the traditional elites an opposition to universal education. These common interests provide a basis for a capitalist-landlord-labor alliance attempting to limit the spread of mass education. [By contrast, in the capitalist centers, the spectre of scarce labor impelled the dominant elements in the capitalist class to support the expansion of mass education.] The landlord class and the traditional elites tended to be isolated in their opposition to universal schooling, which in most of Europe and North America proceeded apace throughout the late nineteenth and early twentieth centuries. Thus the nature of the accumulation process in the modern day capitalist periphery, and the resulting configuration of class alliances, are likely to produce a pattern of educational expansion quite different from the experience of the capitalist center.

However, popular pressure from poorer workers and peasants, as well as ideological considerations, may demand the extension of at least some schooling to all children. The result of these counterpressures is often a dual educational system: a brief and second-rate education for many, and a relatively expensive education for just enough to promote productivity and prevent significant labor scarcity in the capitalist mode. "Nonformal" education, currently popular among international aid-giving agencies, holds the possibility of further institutionalizing the dual educational structure by fostering inexpensive practical manual training for the many and more conventional classroom education for the few.[28]

Evidence of the dual educational structure is not lacking. The disparities in expenditures between rural and urban schools, or between elementary and secondary schools or universities (Table 21), bear witness to it: urban post-primary schools receive a share of the educational budget vastly in excess of their share of total enrollments.[29] So too, does the evidence of conventional economic analysis that poor capitalist countries chronically "underinvest" in elementary schooling relative to other forms of schooling. Estimates of the social rate of

TABLE 21

Resource Inputs per Student Year at Various
Levels of Schooling: Ratios of the
Direct Social Costs of Secondary and
Higher Education to the Direct Social Costs
of Primary Education

Country	Educational level	
	Secondary	Higher
Puerto Rico	1.5	11.6
Mexico	5.0	9.0
Venezuela	3.0	12.5
Colombia	2.7	17.9
Chile	1.5	8.0
Brazil	2.9	18.0
Israel	2.7	16.8
India	5.1	17.6
Malaysia	1.9	13.0
S. Korea	2.4	5.5
Nigeria	7.2	100.0
Ghana	6.2	118.7
Kenya	11.8	160.4
Uganda	14.5	117.6
Unweighted average	4.9	44.8

Source: Computed from Psacharopoulos, *Returns to Education: An International Comparison,* p. 173.

return to schooling exhibit the pattern displayed in Table 22: the rate of return to primary schooling tends to be significantly higher than to higher education.[30] Of course, these estimates may have little to say

TABLE 22

Relative "Underinvestment" in Primary Schooling: Average Social Profitability of Various Levels of Schooling in Poor and Middle Income Countries

Level of schooling	Social internal rate of return (percent)[a]	Social benefit cost ratio[b]
Primary	26	9.50
Secondary	17	2.37
Higher	13	2.00

Notes:

[a]Calculated from Psacharopoulos, *Returns to Education: An International Comparison*, p. 63. The countries in the sample are those in Table 21, plus Singapore, the Philippines, and Thailand.

[b]Hadley, "A comparative study of rates of return to education in less developed nations". Calculated with a 10 percent discount rate. The sample was the same as above plus Zambia. The raw data for this series and that calculated by Psacharopoulos are similar, though not identical. The two authors adjusted the data in somewhat different ways, as well.

about the economic growth maximizing allocation of resources in education: the shortcomings of their conceptual and empirical bases are well known.[31] But given the credence ostensibly afforded by policymakers to the rate of return analysis, the fact that the recent tendency in capitalist countries is to reduce the share of educational resources allocated to primary schooling hardly supports the notion that schooling is being used as an instrument for either growth or equality. Between 1960 and 1973 the growth rate of higher education enrollments in poor and middle income capitalist countries was twice that of primary enrollments.[32] India presents a typical and important example: despite serious unemployment, a low rate of return among college graduates and a high estimated social rate of return to primary schooling (20 percent), planned expansion of primary school enrollments has been consistently less than that of other levels; and target shortfalls have been relatively larger for primary than for other levels of schooling.[33] Equally inexplicable from the perspective of promoting either growth or equality are the allocational preferences of "foreign aid" donors. Typical is the World Bank, which between 1963 and 1974 allocated roughly four times as much funding to higher education as to primary education.[34] The World Bank's recent interest in primary education projects is almost entirely in the nonformal basic education category.[35]

Evidence concerning the relationship between economic structure, class interests, and educational dualism can also be found in cross-country comparisons of the amount of resources allocated to primary education. I will use these data to show that the amount of primary education available in capitalist countries is related to both the extent of the capitalist mode of production and to the power relations between the dominant classes in the two modes of production. To illustrate the restrictions placed on mass education by the capitalist class, I will show that, controlling for relevant differences in the structures of the economies, communist countries tend to provide considerably more primary schooling than do countries dominated by either capitalist or traditional elites.

I have used a sample of fifty-five poor and middle income noncommunist countries and six communist countries. Thirteen of the fifty-five noncommunist countries were classified as dominated by a traditional elite.[36] While there are numerous borderline cases, and none which fits the ideal type exactly, it is hoped that this classification will capture some of the gross differences in the distribution of power and the interests of dominant groups in the countries of my sample. The nontraditional, and noncommunist countries are all classified as capitalist.

I first have to predict the amount of resources allocated to primary education for the entire sample of sixty-one countries, using only two economic structure variables, representing the fraction of the labor force working in agriculture and in wage and salary employment. Equation (1) in Table 23 illustrates the strong relationship between the size of the capitalist sector and the amount of resources allocated to primary education. To identify the importance of the class nature of the state I have reestimated the same equation using dummy variables to distinguish the traditional and communist countries (equation (2) in Table 23). The addition of these class power variables greatly increases the explanatory power of the equation, suggesting that the class with a predominant position in the state is an influence upon the educational resource allocation, above and beyond the direct influence exerted by the economic structure of the society. The signs of the class power variables are as expected, and the coefficients are both quantitatively large and statistically significant. Even taking account of differences in economic structure, the communist countries in the sample devote 91 percent more resources to primary education than the mean for the entire sample.[37] Likewise, dominance by a traditional elite is associated with fewer resources allocated to primary education: an estimated negative deviation from the allocation pattern in the sample as a whole amounting to 21 percent (in absolute value) of the mean for the entire sample.

The estimated coefficients of the political variables underestimate the real impact of class power in the case of the traditional elites: because the preservation of a large agricultural sector and the limitation of the modern wage earning sector are presumably part of the economic strategy of these elites, some of their power is measured in the two economic structure variables held constant in these estimates. Thus, in a more adequate analysis, neither the political power variables nor the economic structure variables would be exogenous.

The evidence from this sample of sixty-one countries is consistent with my interpretation of the forces affecting the allocation of resources to education. Yet in the empirical analysis, important influences on educational resource allocation have been excluded. In particular, the adoption of a static analysis, the use of cross-sectional data, and the assumption that a single class or group is dominant at any one time, have diverted attention from the historical development of the educational system.

The demarcation of class boundaries can never be exact, even in a static analysis. Moreover, class composition is constantly changing. In the above analysis, two competing modes of production, capitalist

TABLE 23

Resource Allocation to Primary Education: International Comparisons

Dependent variable	Coefficient of independent variables (t-statistics in parentheses)				Percentage of variance explained: R^2
	LFRAG	LFRAWE	COM	TRAD	
(1) PTPCH	-.0058	.0035			.38
	(2.7)	(2.7)			
(2) PTPCH	-.0069	.0020	.0157	-.0035	.67
	(-4.0)	(2.0)	(6.2)	(-1.9)	

Notes:

PTPCH = primary school teachers per child of school age in the population.
LFRAG = log of the fraction of the labor force working in agriculture.
LFRAWE = log of the fraction of the labor force working for wages and salaries.
COM   = dummy variables set equal to 1 for communist countries, 0 otherwise.
TRAD   = dummy variables set equal to 1 for countries dominated by traditional elites, 0 otherwise.

Education, Class Conflict and Uneven Development 225

and traditional, give rise to competition between the dominant classes in each mode. Groups on the margin of power and wealth seek access to higher positions. Poor and excluded groups seek greater income and political influence. An econometric analysis based on the assumed hegemony of a particular class fails to recognize some aspects of educational policy which result from the unresolved conflict between classes. Further, it omits elements of educational policy designed to co-opt recalcitrant groups and buy their acquiescence to the class in power. For example, the apparent "overinvestment" in higher education relative to primary education which is characteristic of many poor countries may not be the result of a conscious plan to maximize elite incomes. Rather, it may be that families of children who stand to benefit from the expansion of university facilities are often the most politically vocal and powerful groups outside the elite.[38] In this case, university expansion may well be a concession to them in the interests of stability. Similar pressures occur at all levels of the school system although the political influence of those families that are denied access to primary education is ordinarily minimal.

A static econometric analysis may also contribute to the impression that the educational strategies of the dominant groups are necessarily successful. But the many instances of unemployment among the educated in poor countries suggest that this need not be the case. The use of the educational system to buy off excluded groups may have unintended consequences if the expansion of a particular level of schooling proceeds without reference to the employers' demands for educated labor. With the continued expansion of enrollment it becomes increasingly costly to gain admission to the capitalist mode: first it required literacy, then primary school graduation, then a secondary school diploma. In part, this credential inflation is due to the internal contradictions of the school system itself. Because popular demands for educational expansion cannot be resisted forever, many school systems end by producing more graduates than there are jobs in the capitalist mode. This oversupply of schooled workers leads to an escalation in qualifications for a job. This in turn leads to disappointed expectations and demands for access to the next educational level. And so on. Expansion of the next level takes these graduates off the labor market and blunts their discontent, only to reproduce the problem

at a higher level when they graduate. As long as the significant political power of the urban white collar workforce is reflected in generously
administered salary schedules and inflated credential requirements for
job access which bear little relationship to job content and real scarcity of labor, the overexpansion of higher education will continue to
be fueled by popular demand.

Conclusion: The Limits of Educational Policy

I have argued that the school system plays an essential role in capitalist growth: (a) regulating the labor flow between the capitalist and
traditional modes of production, (b) raising productivity in the capitalist mode, (c) thwarting the development of either a large and class
conscious proletariat or a peasant-worker coalition, and (d) undermining
the ideological and political hegemony of traditional elites. Where,
as in most poor countries, the state represents primarily the interests
of the capitalist class, it is these objectives—not a commitment to
equality or to maximizing the rate of growth of per capita output—
which dominate educational policy. Egalitarian or economic growth
promoting education thus confronts its limits in the imperatives of
the reproduction of the class structure, the logic of the accumulation
process, and the capitalist domination of the state. The primary
obstacle to more bountiful and broadly shared economic rewards is
the distribution of power, not the distribution of human capital.

As part of a popular political movement to challenge the class structure and the uneven development of the capitalist social formation,
educational programs might be used to further social equality or to
contribute to a more rational growth process. Paulo Freire's politi-
cized literacy training in the Brazilian Northeast and Mao-Tsetung's
Rectification Movement of 1942-4 come readily to mind. But to
discuss these possible functions of education, in the absence of rebellion
against the capitalist order, is worse than idle speculation. It is to
offer a false promise, an ideological palliative which seeks to buy time
for capitalism by envisioning improvement where little can be secured,
and by obscuring the capitalist roots of inequality and economic
irrationality.

Notes

1. World Bank, "Education Sector Working Paper" (Washington, D.C.: World Bank, 1974), pp. i, 13.
2. Growth maximizing models of educational resource allocation in the poor countries reveal without exception, to my knowledge, massive discrepancies between actual and growth-optimal educational plans. See, for example, Samuel Bowles, *Planning Educational Systems for Economic Growth* (Cambridge: Harvard University Press, 1969). The contribution of schooling to inequality is indicated by the World Bank's studies of Tunisia, "Report of the basic economic mission" (Washington, D.C.: World Bank, 1974) and Pakistan, "Report of the basic economic mission" (Washington, D.C.: World Bank, 1977), and by Asim Dasgupta's study of India and Colombia, "Income distribution, education, and capital accumulation", mimeograph (Washington, D.C.: World Bank, 1974).
3. See Philip Coombs, *The World Educational Crisis* (New York: Oxford University Press, 1968) and *New Paths to Learning* (New York: Praeger, 1975).
4. Abba Lerner captured this aspect of conventional economics aptly: "An economic transaction is a solved political problem. Economics has gained the title of queen of the social sciences by choosing solved political problems as its domain." In "The economics and politics of consumer sovereignty", *American Economic Review* (May 1972). See also the admirable Presidential Address to the American Economic Association by J. K. Galbraith, "Power and the useful economist", *American Economic Review*, LXIII, no. 1 (March 1973): 1-11.
5. Paul Samuelson, "Wage and interest: a modern dissection of marxian economic models", *American Economic Review* (December 1957).
6. This optimistic stance is nowhere more prevalent than in the economic and social planning documents of international agencies such as the World Bank and the U.S. Agency for International Development. See Hollis Chenery, et al., *Redistribution with Growth* (Oxford: Oxford University Press, 1974).
7. The theoretical underpinnings of this approach are presented in Gary Becker, *Human Capital and the Personal Distribution of Income* (Ann Arbor: Institute of Public Administration, 1967). Dasgupta's work (1974) represents the most full developed empirical application in a poor country. For a critique, see Samuel Bowles and Herbert Gintis, *Schooling in Capitalist America: Educational Reform and the Contraditions of Economic Life* (New York: Basic Books, 1976), and Lester Thurow, *Generating Inequality* (New York: Basic Books, 1975).
8. Ralph Miliband, *The State in Capitalist Society* (London: Weidenfeld and Nicolson, 1969), Gabriel Kolko, *The Triumph of Conservatism* (Chicago: Quadrangle, 1963), and James Weinstein, *The Corporate Ideal and the Liberal State, 1900-1918* (Boston: Beacon, 1968) are representative of the literature.
9. Specifically on schooling, see Bowles and Gintis (1976), Michael Katz, *The Irony of Early School Reform* (Cambridge: Harvard University Press, 1975), Brian Simon, *Studies in the History of Education, 1780-1870* (London: Lawrence and Wishart, 1960), Christian Baudelot and Rober Establet, *L'Ecole Capitalist en France* (Paris: Maspero, 1973), Paddy Quick, "Education and industrialization in 19th century England and Wales", unpublished doctoral dissertation (Harvard University, 1975), Andrew Zimbalist, "La Expansion de la education primaria y el desarrollo capitalista: el caso de Chile", *Revista del Centro de Estudios Educativos*, vol. III, no. 2 (1973): 51-72, David Tyack, *The One Best System: A History of*

Samuel Bowles

American Urban Education (Cambridge: Harvard University Press, 1974), and Martin Carnoy, *Education as Cultural Imperialism* (New York: McKay, 1974).

10. Various themes of the Marxian theory of the state are developed in V. I. Lenin, *State and Revolution* (New York: International Publishers, 1932), Louis Althusser, *Lenin and Philosophy, and Other Essays* (London: New Left Books, 1971), Nicos Poulantzas, *Pouvoir Politique et Classes Sociales* (Paris: Maspero, 1968), and Miliband (1969).

11. Karl Marx and Friedrick Engels, "The Communist Manifesto", in R. C. Tucker, ed., *The Marx-Engels Reader* (New York: Norton, 1972), pp. 331-61.

12. The defining characteristics of the capitalist economy are characterized by Maurice Dobb, *Studies in the Development of Capitalism* (New York: International Publishers, 1947), Chap. 1.

13. On precapitalist modes of production, see Karl Marx, *Pre-Capitalist Economic Formations* (London: Lawrence and Wishart, 1963), and Barry Hindress and Paul Q. Hirst, *Pre-Capitalist Modes of Production* (London: Routledge and Kegan Paul, 1975).

14. It may well be that the development of a wage labor system produces endogenous increases in fertility insofar as it effectively severs the family fertility decision process from the limitations of (and therefore diminishing returns to) its owned land and other resources. See William Lazonick, "Karl Marx and enclosures in England", *The Review of Radical Political Economics,* vol. 6, no. 2 (Summer 1974): 1-32, and Nancy Folbre, "Capitalist development and population growth in Zongolica, Vera Cruz", *Latin American Perspectives* (Summer 1977).

15. For an alternative analysis based on a more fully developed treatment of the international aspects, see the insightful paper of Alain de Janvry, "The political economy of rural development in Latin America: an interpretation", *American Journal of Agricultural Economics,* vol. 57, no. 3 (August 1975): 490-499. In effect, I assume that all goods or their close substitutes are to some degree traded.

16. Simon Kuznets, "Quantitative aspects of the economic growth of nations: distribution of income by size", *Economic Development and Cultural Change* (January 1963), and S. Swamy, "Structural changes and the distribution of income by size: the case of India", *Review of Income and Wealth* (June 1968): 155-74. If V_T and V_C are the coefficients of variation of income in the traditional and capitalist mode of production respectively, h is the average income per recipient unit in the capitalist mode relative to that in the traditional mode, and W_T and W_C are the fraction of households, respectively, working in the traditional and capitalist modes, then the coefficient of variation for the social formation V can be expressed

$$V = \frac{[W_T V_T{}^2 + W_C V_C{}^2 h^2 + W_T W_C (h\text{-}1)^2]^{1/2}}{W_T + W_C h}$$

17. The small surplus, of course, does not "explain" the relatively equal income distribution. While I do not attempt this here, both may be understood as expressions of the underlying mode of production. The relatively equal distribution of real income in the traditional mode of production yields the positive correlation found in cross-section studies of poor and middle income countries between the gini coefficient and the percentage of the labor force working for wages. See Jerry Cromwell, "The size distribution of income: an international comparison", Department of Economics, Harvard University (mimeograph, 1976).

18. See Samir Amin, *Unequal Development: An Essay on the Social Formations of Peripheral Capitalism* (New York: Monthly Review Press, 1976) for a full discussion. This interpretation of the distribution process provides, I think, a good explanation of the apparent tendency for income inequality first to increase (Kuznets' famous inverted U-shaped pattern) and then to decrease in the course of capitalist development, the eventual decrease being the result of the relative depletion of the reserve army with the declining relative size of the traditional mode of production.

19. The assumed open nature of the economy—all goods or their close substitutes are available through international trade—is critical here. Further, to the extent that different family members work in different modes of production *and* the family remains the relevant consumption unit, this analysis is incomplete. See Carmen Diana Deere, "Women's subsistence production in the capitalist periphery", *Review of Radical Political Economics,* vol. 8, no. 1 (Spring 1976): 9-17, Marjorie Mbilinyi, "Women: producers and reproducers in underdeveloped capitalist systems", mimeograph, University of Dar es Salaam, 1976, and Calude Meillassoux, *Femmes, Greniers, et Capitaux* (Paris: Maspero, 1975). When this phenomenon is prevalent, increases in productivity in the traditional mode may contribute to pressure for lower wages, as more of the family's subsistence is procured through direct production in the traditional mode. In this case, the direct relation of the two modes of production through the family unit complements or even supersedes the indirect relation through the markets, thus undermining the salience of the assumed external determination of prices.

20. This is suggested in Folbre's (1977) Mexican case study.

21. One can think of a number of exceptions to this rather widely accepted proposition. Values and skills based on the precapitalist economy have evidently been central to the success of the capitalist economy in Japan. See Thomas Smith, *The Agrarian Origins of Modern Japan* (Stanford: Stanford University Press, 1959), James Abegglen, *The Japanese Factory: Aspects of its Social Organization* (Glencoe: The Free Press, 1958), and Robert Bellah, *Tokugawa Religion: The Values of Pre-Industrial Japan* (Glencoe: The Free Press, 1957). Clifford Geertz makes a similar argument in his comparative study of development in Indonesia, *Pedlars and Princes: Social Change and Economic Modernization in Two Indonesian Villages* (Chicago: University of Chicago Press, 1963).

22. The arguments in this and the next section are presented in greater detail and with empirical support in Bowles and Gintis (1976).

23. See E. P. Thompson, "Time, work-discipline and industrial capitalism", *Past and Present,* no. 38 (December 1967): 56-97; Herbert Gutman, "Work, culture and society in industrializing America, 1815-1919", *American Historical Review* (June 1973): 541-88, and Wilbert Moore, ed., *Labor Commitment and Social Change in Developing Areas* (New York: Social Science Research Council, 1960).

24. Stephen Hymer, "The multinational corporation and the international division of labor", Department of Economics, Yale University (unpublished paper, 1970).

25. See T. W. Schultz, *Transforming Traditional Agriculture* (New Haven: Yale University Press, 1964).

26. The "labor aristocracy" theme has been developed in Marxian literature since Lenin. See Giovanni Arrighi, "International corporations, labor aristocracies, and economic development in Tropical Africa", in Giovanni Arrighi and John Saul,

Essays on the Political Economy of Africa (New York: Monthly Review Press, 1973).

27. Karl Marx, *The Eighteenth Brumaire of Louis Bonaparte* (New York: International Publishers, 1963), p. 125. A similar struggle took place between the Church of England and the educational programs supported by capitalists and Dissenters. See Quick (1975).

28. See John Simmons, "Can education promote development?", *Finance and Development*, vol. 15, no. 1 (March 1978).

29. For evidence on urban-rural differences in wastage rates, see World Bank, "Education Sector Working Paper" (Washington, D.C.: World Bank, 1974). On urban-rural disparities in the percentage of elementary schools offering the complete number of grades, and primary-secondary differences in student-teacher ratios see UNESCO, *Statistical Yearbook* (1972).

30. See Bowles (1969). In Samuel Bowles, "Class power and mass education", Harvard University, mimeograph (1971), I consider the likely biases in the rate of return estimates, and present alternative series of estimates, similar in overall pattern to the Psacharopoulos and Hadley estimates found in George Psacharopoulos, *Returns to Education: An International Comparison* (San Francisco: Jossey Bass, 1973), and Lawrence Hadley, "A comparative study of rates of return to education in less developed nations", mimeograph, University of Connecticut, (1976). It seems doubtful that the biases in these estimates can explain the systematic finding of higher rates of return to primary education. While the direction of bias cannot be confidently indicated, if anything the biases on balance would suggest an overestimate of the social rate of return to higher education (due to administered civil service salaries for high level bureaucrats and noncompetitive politically "necessary" high salaries for the indigenous management component of foreign firms) and an underestimate of the rate of return to primary education (due to the use of income estimates that overvalue the social marginal productivity of unschooled workers in a labor surplus economy).

31. For a review, see Bowles (1969). Alternative interpretations of these data are offered in Martin Carnoy, "Class analysis and investment in human resources", *Review of Radical Political Economics*, vol. 3 (Fall-Winter, 1971): 56-81, and in Jagdish Bhagwati, "Education, class structure and income inequality", *World Development*, vol. 1, no. 5 (1973).

32. UNESCO, *Statistical Yearbook* (1976).

33. Mark Blaug et al., *The Causes of Graduate Unemployment in India* (London: Allen Lane, 1969).

34. World Bank (1974).

35. World Bank (1974), Annex 5.

36. The basic data on the labor force are primarily from the International Labor Organization, *Yearbook of Labor Statistics, 1965* (Geneva: ILO, 1966). Those on schooling are from UNESCO, *Statistical Yearbook* (1966, 1968). The classification of traditional elites is a slight modification of Irma Adelman and Cynthia T. Morris, *Society, Politics, and Economic Development* (Baltimore: Johns Hopkins Press, 1967). Classed as "traditional" are "countries in which traditional and land-owning and/or other traditional oriented national elites were politically dominant during the greater part of the period 1957-62". A full description of the criteria used by Adelman and Morris is their statement that "traditional elites . . . include both traditional land-holding elites and bureaucratic, religious, or military

elites who favored the preservation of traditional political, social, and economic organization, institutions, and values". My classification differs somewhat in laying greater stress on the economic base of the elite and in particular the relative absence of wage labor in its production, and the lack of integration into the world economy.

37. The importance of the communist variable is suggested, also by the educational histories of particular communist countries. See, for example, my analysis of Cuban education since 1959 in Samuel Bowles, "Cuban education and the revolutionary ideology", *Harvard Education Review*, vol. 41, no. 4 (November 1971): 472-500.

38. This may well be the explanation of the persistent unemployment of university graduates resulting from the "overexpansion" of higher education enrollments in India. See Blaug et al. (1969).

What Can be Done?

CHAPTER 15

Steps Toward Reform

JOHN SIMMONS

"Incremental reform is both necessary and inadequate."
Michael Harrington

The preceding chapters suggest that, for most developing countries, adherence to the current policies of educational investment will result in increasing inequality between the rich and the poor and little improvement in the efficiency of school systems. The alternative is to implement a package of reforms which extends beyond the educational system to the labor market and political arena. If the objective is greater equality and efficiency, then a central problem is how to redefine the relationship among the actors in the reform process— the haves and have nots—to assure that both groups participate in the identification of their needs and the management of the investment programs. Robert McNamara has emphasized that the governments of developing nations "must recognize the necessity of assuring broader participation of their peoples in the process of development".[1] Although this chapter suggests a range of strategy options available to the reformer, it focuses on the process, or steps, required to truly attack inefficiency and inequity rather than on specific reforms.

Strategies for Reform

Reforming social institutions is never an easy task, and institutions engaging in mass education are no exception. Reforms are major changes in budget allocations among different levels of education, in what students learn in school, or in the percentage of low income students of the total who graduate from the university, which affect schooling across the nation, in contrast to innovations which are often local and have little impact on educational outcomes. Although reforms often take place after revolution, it is not a necessary condition for effective reform. Two theories of educational reform define options available to the developing countries. The first theory of the technical school concludes that educational structures and processes are relatively independent of political and economic forces. Thus potential reformers need only wait for the technical prerequisites to be met before transforming the educational system. The second theory of the structural school argues that the educational system cannot be reformed without changes in the political and economic institutions. Beyond studying and experimenting with the most promising reforms, national reforms cannot precede a basic socioeconomic transformation.

These two schools of thought are associated with two different development goals, both in theory and in practice. The technical school's concern with efficiency and other technical concerns corresponds to its identification of economic growth. Thus members advocate educational programs that will contribute to the growth in national output, often regardless of the impact on social equality or democracy. Adherents to this school are currently proposing cutbacks in some countries for secondary and higher education, and even for primary education beyond the fourth grade. They propose more investment in early primary education and vocational training.

The structuralist school's concern with the process of education, the relative rigidity of the wage and employment structure, and the school system's role in preparing people for and rationing them to an hierarchical job structure parallels their development goal of greater social and economic status for the poorest members of the populations of the developing countries. Adherents to this school are critical of the dual system of education effectively proposed by the incrementalists—public primary and vocational education for most; public and private secondary and higher education for the few. Instead they propose changes in the distribution of income, restructuring of jobs and the actual process of work-life, and in the educational system. Specifically they advocate a more democratic job process to spread out managerial functions. They then propose a closer integration between schooling and working. Thus in addition to arguing strongly for universal primary education through the ninth grade, so that adequate levels of reading comprehension can be reached, structuralists suggest a heavy component of practical experience, including workshops to train children in certain skills and especially job processes. Then, after two or more years of work, secondary and higher education slots could be filled by part-time students who also work part-time, so as to ensure that further manpower development matches job requirements. For the most part, these changes are only practicable in the context of wide-ranging reforms including educational, economic, and social structures.

Based on an understanding of these two sets of theories, goals for development and types of options for change, the educational policies of the developing countries can be classified. The number of countries which are aggressively pursuing the objectives of equality and efficiency through national programs with comparative success is small, but growing. It includes China, Cuba, Tanzania, and Somalia. Other countries like Algeria, Ecuador, Ethiopia, and Sri Lanka are implementing national reforms, but their policies are either not sufficiently comprehensive or insufficient time has passed to determine if they are having the desired effect. Some countries like Liberia, Pakistan, and Tunisia have specified equality and efficiency as reform objectives in their national development plans, but have only introduced pilot projects.

The history of educational reform, both in the developed and developing countries, provides weighty evidence for the structuralist position.[2] It appears that innovation, but not reform, is the limited achievement of the human capital or technical school. The industrial revolution, the installation of democratic governments, and the imposition of colonial rule brought major reforms to existing educational systems. Since World War II, effective educational reforms in the developing countries, in addition to the expansion of enrollments, have usually resulted from the rise of new political leadership with a major commitment to reducing poverty. As has been noted, this has been the case, for example, in Cuba, China, Somalia, and Tanzania.

An educational strategy, as opposed to a comprehensive program detailing specific projects, would first identify the reform objectives and the obstacles to achieving them, and then select the processes appropriate to remove the obstacles. Next, criteria are needed to determine if a proposed reform is consistent with the objectives. If the objectives are the reduction of inequality and improvement of efficiency, then one criterion might be the extent to which a reform would assure that the poor as well as the rich complete primary school, and that an increasing proportion of students graduating from the universities are from poor families. Other criteria might review the extent to which changes in the school experience would promote the skills needed for employment, self-reliance, community participation, and family development. This is the logical starting point for reform. The objection might be raised that this kind of general strategy would not be useful if individual nations' needs and situations were vastly different from each other. The differences, however, are usually more a question of degree than kind. The characteristics of the demand for more school places, unemployment of the educated, wage structures, examination systems, and classroom organization tend to be similar in most countries.

A critical problem of strategy that many countries face is how to plan and implement effectively a national reform plan. What is the process? A two-phase approach to developing a national plan is suggested. The first phase involves establishing an awareness of the problems of the current system and eliciting popular participation in their study; the second is a reorganization of the educational system. Each phase has several reference points which enable planners to check their progress, and which could be used to construct a national plan. The phases are outlined below; a discussion follows.

Phase I, which might be called "awareness and transition", involves an understanding of (a) the demand for skilled manpower, (b) the supply of skilled manpower, (c) the effect of previous educational investments on equity, (d) the resources required for transition, and (e) a model for the future. Phase II, which involves a reorganization of the educational system, covers the following four issues: (a) innovation and experimentation; (b) technical changes; (c) legal revisions; and (d) commitment of resources.

My purpose is to suggest some of the questions to ask which would facilitate a reform process. Discussion of the answers should be part of the detailed planning process by the people who will have responsibility for preparation and implementation. It is my central contention that traditional attitudes toward investment including those which are realized in the current pattern of educational investment, are so misguided that any solution to the problem must necessarily be preceded by a definition of the pertinent questions. Thus, a necessary condition for deciding whether or not countries need reform is identifying an initial set of questions the planners feel are relevant to their specific problems.

Phase I. Awareness and Transition

The forces that can be allied to resist changes in the structure and operation of educational systems are among the strongest in a society. It is for this reason that basic economic or political changes usually have to take place in society before fundamental educational reforms can occur. Hence, Phase I is the crucial first stage in determining whether or not a country is ready for basic reforms. In it, questions may be organized into five policy issues: manpower demand, manpower supply, equity, resources, and a model for the future.

The Demand for Manpower

The economic demand for manpower is mainly generated by the creation of new jobs and by the replacement of expatriates and workers leaving the work force. However, the total demand for school places reflects parental and student as well as employer desires. Further, economic demand is for both experienced and inexperienced workers. Too often in the past, manpower planners have assumed that new school leavers could satisfy the demand for experienced workers. The failure to specify job characteristics is another reason for inaccurate manpower demand predictions by planners. What are the abilities needed to succeed at a job? Which are best learned in school and which on the job? To what extent do employers use the amount of schooling or the certifications candidates have simply to limit the number of job applicants, with little or no reference to the skills that the years of schooling may imply?

Supply of Skilled Manpower

The supply question involves two basic issues. The first is the extent to which worker characteristics required by occupations are improved by schooling. The second is the extent to which nonschool experiences, like learning on the job, shape the desired traits. With regard to the first issue, reformers must address questions such as these: (a) Are primary school graduates able to read the national newspapers and retain this ability? Are they learning how to learn, and are they enjoying the learning process? (b) Is rural education generating skills which meet the needs of the poor? (c) Is the political socialization and modernization desired by the nation's leaders taking place, as has been assumed, or are schools having the opposite effect and alienating the younger generation from manual labor and national objectives?

With regard to the second issue, the influence of nonschool factors such as family and job experience, there are several questions to ask: (a) Can the skills desired by employers be acquired more efficiently through apprenticeships or on-the-job training than in the classroom? (b) Can skill training, including the acquisition of important affective traits, be made more explicit in the curriculum? (c) Are school examinations a good indicator of useful job abilities? Is there an excess or a deficit of manpower for different kinds of jobs? Answers to these questions will begin to describe the characteristics of the supply side.

Design of Increased Equity

The major issue of equity in Phase I is to study the effect of investment in education on the distribution of income. The pertinent questions are: (a) Is the tax system regressive, falling more heavily on the poor as a proportion of their total income than on the rich? (b) Do fewer poor students complete each level of schooling than one would expect from their proportion in society? The null hypothesis should be that schooling has a negative effect on income distribution. A plan for at least neutralizing these effects should be designed during the transition phase.

Resources for Transition

Leadership and expertise are required to initiate and sustain discussion on the above issues. Expertise without leadership will not suffice. Leadership provides the inspiration and management required to raise public awareness of the issues and to encourage the maximum feasible participation of the public in proposing solutions. This assumes that individuals, with or without formal training, will be willing to explore the above questions with open minds, and then design and implement experiments with attractive solutions. The existence of research institutes, while advantageous, is not a prerequisite to reform planning.

In most systems of technical education, there are no mechanisms or incentives for employers to participate in educational policy decisions.[3] An important first step in all phases of the transition to a more effective system would be to hold discussions among employers, craftsmen, students, and teachers about the kind of workers that employers need. Now almost no information flows systematically between these four groups, which are also not consulted by the educational planners about the kinds of abilities which jobs require and school might teach.

Models for the Future

The planners and the public need an idea of what the new educational objectives and processes will look like, before they enter Phase II. This will also assist in building a constituency among the different groups of beneficiaries. Given the deficiencies of the present system for meeting the needs of the poor majority, the models which emerge through country discussions are likely to emphasize universal schooling through the ninth grade, adult education for awareness and organization, work-study programs, and village and neighborhood participation in the planning and management of school decisions.

When the questions raised by the above five policy issues have been studied, when an awareness of the problems of education is widespread, and when the producers and consumers of formal education feel the urgency for reform and understand the implications based on their analysis, then it is time to consider moving to Phase II.[4]

T.E.D.—R

Phase II. Reorganization of the Educational System

Innovations and Experimentation

Whether planning in agriculture, education, or in other sectors, most countries seem unable to profit from the experience of others when dealing with similar problems. The relatively rapid spread of the new wheat and rice strains is one of the exceptions; the spread of Coca Cola is another. Some potentially useful innovations have not been widely diffused. They range from primary-level science curricula adapted for use by semiliterate teachers,[5] to farmer-oriented radio programs,[6] and short course paramedical training.[7] These innovations have not spread, partly because they were not supported by the massive commitment, experimentation, and organization that promoted the new wheat and rice varieties. Unless countries have access to ideas and innovations that have been used successfully, they risk repeating unnecessary years of trial and error.

If they could understand how innovations are successfully propagated, developing countries could reduce their dependence on foreign consultants. Common sense, supported by the findings of innovation research, suggests that hearing of a new idea is not enough.[8] It has to be seen in action, thoroughly discussed, and experimented with on a small-scale, where the costs of failure are small, before a decision can be made to adopt it.

But knowing that an innovation has succeeded in other countries is not enough. It has to be adapted to local needs, and experiments must be designed to test the proposed innovation. The process of experimentation serves two purposes basic to reform: first, it tests the innovation and resulting adaptations and second, through the learning experience itself, it also develops that self-confidence in the experimenters which is essential to expand past the pilot phase. The innovation must not only be thoroughly understood by those who adopt it, but must also be adapted to local needs. An essential link in the successful spread of the new wheat and rice varieties was the training of experts at Chapingo, Mexico, and Los Banos, Philippines, to participate in testing the innovation in their own country. Rarely can outside experts achieve the required effectiveness in either experimentation or instilling confidence. The experience of Swedish reformers who used educational research to test and diffuse reform provides an important lesson about the process of change. Research results were used to resolve issues over which there was conflict, like the effects of mixing fast and slow learners in the same classroom.[9] The successful completion of educational experiments and innovations and the national diffusion of the results rely on each nation's willingness to undertake reform.

Technical Change

Schools embody a technological process in the sense that they combine labor and capital to produce output. The evidence presented in the earlier chapters has suggested that schools are not as efficient a technology as had been hoped. Therefore, it is important to explore other learning methods, such as apprenticeship systems, integration of schooling and working, and improved parent-child interaction which may be more appropriate to a country's problems of human development.

An equally important consideration in effecting technological change is the scale and complexity of equipment and systems that individuals will have to operate and repair. Economically appropriate technologies which stress practicality and ease of repair, not engineered obsolescence are being created for and in the developing countries. Their use needs to be encouraged.

Until about fifteen years ago, small-boat fishermen in Peru had little trouble repairing their outboard motors. Then tolerances became finer, parts more fragile, and the mechanisms more complex, making local repairs lengthy, expensive, or impossible. Unnecessarily sophisticated and fragile equipment is usually not economically profitable for the owner or developing nation, even if it is financially profitable for the supplier or manufacturer. The use of appropriate technologies reduces a nation's dependence on imported repairmen and spare parts. With more appropriate technology, vocational skills could be accessible to virtually anyone with curiosity, motivation, and basic psychomotor skills, rather than left to the domain of a few experts. The successful spread of appropriate technology and the allied training would demonstrate a country's ability to undertake reform.

Legal Changes

The law often supports mandatory formal education and gives a monopoly to the state. Private, as well as public, education is usually under state supervision and examinations for certificates are the same as in the state schools. When the effect of these laws is combined with the prevailing social goal to attain as much formal education as possible, there are usually neither the possibilities nor incentives to develop more effective alternative ways of learning.

The evolution of education in Anglo-American law is enlightening. English common law had given parents virtually complete control over the education of the child. But by the beginning of the twentieth century, in the United States, "the education of youth (was said to be) a matter of such vital importance to the democratic state . . . that the state may go very far indeed by way of limiting the control of the parent over the education of his [sic] child".[10] This statement should be contrasted with the United Nations Universal Declaration of Human Rights, adopted in 1948, that "parents have a prior right to choose the kind of education that should be given to their children" (Article 26-3).[11] With the desire to improve learning, laws on mandatory schooling should be considered for revision.

It is possible that ending forced school attendance would reduce the proportion of the six to eighteen age cohort in school, and that more poor students than rich would drop out. This effect could have certain social costs, but the benefits might outweigh the costs. For example, if students who repeatedly fail, but are forced to stay in school, are socialized to think of themselves as failures, this may destroy the development of sufficient self-confidence and self-esteem to hold a steady job, or initiate a career. If students become delinquent because they resent school, then surely there are benefits from staying out of school. Finally, the opportunity costs of the labor of older children may be significant and a reason why poor parents keep their children out of school.

Hiring practices of employers, which screen applicants on the basis of formal education, have assumed the status of *de facto* law. These practices make sense when the skills taught in school are a major requirement for the job, such as simple arithmetic for carpenters or anatomy for doctors. But when only primary school certificate holders will be considered for jobs as street-sweepers, while students with the same years of schooling but without the certificate because they failed the examination are refused, the hiring practices are clearly unfair and wasteful. Some firms no longer request information about schooling when interviewing candidates for certain blue and white collar jobs, and substitute simple tests of the skills the job requires. If the job skills cannot be adequately tested, they allow a trial period in which the candidate must either demonstrate or learn the essentials of the skills on the job. Other firms have been forced by the courts to stop using education as a requirement for hiring. The United States Supreme Court found that the use of education as a criterion for employment discriminated against the low income groups because the poor had not had an equal opportunity to gain schooling. The court found that jobs did not require most of the knowledge for which schools test students.[12] Thus, legal means may be used to change employer hiring practices. If a country can reform its legal monopoly on education, reevaluate forced attendance regulations, and change the discriminatory hiring practices of employers, then substantial changes can happen.

Resources for Reform

In discussing Phase I, I suggested the importance of expertise and leadership. Both can play an important role in providing information on alternative forms of education and making consumers and producers of education aware of deficiencies in the formal system. This information process is broadened in Phase II to include the results of experimentation with the alternatives. But there are three more requirements of the resources needed for reform, preconditions for successful completion of Phase II. First, basic changes in society usually have to precede, and thus induce, changes in educational processes and structures. As long as large or artificial wage differentials continue to exist, the private demand for schooling will not decline. Second, considerable political courage and power is required to implement reforms of formal education intended to equalize the income distribution. Third, because some of the reform decisions will be unpopular among some groups, strong constituencies have to be organized to support the reforms especially among low income groups. Without these political prerequisites, countries may decide not to undertake either Phase I or Phase II. But successful completion of Phase I may create political pressure to move to Phase II.

Planners in many countries may have already considered the issues raised in Phase I, and have considerable information about their resolution. But do they have the support of the administrators, teachers, and parents who are crucial to the successful implementation of the reforms? A major objective of Phase I is to encourage popular participation in studying the issues and planning the reforms. Educational reforms imposed from the top have a poor record.

The issues raised in Phase I enable a country to face the difficult questions, but without commitment to change. Thus, at the end of Phase I, a country can decide that the costs of the reforms outweigh the benefits and stop the process. Work on Phase II will require sustained commitment by both the leadership and the people. It will raise hopes but also create conflict; successful completion of Phase I will prepare the people and the leadership for the necessary struggles of Phase II. The two-phase process may be seen as contradictory to the assumption that educational reform is usually preceded by political and economic change. I think not, for three reasons. First, the process is applicable in those countries where the political and economic changes have already taken place. There, implementation of the process should be easier, but each issue would still require careful consideration by the people and the leadership. Second, what constitutes "sufficient" political and economic change? China and Cuba required revolutions, but Tanzania did not. All three have had substantial political and economic change, and reformed education systems. "Socialist" government is not a sufficient condition for appropriate educational reform, as the experience of countries like Guyana, Tunisia, Pakistan, and Equatorial Guinea illustrate. Third, it is possible that some countries like Sweden without such political and economic change may be able to plan and implement effective education reforms. The two-phase approach could assist their efforts.

A Range of Options

The preceding sections have attempted to analyze the basic issues of educational systems in developing countries. The analysis, however, is not a blueprint for educational reform. Each country has to develop its own educational program. At the same time, the similarities in the issues across countries suggest that reviewing existing options might benefit individual countries' planning efforts. In fact, social investments made without a careful analysis of the options have often been wasteful or useless. For example, national programs ranging from lengthening teacher training to reducing class size have been instituted in certain countries without prior knowledge of their effectiveness or economic benefits. Now is the time to begin designing and testing educational options for achieving objectives of economic growth, educational efficiency, and social equity. The process of educational reform is difficult. While some countries may be able to design and implement true educational reforms without basic changes in the structure of production and wealth of their economies, others will require structural reform.[13]

Based on the policy implications of the research and experience discussed in the preceding chapters, a range of policy options emerges. Although they are not consistent, they deal with the issues of demand for schooling, development of alternative learning models, and equality.

To reduce the private demand for more schooling at the upper secondary and higher levels and to reduce the inefficiency of the allocation of educational resources:

(a) Wage differentials should be narrowed as soon as possible by stabilizing or reducing higher level salaries and gradually increasing lower salaries. Furthermore, distortions in factor and product prices should be reduced to encourage use of labor intensive technologies. International trade in skilled workers implies the need for better controls to limit the export of highly skilled manpower from the developing countries.

(b) General school certificates should not be required for most occupations. When employers become more specific about the skills they need, a more diversified educational structure will emerge to meet the clearly specified demand. Then the certification of specific job skills can be introduced.

(c) Middle and upper income students should pay a greater share of the cost of their secondary and higher education. The advantages of establishing an educational bank to shift the costs of post-primary education to the consumer should be explored. Time spent in public service could count as a form of repayment, and should be encouraged. School taxation and expenditures should be localized, so that the costs and benefits are better understood locally. Low income groups should have subsidies drawn from a progressive tax system to overcome the private costs of schooling.

(d) A quota system should be introduced by which the absolute number of students at the upper secondary and university levels could be restricted. The quota could be combined with existing examination systems. In some countries, rationing is already taking place on the basis of geographic location, which usually serves as a proxy for parental social status. Quotas should allow the percentage of the national budget and GNP allocated to education to drop in many countries and level off in others. Misallocation will be reduced.

In order to encourage the development of alternative education which could be more relevant to the needs of family, community and employment countries could:

(a) Eliminate the monopoly of central governments in the field of education, and support community participation in planning and managing school decisions. If creative and efficient alternatives to formal schooling are to develop, incentives are needed to encourage innovative teaching methods and learning opportunities. Apprenticeship may be the most efficient system for learning many manual and mental skills.

(b) Make the teaching of basic skills more effective by training teachers from the community who are more committed to their own people than outsiders are. This would assist in reducing the production of semi-literates by the primary schools.

(c) Explore the opportunities of informal education—learning by experience—using adults and more advanced students as teachers, to teach poor adults the skills required to start and manage organizations which will work to meet their needs.

(d) Finally, require all students to work or do national service for several years before they could apply to enter the last three years of secondary school, or between secondary school and the university.

To compensate for the inequality in future incomes which is reinforced by most existing formal school systems, countries could:

(a) Establish quotas for admission to upper secondary school and the university on the basis of social class, geographic location, or school to assure that the proportion of low income students is at least equal to their representation in the population.
(b) Consider the use of automatic promotion from one grade to the next.
(c) Deemphasize the role of examinations for promotion.
(d) Encourage dropouts to reenter the formal system at a later age by providing them time off from work and low cost courses.

In conclusion, I should emphasize that the options are intended only as a starting point for discussion between the producers and consumers of formal education with the aim of improving the efficiency, effectiveness, and equity of educational systems. Effective dialogue and political commitment are necessary conditions for successful reform.

Notes

1. "Poverty and population in the developing world", Lecture (Washington, D.C.: World Bank, 1977).
2. Michael B. Katz, *The Irony of Early School Reform* (Cambridge, Mass.: Harvard University Press, 1968); and John Simmons, *Lessons From Educational Reform* (Washington, D.C.: World Bank, 1979).
3. For examples of some exceptions, see Aurelio Cespedes, "In Colombia, it's SENA", *American Vocational Journal* (December 1972), and Manuel Zymelman, *The Relationship Between Productivity and Formal Education of Labor Force in Manufacturing Industries* (Cambridge, Mass.: Harvard Graduate School of Education, Occasional Papers in Education and Development, 1970) on tax supported in-plant training programs in Brazil and Chile.
4. The planning and management of change has been subject to extensive research. For an example of valuable guidelines see Douglas McGregor, *The Human Side of Enterprise* (New York: McGraw Hill, 1960).

5. E. R. Duckworth, "A comparative study for evaluating primary school science in Africa" (Newton, Mass.: Educational Development Center, 1971).
6. For an analysis of the India Radio Farm Forum, see Prodipto Roy, Frederick B. Waisanen, and Everett M. Rogers, *The Impact of Communication on Rural Development; An Investigation in Costa Rica and India* (Paris: UNESCO, 1969).
7. Examples are the Chinese "barefoot doctors" and paramedics in the U.S. Army.
8. Everett M. Rogers and F. Floyd Shoemaker, *Communication of Innovations,* 2nd ed. (New York: Free Press, 1971).
9. See Arnold Heidenheimer, *Major Reforms of the Swedish Education System* (Washington, D.C.: World Bank Working Paper, 1978).
10. Newton Edwards, *The Courts and the Public Schools: The Legal Basis of School Organization and Administration* (Chicago: University of Chicago Press, 1955), p. 24.
11. See David Bakan, "Adolescence in America: from idea to social fact", *Daedalus* (Fall 1971), for further discussion of the implications.
12. The United States Supreme Court made such a decision in *Griggs v. Duke Power* in March 1971. Subsequent lower court decisions have had important implications for removing the schooling requirement for hundreds of skilled jobs.
13. For a review of the causes and consequences of educational reforms, see John Simmons, *Lessons From Educational Reform*.

Notes on Contributors

Leigh Alexander

Mr. Alexander is an Economist with the International Monetary Fund in Washington, D.C. Previously he worked as a Research Fellow at the Brookings Institution. He took his undergraduate degree at the University of Melbourne and his Masters in Economics from Monash University, Australia. He is writing his Ph.D. dissertation for the Johns Hopkins University on the subject of schooling benefits for workers.

Mark Blaug

Dr. Blaug is Professor of the Economics of Education and Head of the Research Unit in the Economics of Education at the University of London, Institute of Education. In addition, he is a lecturer at the London School of Economics and has been a consultant to OECD, UNESCO, IBRD, ILO, and The Ford Foundation. He is the author of several books, including *Education and Employment* and (with Richard Layard and Maureen Woodhall) *The Causes and Consequences of Graduate Unemployment in India,* and has published articles on both economic theory and education. Dr. Blaug graduated from Columbia University with a Ph.D. in Economics.

Samuel Bowles

Dr. Bowles is a Professor of Economics at the University of Massachusetts at Amherst. Prior to that he worked as Associate Professor of Economics, Harvard University, as visiting lecturer at the Universidad de la Habana and as Education Officer in the Nigerian Civil Service. He is the author of several articles on economic theory, econometrics, and education. Dr. Bowles is a graduate of Yale University and Harvard University, where he earned a Ph.D. in Economics. His books include *Planning Educational Systems for*

Economic Growth and (with Herbert Gintis) *Schooling in Capitalist America: Educational Reform and the Contradictions of Economic Life.*

Martin Carnoy

Dr. Carnoy is Professor of Education and Economics at Stanford University and Director of the Center for Economic Studies, Palo Alto, California. Prior to that he worked as a Research Associate in Economics at the Brookings Institution. He has written many books, including *Education as Cultural Imperialism, Cost-Benefit Analysis in Education: A Case Study of Kenya,* and *Schooling in a Corporate Society: The Political Economy of Education in America,* as well as articles focusing on the economics of education. Dr. Carnoy holds a Ph.D. in Economics from the University of Chicago.

Remi Clignet

Dr. Clignet is currently a Professor of Sociology at Northwestern University. He has been Head of the Psychological Section, Education Ministry, Ivory Coast, and Lecturer, Advanced Training Program, Peace Corps, Dartmouth College. He is the author of several books, including *Liberty and Equality in the Educational Process: A Comparative Sociology of Education,* and articles on education and sociology. Dr. Clignet received his Doctorate from the University of Paris.

Ronald Dore

Professor Dore is currently with the Institute of Development Studies, University of Sussex. He has been an Associate Professor of Asian Studies, University of British Columbia, Professor of Sociology, University of London, and a Visitor, Institute for Advanced Study, Princeton. He is the author of several books and articles on land reform and education in Japan. His most recent book is *The Diploma Disease: Education, Qualification, and Development.* He is a graduate of the University of London and did post-graduate research at the School of Oriental and African Studies, University of London.

Edgar O. Edwards

Dr. Edwards is Professor of Economics at Rice University. He has been Economic Advisor, Asia and Pacific Program, The Ford Foundation, and a member of the faculty at Princeton University. He has been Director of Planning and Principal Economic Advisor, Ministry of Economic Planning and Development, Government of Kenya. His publications include *Employment in Developing Nations, The Theory and Measure of Business Income,* and *The Nation's Economic Objective,* and articles on both economics and education. Dr. Edwards is a graduate of Washington and Jefferson College and Johns Hopkins University, where he took a Ph.D.

Arnold Harberger

Dr. Harberger is Professor of Economics, University of Chicago. He has been a consultant to The Ford Foundation, the India Planning Commission, AID, the Ministry of Planning and Economic Policy of Panama, and the Department of Regional Economic Expansion of Canada. He was a member of the Board of Editors of the *American Economic Review* and the *Journal of Economic Literature,* and a member of the Executive Committee of the American Economic Association. He is the author of many articles and studies in the fields of public finance, materials policy, economic theory, international trade, economic development, and econometrics. His books include *Project Evaluation* and *Taxation and Welfare.* Dr. Harberger holds a Ph.D. in Economics from the University of Chicago.

Dean T. Jamison

Dr. Jamison is an economist with the Population and Human Resources Division, the World Bank, Washington, D.C. He previously served as Chairman of the Economics and Education Planning Group, Educational Testing Service, Princeton. Prior to that he was Assistant Professor of Management Science at Stanford University. He is the author of several articles on economic theory, communications, and education and has written two books: *The Cost of Educational Media: Guidelines for Planning and Evaluation* (with S. Klees and S. Wells) and *Radio for Education and Development* (with E. G.

McAnany).   Dr. Jamison is a graduate of Stanford University and received his Ph.D. in Economics from Harvard University.

Joanne Leslie

Ms. Leslie has a MSc. from the Department of International Health of the Johns Hopkins School of Hygiene and Public Health and is currently a doctoral student in that program. After completing her undergraduate work at Reed College, she worked for a number of years at Stanford University's Institute for Mathematical Studies in the Social Sciences, where she studied uses of technology in education. She is also a research associate with EDUTEL Communications and Development, Inc., for whom she has recently completed a survey of the use of mass media for health and nutrition education.

Ernesto Schiefelbein

Dr. Schiefelbein is currently a specialist in Education and Vocational Planning, Regional Employment Program for Latin America and the Caribbean under the United Nations Development Program. He has been a Visiting Professor at Harvard University, teaching Planning Education in Developing Countries, and a consultant, Economic Development Institute, at the World Bank. A graduate of Universidad de Chile, Dr. Schiefelbein received his Ph.D. from Harvard University. He is the author (with Russell G. Davis) of the book *Development of Educational Planning Models.*

Marcelo Selowsky

Dr. Selowsky is currently an economist with the Development Research Center, the World Bank, Washington, D.C. Prior to that he served as Assistant Professor of Economics at Harvard University. He is the author (with Shlomo Reutlinger) of *Malnutrition and Poverty: Magnitude and Policy Options* and of several articles on human resources, particularly on the subjects of infant malnutrition and educational planning. He was awarded his Ph.D. by the University of Chicago.

Johns Simmons

Dr. Simmons is an economist with the Policy Planning Division, the World Bank in Washington, D.C. He has taught and been a research fellow at Harvard and Princeton Universities. In addition, he has been a consultant to UNDP, World Education, Inc., Stanford Research Institute, USAID, The Ford Foundation, UNESCO, and the Adlai Stevenson Institute. He is the author of the books *Cocoa Production* and (with Russell Stone) *Change in Tunisia* and of articles on education and rural development. A graduate of Harvard University, Dr. Simmons received his Ph.D. from Oxford University.

Michael P. Todaro

Dr. Todaro is currently Deputy Director and Senior Associate of the Center for Policy Studies at the Population Council in New York. He was formerly Associate Director, Social Sciences, The Rockefeller Foundation. He has been a lecturer on economics at Yale University and Makerere College, Uganda, a research fellow at the Institute for Development Studies, University College, Nairobi and, most recently, Visiting Professor of Economics at the University of California, Santa Barbara. His books and articles focus on both migration and education. A graduate of Haverford College, Dr. Todaro received his Ph.D. from Yale University. His most recent books include *Internal Migration in Developing Countries, Economics for a Developing World,* and *Economic Development in the Third World.*

Index

Page numbers in italics refer to figures and tables.